Abducted

A Novel by

James W. Murphy

At this point I'd like to thank a few people for their significant input into this work. Without their assistance and expertise this work would not be the product it is:

My wife Jean, who has for the last God-given forty-nine years, has been my constant companion and friend. Her patience and support through the times I sat glued to a typewriter, and her 'keep going' attitude encouraged me throughout the process, not only with this book, but the previous five novels. Thanks, babe! (15)

I interviewed two officers of the law, one a retired police chief, and one a retired sheriff's deputy, and received invaluable advice and insight into this piece of fiction. Their patience with me during the interview process (all five pages of questions) is greatly appreciated. Gentlemen, my eternal thanks:

Don Hollingshead, Retired Captain, Laramie County Sheriff's Office, Cheyenne, Wyoming; 27 years

Jeffery C. Johnson, Retired Chief, Worthington, MA Police Department; retired Chief Master Sergeant, United States Air Force, Security Forces; 32 years (and he's a former US Marine! Semper Fi my friend)

The cover photos were taken by yours truly, however, thanks to the expert skills and artistic ability of Ann Lauwers, of *An Artist's View Photography*, the cover would not be what it is. Ann has now done the covers of all six of my novels. Thanks Ann, and again, great job.

The model for the cover photo is Officer Michael Nelson, Cheyenne Police Department. The photo op was a terrific event on a windy day in Cheyenne. Jean and I thank Michael, and Cheyenne Chief of Police Mark Francisco, who graciously granted permission (and technical advice) for the photo opportunity.

Thank you to Mr. Larry Jacobsen for using his photographic skills to create the photograph of me on the back cover of this book. Jean and I had a swell time during the session. Thanks, Larry, and God bless.

Thank you Ms. Beckie Murway, my Editor in Chief. Great ideas and terrific suggestions brought this piece together.

Once again, this is a work of fiction and I have purposely taken great liberties with the police work depicted in this novel. I intentionally changed many things so the real way things are done in local police work was not portrayed. This is to help protect our courageous men and women in blue, who place their lives on the line for the community at large every day. Thank you for all you do!

Abducted

Table of Contents

Excerpt from Jim's next exciting book

Murder in the Medicine Bow   Page 281

CHAPTER ONE

Cheyenne, Wyoming

April 25, 2029, 1635 Hours

"MY BABY, MY BABY is missing!" the obviously distraught twenty-something year old woman yelled at the Cheyenne Police Department desk sergeant as she burst into the foyer of the squad room.

"Lady, slow down, please lady, just calm down and tell me what happened," the desk sergeant, now standing tried yelling over the woman's screaming and crying.

"My baby is gone…somebody took her."

"Who took your baby?"

"I don't know…I…I put her to bed and then she was…just…just gone," the woman said now crying buckets.

The desk sergeant knew this was way over his head and he hated dealing with crying women, so he called up to the Chief of Detectives and asked for a woman detective to come down and help the poor woman. In the meantime, he called over a female officer to sit with her until the detective could come down.

"Ma'am," the desk sergeant said with a gentleness even he didn't think he had, "this is officer Lucy Stone, please go with her and she'll take you to one of our offices so a detective can help you. Lucy, take her over to number four, kid, and thanks."

"You got it sarge," an obviously very young rookie Officer Stone said. "Ma'am, please come with me," she directed the lady while handing her a courtesy box of tissues. Stone put an arm around the lady's shoulder and walked her to interrogation room four. The room was a drab green over gray color, bare walls, a small table, and three chairs, no windows except for the one in the door with thick, wired safety glass. They sat down and Stone asked, "Ma'am, what's your name, please?"

"Oh, I'm sorry, I forgot my manners, I - forgive me - my name is Margaret, Margaret Pierce," the woman answered between sobs. "My daughter's name is Wanda," she answered which led to more tears.

"Margaret, calm down, please, we'll need to ask you some questions and you need to help us and yourself by calming down," Stone explained.

Just then, Detective First Class Anita Wilson knocked on the door and entered without waiting for an answer. Stone got up and did the introductions then left the room. After she left, Wilson looked the woman over sitting in front of her. Blonde hair, blue, bloodshot, tearing eyes, judging her to be around five foot three or so, nicely figured (not overweight), dressed nicely, medium sized diamond with the wedding band on her left ring finger, mother's ring on the right hand with one stone that looked to be a diamond, and a band aid on her right index finger.

To break the ice, Wilson asked, "How'd you cut your finger?" Anita Wilson, thirty-nine years old, five feet six inches, one hundred fifteen pounds, strawberry blond hair tied up in a bun, blue eyes, no make-up and unspeakable nails, dressed in jeans, a blue cotton, *Carhartt* work shirt with a Warner Brother's, *Marvin the Martian* tie, loose at the neck, and Nike walking shoes, Glock nine millimeter with two spare magazines on her right side, sticking out like a neon light at midnight, and a pair of handcuffs in a holder on the left. She'd been on the force for almost twenty years and had been a detective for eleven. She'd been begging for the last six months for a more intense case because she wanted something more exciting than stolen cars and bicycles. A non-smoker, she enjoyed wine, movies, and homemade breads. She doesn't miss CBS' CSI unless her own duty called, and has a home theatre system that is to die for. "One can splurge when one is single," she was fond of saying. Her movie library contained over nine hundred titles and most of those are classics.

"Huh…what?" Margaret answered with a confused look on her face.

"How did you cut your finger?" Wilson said again, now pointing to her right hand.

"Oh," she said holding her finger up just a bit, "I did it on a piece of paper. Nasty little paper cut that stings more than anything else. Why?"

"No matter, just asking; now, Mrs. Pierce, what happen to your daughter?"

"Please call me Margaret. I put her to bed for her afternoon nap at two-thirty, and about three-fifteen I went in to check on her and she wasn't there. I searched her room, then the whole house. I even went outside and to the neighbors, but no one had seen her."

"How old is she?"

"Wanda just turned two last week. She has blonde hair and blue eyes like me; her dad says she looks like me, too," this statement brought back the flood of tears and more tissues.

Wilson stepped out of the room and got a bottle of water and gave it to the grieving mother.

"Thank you," Margaret whispered between her sobs.

"Yes, ma'am, did you see or hear anyone enter your house while Wanda was taking a nap?"

Swallowing a mouthful of water, Margaret answered, "Heavens no. Everything was normal."

"Do you keep the doors and windows to your home locked at all times?"

"No, in fact I had opened Wanda's bedroom window…it's been so hot lately."

"Yes, ma'am, did you hear anything unusual?"

"No."

"Have you notified your husband yet?"

"Yes, I told him I was coming over here and he's going to meet me here soon."

"Was he at work?"

"Yes."

"Where does he work?"

"He's with Dalton Insurance and Brokerage over on Henderson. He should be here any minute."

"Yes, ma'am, did you have any unusual phone calls or strangers at your door today or within the last few weeks?"

"None today, but we usually get some of those calls from telemarketers, you know the ones that I mean."

"Yes, ma'am, do you know anyone that would want to take Wanda away from you?"

"Heavens no, why would anyone want to take a child from their mother," and the tears began again.

A knock on the door announced the arrival of Bryan Pierce, visibly upset. He went immediately to his wife when he entered the room.

"Margaret, what happened, did you find Wanda," was his first words.

Wilson looked Mister Pierce over while he hugged his wife…late twenties, neatly cut brown hair, light color eyes, not blue, kind of gray-green, nose slightly bent to the left, small scar on his chin, light weight business suit, Sears by the look of it, black penny loafers, and he looked to be five feet ten or so, maybe one-seventy or so.

Wilson let the two of them embrace for a few moments, and then interrupted with, "Sir, I'm detective Wilson. Anita Wilson. Are you Mister Pierce?"

"Yes, Bryan Pierce," he replied, standing and extending a hand to shake. "Any word on our daughter?"

Shaking his hand, he had a firm grip, Wilson answered, "Just started questioning your wife, sir. Nothing to report as yet, may I ask you some questions?"

"Absolutely, what do you need to know?" Bryan asked.

"Do you know of any one that would want to abduct your daughter?"

"No…no one," was his rapid, obviously surprised answer.

"Have you spoken to any strangers or had any unusual phone calls within the last month or so?"

"No…a few new clients at work, I guess I can call them strangers. No unusual phone calls, though."

"Well, sir, what we have so far is just what your wife has told us. She put Wanda to bed for her nap around two-thirty and around three-fifteen went to check on her and found her gone. Your wife said she searched the house and surrounding neighborhood, the neighbors and so forth, then came here after calling you. Can you tell me what time it was she called you?"

"Yeah, it was about four-ten or so. My secretary, Julie Sims, can probably tell you exactly what time if you need it."

"Sir, we need to go over to your home and look around. Would that be all right with you?"

"Absolutely, here's my keys, go on in," he responded handing Wilson his key chain.

"Thank you, sir," Wilson replied taking the keys. "I'm going to have officer Stone come back in and take statements from both of you. While she's doing that, my partner and I will go over and take a look at your home, if that's OK with you."

"Ok, that'll be fine," Bryan Pierce responded.

"Is there someone else we can call for you or is there anything we can get for you or your wife?"

"Actually, can you have someone contact our pastor?"

"Yes, sir, do you have a number?"

Bryan got up and pulled a card out of his wallet and handed it to Wilson.

"Ok, I'll have the desk sergeant call him right now. Officer Stone will be here in a moment."

"Thank you ma'am," the distraught woman answered.

Wilson looked out of interrogation room four and motioned for Stone and the desk sergeant to come over. They both looked at their watches, knowing she was motioning them to come over and witness something. She gave the card to the desk sergeant as he and Officer Stone got to the door, and then once again asked Bryan, "Mr. Pierce, you sure it's OK if my partner and I go into your home without you or your wife being there?"

"Absolutely, we have nothing to hide," he quickly answered.

Wilson withdrew, giving instructions to the desk sergeant to call their pastor straight away; left Officer Stone with the two distraught parents to take statements then went upstairs to the detective's office to get her partner, Detective Samuel Bishop.

"Bish," she yelled, "get your hat, darlin', we're going on a road trip."

"You get something downstairs," the burly detective asked?

"Yeah, we're on a missing person case as of now."

"We don't do missing persons, you ditsy blonde," Sam admonished. Sam had been on the force for twenty-two years. One could find him in the gym most often or on the road jogging or riding his mountain bike or reading a book of some sort. A muscular guy with a large chest, hands like anvils and the beginning of a 'settling of muscle' as he liked to call it, around his waist and under his chin. Quick-witted and intense, he made sergeant at five years on the force and detective at nine and continues to choose not to go higher. "I'm happy right where I am," he tells promotion boards. A loner off duty, he lives in a three bedroom apartment on the west side of Cheyenne, with one room being his library – he owns over six thousand books and has read every one of them. Drinks like a thirsty race horse, but only socially, and never, never beer; just the best bourbons on the market, drinking it on the rocks or with diet, yep, diet, 7Up. He enjoys good scotch also. Sam being a non-smoker chose instead to have as his only other major vice a passion for peanut M&Ms. He always has them at hand, and God forbid if he runs out or someone takes one.

"We do when they're two years old, were put down for a nap and forty-five minutes later is gone without a trace."

"Oh my God; where we goin'?" he asked her.

"Almost just around the corner, just four blocks over on the West side, this side of your place. The mother ran over here to make the report."

"No kidding, ran? She a suspect… or the father?"

"Don't think so, both are pretty shaken up and very cooperative, and yeah, she ran over here," she replied dangling the house keys in front of Sam's nose. "Dad gave me these and said we could go right in, and yes, I got witnesses to that fact," answering his next question before he could ask. "And you want to know what he said when I asked?" Not waiting for an answer she continued, "He said, 'absolutely, we have nothing to hide'. He wasn't worried that we'd take anything. He wants us to find his kid."

"That's sweet of him, and quit reading my mind."

"Behave, boy. The first thing the dad asked for was their pastor – my gut feeling is they're on the up-and-up. So lay off the wise cracks. This couple is right out of the *Father Knows Best* play book."

"Ok. I've learned to trust your gut feelings, so let's go over and see what we can see."

They grabbed their coats and hats and went down stairs to the underground garage and got into their chocolate brown, "unmarked" police car with its black-walled tires and spotlights on both sides. Started the engine and pulled out. Heading north, they turned left just a block from the station and went west for another four blocks.

"There's the house, the one with the white gate," Detective First Class Anita Wilson pointed.

Detective Samuel Bishop, pulled up and parked across the street and they sat in the car for several minutes just observing the area. A nice looking old style New England home with a huge front porch, Adirondack chairs, a small table, and little girls' outdoor toys scattered about. The home was painted light brown with off-white, cream-colored trim, shutters on the windows, and soapstone for the base. The lawn was neatly trimmed and a nice big cottonwood tree with a swing gently swaying with the breeze. The house faced north. They got out of the car.

When they got to the gate, Wilson went left, Sam going right, both knowing they'd meet at the back of the house. No words were spoken as both professionals trusting their partner, went their separate ways looking up, down, and sideways, taking in everything as trained investigators were supposed to do.

Wilson noted two windows on her side of the house, both open with screens in place. No signs of obvious forced entry. No mud for tracks, no shrubs, no signs of shoe scrapings on the wall. Two basement windows closed and obviously not opened in quite some time. Looking closely at the ground she could find no evidence of anything out of the ordinary. Looking through the first window, it looked like part of the living room or sitting room. The second was the girl's room. Dolls, and pink walls, Barbie bed spread and horses. Upon close inspection she found scrapes where someone had pried the screen with a knife or screwdriver. She could just get her elbows up to the window ledge. Not wanting to disturb any evidence, she continued to the back of the house.

When she turned the corner, Sam was already there looking around the back yard. "Nothing interesting on my side," he said. "How 'bout you over there?" he asked, pointing.

"Found the girls room. Screen had been pried with a blunt instrument like a knife or screwdriver or something. No tracks, no scrapes on the wall and I can just get my elbows up to the ledge."

"You're too short to be a criminal," Sam kidded.

"Shut up."

"Can't find any sign of entry through the back yard; fence and hedges all intact."

"You don't suppose whoever did this just stopped on the street, pried open the screen, went in and took the girl, replaced the screen, and right back out to the street and calmly drove off?"

"Maybe there were two of them…one to take off and replace the screen and another to grab the girl and head for the car."

"Makes sense; next question is motive. Why would you abduct a child from a middle-class family that's obviously living from payday to payday?"

"I wouldn't, but it can't be for money. Maybe mom or dad has really ticked off someone, maybe a bad business deal or something from dad's standpoint. More questions to ask the Pierces'. What business is the dad in anyway?"

"He's in insurance and brokerage, a junior agent by the looks of him, and yeah, I'm sure we'll come up with more questions to ask them and we'll need to dig into their background real deep. However, I can't see either one of them being part of this right now. They're too broken up. Might be a swell show, but I don't get that feeling. Someone may be ticked off at the dad for a busted business deal of some sort like you said, but I wouldn't bet the bank on it."

"Let's go inside."

"Yeah, come around this way and look at that window first."

They went back out to the front, stopping long enough for Sam to check out and agree with Wilson's assessment of the window scrapings. As they climbed the front steps, they donned gloves, then both stopped and looked around. Wilson checked the mail slot in the door - it opened with a creek – not a thing. She knocked hard, three times. No answer and no noise…no dog. She quietly inserted the key, and they both pulled weapons. She slowly turned the door knob and began slowly pushing the door open. Sam standing taller was near her left side with his weapon up and covering her right side and she covering the front and left. The door quietly opened and they just stayed there for a moment listening…nothing but their radios with the usual traffic noise. They entered. Just as she thought, the first window was the living room. The place was a typical middle-class home. Clean and tidy - couch, chair, recliner, TV, stereo, family pictures on the walls, kids' toys. It was odd there was no gun cabinet. They moved down a central hallway, he covering left and her right. On her right, the first door went into the kitchen; the next into the main bath and the third the master bedroom.

Sam pointed with his weapon towards the girl's room and they both went in…nothing. They holstered their weapons and began looking around. Nothing really seemed out of place. This was a little girl's room. Toys everywhere, dolls, blocks, kids' books, blanket.

"Look," it was Sam.

Wilson went over to look where he was pointing and there on the floor was a stalk of grass lying just under the window sill. "I bet this is definitely where they entered."

"Ok, let's call in the Crime Scene Team (CST) and see if they can lift any prints. I'll have them dust the whole room and the wall outside, the window and screen. I'll have them be real careful and look out there to see if they can find any shoe imprints."

"I'll go check the street for tire marks, might be some in the crap alongside the street gutters, and I'll call in to have the desk sergeant print mom and dad."

"Good idea, I'll make the call for CST," and she brought her radio out.

Not long after Wilson made the call, the CST arrived with another unit for back-up and crowd control, not that there would be much in Cheyenne, and Sam gave the CST a briefing on what and where they wanted them to search for evidence and told the other officers to control the scene.

"Make sure you bag that piece of grass in the bedroom," Sam told the CST.

"No problem, we'll get everything we can," the CST team leader, a lieutenant, assured him.

"Sam," Wilson yelled.

"Yeah, out here," the big guy answered her call.

"Come in here will ya?"

"Yep, on my way," he said as he took the front porch steps in two bounds, Wilson opened the screen door for him. "Nothing's interesting in the street or on the sidewalk. What's up, doc?"

"Got a call from Stone and she said the mom told her to have us look for a hand-made, pink blanket with little bears on it and a brown and black stuffed horse. The kid never went anywhere

18

without those two things. If they're gone, then whoever took the girl knew they would keep her quiet. And that means familiarity."

They both shot down the hallway to Wanda's room and searched everywhere, including under the bed sheet; both were missing.

"Let's check out the rest of the house. Maybe the kid left them somewhere else," Sam said.

"Not likely going to take a nap, but just to be sure," Wilson agreed.

After telling the CST team what to look for, a search of the entire house turned up the same as the Wanda's bed room – no blanket or horse.

"This or these persons knew this family," Sam noted the now obvious out loud.

"Yeah, I think so, too," from Wilson. "OK, let's hit some neighbors with some questions. Somebody's got to have seen the vehicle."

"East or West," Sam asked?

"Let's go look."

As they left the house, they stood on the porch and looked over the surrounding area. There was a small park just across the street; nice look alike *Ozzie and Harriet* homes to the left and right.

Sam broke the silence with, "My dad always said follow your heart, so let's do left first."

"So be it; lead on detective," Wilson answered with a slight bow and a wave of her arm and hand towards the steps.

Opening the gate to the yard next door they noticed a lady open the door of the home and step out onto the porch. She was wearing a bright yellow sun dress and a wide brimmed hat covered with faux flowers, sneakers on her feet with white socks and dirty, well-used gardening gloves on her hands. "Hello, I'm Jena Hullinger," she introduced herself, taking the glove off of her right hand and offering it to Sam. "I figured you'd be over pretty soon. Like some ice tea?"

Sam took her hand and shook it and said, "Uh, no thank you, ma'am. I'm Detective Sam Bishop and this is my partner Detective First Class Anita Wilson."

"Ma'am," from Wilson with a nod, also shaking her hand.

"Good afternoon, nice to meet you. Not the best of circumstances, I gather," Jena observed shaking Wilson's hand.

"Yes ma'am," answered Wilson. "Can you tell us what you know about what went on with the Pierces' this afternoon?"

"Sure. Please have a seat," she invited, motioning to some lawn chairs on the porch. "Margaret came over about an hour and a half ago, I guess, and she was all in a tizzy saying Wanda was missing and wanting to know if she was over here. I watch her sometimes, you see. I told her no, and we looked all in the house and out in the back yard but couldn't find her. I told Margaret to go call the cops, err, excuse me, I mean police…"

"No problem, ma'am, please continue," Sam told her.

"Thanks. She just yelled she was going down to your station and told me to look around some more."

"Did you look around some more?" from Wilson.

"Why, yes, I did. I went over to Missy's house on the other side of Margaret's but they're not home. Went shopping I guess."

Wilson was writing in her notebook and Sam asked, "Did you see any strange vehicles parked in the street earlier today?"

"Always do, because of the park; folks coming and going all the time over there. I don't pay too much attention to them, you see."

Sam nodded and Wilson wrote.

Wilson asked, "Did you hear anything out of the ordinary earlier today, between two-thirty and three-thirty?"

"Why no, what would you suppose that I'd hear?"

"Don't know, ma'am, anything really. Car backfire, tires squealing, child screaming, anything like that," Sam explained.

"Why, no, I don't remember anything like that at all. I was out in my garden in the back yard most of the afternoon. Only reason I knew Margaret was over was I could hear her yelling, poor child."

"Jena," Sam asked, "do you think the Pierces take good care of Wanda?"

"Oh heavens yes. That little child is plenty spoiled. They take her to the park almost every evening after they have supper. Both Margaret and Bryan play with her out in the yard. Just look at all those toys over there. If something terrible has happened to that child, it'll just kill those two."

Wilson continued writing. Sam said, "Yes, ma'am. Sounds like a real nice family. You know of anyone that may want to harm them for some reason or another?"

"Goodness, no, they're real nice people. Bryan came over this last winter and fixed my furnace. He's such a nice young man, always asking if I'm all right. And Margaret always asks if she can pick up anything at the market for me when she goes - just plain nice people."

"Yes, ma'am," Sam answered. He looked at Wilson and shrugged.

"Jena, if you remember anything, anything at all no matter how trivial it may seem to you, please, give one of us a call at this number," Wilson instructed handing Jena a business card. "Are you married?"

"Widowed for these past eight years," she answered, looking at Sam.

"I see," said Wilson as Sam quickly looked out towards the street. "Again, if you remember anything at all, give us a call and thank you for your cooperation and time."

"Oh, you're very welcome. Drop by anytime," Jena said with a smile and a look obviously meant for Sam.

The two detectives left the yard and went down into the street to look around some more.

Wilson took the opportunity to goad Sam just a bit with, "So, the older ladies really go for you young'uns, huh?"

"Can it, Wilson, you freak-of-nature cop."

"Ohh, touch a cord, did I? You got the hots for the sun-dress widow next door? I'm gonna start singing a Beatle tune any minute, how about '*When I'm Sixty-Four*.'"

"Shut up…you're just jealous…" and the bickering went on and on while they searched for any evidence. They always goaded and taunted each other when on an investigation. Both said it made their minds sharper. The other cops thought they were crazy and in love with each other. Crazy maybe…in love…far from it. They did love each other, but not in a "lovers" way, rather in a brother and sister sort of way. Both had a healthy respect for one another.

The bickering began day one when they met and were introduced as new partners. When Wilson was introduced to Sam, Sam shook her hand and looked her over from top to bottom and from side to side. Then he looked her in the eye and said, "Funny, you don't look anything like the actor."

She Asked, "What actor?"

And he replied, "The one in that movie with Tom Hanks, where they were stranded together on that island…"

Well, that had started it all. She had been stunned for just a few seconds, but when he smiled at her they both laughed. The ice was broken. Now, they knew each other like the backs of their hands; knew each other's moves and moods; could read each other and their thoughts just from a look. The best natural match for this kind of work the chief had ever seen. A real team that worked so well together that everyone from the Chief on down left them alone and knew that with them on a case a crook was just buying time until they were arrested and put away.

This case was different, however. After two weeks of intensive investigating, phone calls, interviews with family, friends and acquaintances of the Pierces' by both them and the FBI's kidnapping/missing person experts, no clues, other than the scrape on the screen, the blade of grass, and the fact of the missing blanket or stuffed toy had not been found. It was as if

Wanda Pierce, age two, had dropped off the face of the Earth without a trace.

Mom and Dad had posted photos of Wanda all over Cheyenne. News casts on the local TV and radio stations and on the nation-wide "Amber Alert" system had been broadcast. The newspaper had done an article and published Wanda's photo as well. Local schools passed her photo around to all the students and asked them to keep an eye out. Still nothing.

That's where partners Anita Wilson and Sam Bishop sat after lunch on the third Monday, May 14, 2029, following their initial investigation.

"Sam, you ever heard of anything like this before," Wilson wanted to know? "I mean no clues to speak of, no calls from the kidnappers, no contacts, nothing?"

Sam had his head down with his chin on his chest, hands folded in his lap, thinking about the question. Finally he raised his head, looked at her and said, "Seems I do remember a case similar to this one several years ago. Down in Wellington, Colorado, I think. Sometime in the spring or early summer I think, like this one. Why?"

"I don't know. I just got a feeling that's all."

"Oh, I hate it when you get 'feelings'," he said motioning the quotes with his hands.

"Don't get me wrong, I'm not trying to be sarcastic or macabre or anything. Just that I got this feeling this may just be something else."

"Like what, for instance," Sam asked sitting forward in his chair.

"Well…honestly…I don't know. I just think we should do some checking that's all."

"Come on, toots, let it all out, where you going with this?"

"Let's check and see how many 'like cases' we can come up with in…say Colorado and Nebraska. Don't want to say it, but maybe this has happened before, you know?"

"OK, let me get this straight. You think we're on to something else, a 'trend' or a serial type of abduction case or something, right?"

"God, I hope not. But I got this feeling we need to keep checking and looking for a possibility like that."

Sam's head tilted to the side as he looked at her. He suddenly had a very serious look on his face and said, "This one has gotten to you, huh?"

She looked up from her desk at his face and simply said, "Yeah, partner, you know me when a kid is involved."

Sam met her gaze for another moment, then straightened up and became plain old Sam again and said, "OK, I can start with the one I think I know about down in Colorado. Have a friend down there I can call to see if she can enlighten me."

Knowing Sam was on her side even now was a blessing for Wilson. She cracked a small smile and, looking at him, said, "You don't have friends, especially female. Anyway, while you call I'll get on the computer and see what I can conjure up."

"You're a female, I think. Must be if you can conjure. Get back with you in a bit."

"Watch that witch innuendo or I'll turn you into a frog."

"Hey," he shot back, "how 'bout a tadpole. I'd live longer and you couldn't get to me that fast with your broom…"

That's when the phone book flew past his head and smacked against the wall behind him. "Get to work, detective and stop harassing the boss."

"Boss…boss…talk about harassment…getting stuff thrown at you by the 'boss'," Sam said sarcastically with pursed lips and flinging his hands into the air.

"You'd better get moving before I throw something more substantial at you," Wilson shot back with a smile on her face. She turned to her computer desk and began by bringing up the national crime data base file. She entered the unsolved missing person's window and as that came up, input her creds. While the system digested her information, she began writing down information to search for – female, infant to five years old,

Caucasian, Hispanic, Native American, Oriental, African American, nationwide, twelve month cycle, going back say ten years, no contact from abductor – these questions just to start.

The window finally came up and she entered her location, badge number, phone number, and began inputting the information she wanted the database to collect and print out when the system was finished compiling the data. Satisfied with what she had put in, she hit enter, turned around to her desk and picked up her coffee mug.

She noticed Sam on the phone. He had a flirtatious smile on his face and that made her think about the woman on the other end. Wilson had never really looked at Sam as a ladies man, but, in his own way, he was desirable. He might just be one of those diamond-in-the-rough guys she had heard about. He was always a gentleman with her and other women she'd seen him with, opening doors, and such, never tried to date her, and always seemed more concerned when a crime they investigated involved children or women. He took much more interest in those cases she had noticed. Sir Galahad, one of the female detectives in K9 had called him.

Oh, sure, they had eaten together, lunch and such. They had had dinner with each other as well, but only in conjunction with an investigation. They had partied with other officers too, especially after successfully solving a case. She had never really thought of Sam as a 'guy' until this moment. Tilting her head and casting him a sideway glance, she wondered why now. Was it because of the look he gave her when he suggested he call the woman friend in Wellington? Or was she just being naïve? Her eyes dropped from him to rest on his desk and she actually began to day-dream about what would happen if…

"Hey, Wilson," Sam practically yelled as he hung up the phone. "Mary, down in Wellington said the case they had was two years ago and almost exactly like ours. It was on the west side down there, on a ranch no less. And get this, it happened in the same month as ours and the kid was a two year old with blonde hair and blue eyes. I think you may have hit on something."

When he began speaking she had almost jumped out of her skin she was so startled. She looked like a kid that got caught with her hand in the cookie jar…and he noticed. She wasn't really listening. She just sat there shaking her head at him acknowledging what he was saying but not really hearing.

"WILSON," he yelled. "You really getting any of this or what?"

"Yeah, got it, two years old, blonde hair, blue eyes, just like our case," she responded almost angrily. "I got it!"

"Wa'sa matter," he said looking at her with a somewhat concerned look on his face.

"Nothing - you got anything else to add?"

"No, you got anything on the computer yet," he asked still looking at her funny.

"No, it'll start printing as soon as it's done compiling the information."

"Cool. Hey, you really think we may be on to something with this?" Sam asked earnestly, getting back to normal.

"Don't know, Sam, but do you really want to find out if little girls are being abducted all over the place?"

Both stopped and thought about that. They looked at each other and both knew by each other's look that if they had stumbled onto something, it was going to be bigger than both had ever imagined. And probably more horrifying than either wanted to realize.

"Sam, I'm going to go home, pop a cork on a real nice hearty burgundy and get in a hot tub full of bubble bath and think about this. I'll see you tomorrow," Wilson suddenly said getting up, getting her coat, and heading for the door. "The computer will automatically print what I asked for so just let it go. It'll be ready in the morning I s'pect. Go get some time off yourself; I'll see you tomorrow morning."

Sam just watched her as she got her stuff together and left. He wondered to himself what she would look like in a bubble bath holding a glass of wine…he sat bolt upright in his chair and shook his head in surprise at the thought he was having. He looked around the room checking that no one saw him thinking like that. Seeing no one was around to catch him, he jumped up, grabbed his hat and coat, and headed out the door himself.

When Sam got home, he threw his hat and coat on a parson's table in his foyer, retrieved his newspaper and headed for the kitchen. He knew that if the information Wilson asked the computer to compile was what they both suspected it might be, that meant they wouldn't get a good meal or rest for quite some time. So, he opened his freezer, took out a T-bone steak, and threw it in the microwave to thaw. He went out on his patio, pulled out his grill, poured in some charcoal, doused it with lighter, and lit it. Then he went into his library, got his new book, *Shadows of Steel* by Dale Brown, and opened his liquor cabinet. He stood there for a moment deciding on what to drink with dinner and finally selected a bottle of fifty-seven year old Glenfiddich single malt scotch he'd been saving and poured a very healthy three-fingered amount into a crystal brandy snifter.

He went back into the kitchen and prepared some fresh vegetables – green, yellow and red pepper chunks, mushrooms, onion cubes, crushed garlic, and two carrots sliced in chunks. All this he placed in some aluminum foil, added butter and some other seasonings, closed up the foil sealing in the mixture and placed it on the grill once the briquettes were ready. He opened a can of peas and poured them into a sauce pan and set that next to the stove as the microwave beeped. He took his steak out, sprinkled it with pepper and some other spices, and put it on the grill also.

He went back into the library and fired up his stereo system and put in five CDs worth of Black Sabbath, Pink Floyd, Grand Funk, and The Doobie Brothers. He would feast, drink, read, and listen well this night. He thought all this would take his mind off Wilson…Anita. Hmmm, he thought to himself that he had never called her by her first name before… "Anita," saying her name out loud for the first time and smiling.

About the same time, Wilson was placing a halibut steak with pasta and white wine sauce on a plate, poured herself a glass of burgundy and sat down to eat and read the paper. Her meal went rather quickly as she really wanted to get into that tub of hot water and relax. She cleaned up her dishes and went to the bathroom. She started the hot water in the tub and poured in her favorite bubble bath, a mixture that smelled like pears and strawberries. She added some cold water to the flow and went back to the kitchen to fetch her bottle of burgundy and her glass.

She lit the candles and incense, stripped, and slid into the steaming bath. In the background the music of Mozart floated throughout her apartment as she reclined in the tub, enjoying the atmosphere and sipping her wine. All was well in her world for the moment.

Both of their alarms went off precisely at five in the morning. Both practically jumped out of their beds, his head pounding, and her mouth as dry as a cob web. They both hit the station house at the same time. She looked at him and all he said was, "Eight fingers of the good stuff…you?"

She swallowed hard and replied, "Three quarters of a bottle of burgundy and a bottle of port."

"Yuk. How can you mix stuff like that?"

"Must've been the bath and the Mozart."

"Don't say no more. I don't even want to hear it. Mozart…yuk. I read Dale Brown last night 'till I dropped. I learned a long time ago to turn on the alarm clock before I start an evening like that. It pays."

"Truer words were never spoken as I do the same. S'pose you listened to rock-n-roll all night?"

"Yep, sure did."

When they finally made it upstairs to their office, both felt like they had already put in a full day. Wilson opened the door and stopped short. Sam rear-ended her, staggered back some and surprised said, "Your break lights broke? What's the hold up, sister?"

Pointing to the pile of computer paper on the floor, she answered, "Will you look at that? We must have hit the mother lode with that request on the computer last night."

"Wow, what did you ask for?" Sam asked incredulously, looking over her shoulder at the pile of paper strewn about the floor. He was about to move away but stopped when he noticed the fruity smell of Anita. He caught himself and moved away.

She answered his question with, "Did a nation-wide search like I said I was going to. Didn't think I'd get this much stuff, though. Wow."

"You said it, sister," Sam voiced.

Wilson bent over and began straightening up the mass of paper that had spilled itself out on the floor. "You make the coffee while I clean up this mess, will ya?"

"Way ahead of you darlin'. If I don't get more coffee in me soon I'm gonna curl up and die, ohh my aching head. Got any aspirins or Motrin or something?"

"Yeah, top left under the pen holder. Watch the lip stick."

"Gross! Always hated getting into my mother's purse for something - no telling what she had in there. Always thought I'd draw back a bloody stub of a hand when I got in her purse. That gonna happen now," a nervous Sam asked looking up at her?

"Only thing in there that might bite you is the odd spider that may have happened by. Your hand may come out smelling better, though."

"OK, nuff said, I'll take your word for it that I'll come out whole. Need the aspirins worse. No critter in its right mind would get in my way right now the way I feel. Would be the last thing it ever did. And speaking of smell, why do you smell like a fruit tree this morning?"

This made her look at him as he was rummaging around in her desk drawer. Sam had never commented on the way she smelled before and it brought a smile to her face knowing that he'd noticed.

"It's from my bath last night. The mixture is pear and strawberry…"

"Nuff said. Already more than I really wanted to know," he said throwing three aspirins in his mouth, chewing them.

"Oh my God, you're sick. How can you chew those things?" Wilson with a sour face asked.

"Gets into your system faster this a way; now, you want coffee or you gonna keep grilling me on my habits?"

"Do the coffee, please," Wilson said as she returned to picking up the pile of computer paper. While she straightened up the pile she again thought of how Sam had noticed her aroma and again had a smile on her face. *He noticed*, she thought to herself.

She finally placed the stack of paper neatly on her desk. Each page listed a case, showing case number, location, investigating officer's name or names and any other agencies that may have been involved, child's name, date of birth, description, name, address and phone number of the child's parents and their occupations if any. Also listed were the suspects, if any, and their current locations.

She remembered she had requested ten years' worth of information and looking at the page numbers, turned to the last page…number two hundred seventy-one. An average of twenty-seven cases a year nationwide.

"Sam, there's two hundred seventy-one cases listed here. That's nationwide over the last ten years. Where do you think we should start? I never dreamed it would be this big."

"Me neither. Let's think on it for a while, while the coffee's brewing. After a few slugs of 10W30 caffeine, I'll be able to think better."

"Yeah, Okay with me. I'll go down and get us something to snack on. How about bagels?"

"Swell, that'll be fine; one wheat, one sesame seed, and both with honey butter for me, please."

"Okay, back in a bit."

She went down stairs all the while thinking about the computer run - so many cases. She never dreamed there would be that many. She wondered if any would be similar to their current case. Then wondered how they should compile all the information so it could be more easily researched. Then she remembered what Sam had said about the Wellington case. The kid was two years old, blonde hair, blue eyes, and abducted in April, just like little Wanda. Maybe that would be their key, then, use the month of April as a starting point.

She got the bagels; hers was an apple sauce with cream cheese, and headed back upstairs in a hurry. When she got there, Sam was sipping hot coffee and had poured her a cup as well. Both liked it black or 'straight up' as they liked to say.

"Hey, chickie poo, I think we should start with April as a place to start putting all this stuff together, then go from there," Sam said between sips.

"Man, we really do think alike. I came up with the same idea downstairs. The computer keeps all this information for twenty-four hours so it'll be faster to compile than yesterday," she said sitting at her desk and grabbing her coffee. "Mmmmm, this is good stuff."

"Only the best mountain grown for my partner."

"Really, what is this?"

He shrugged his shoulders and said, "Cheapest I could find at the market. I always get the cheapest and it always tastes best to me, go figure."

"Hmmmm, that's nice. Look, I'll start putting this in the computer," Wilson said then took a big bite of her bagel. Fifteen minutes later they had a list that went from two hundred seventy-one down to thirty-seven. "OK, dude, we're down to thirty-seven. How do you think we should break it up now?"

"How's age sound," he answered. "We got two kids for sure that are two years old. Let's harp on that angle and see what we get."

"OK, Kemo Sabe, let's see what we get."

This time it only took seven minutes.

"Hey, look at this," she said. "We're down to six, counting Wanda, all in April, all two years old, and look at this, all their birthdays are real close together and all in April. We really have something here. Let's look at locations."

"Here, give them to me, I got a US atlas book. Five in ten years, not counting Wanda, she's not on the list yet, I already checked. So that's six in ten years. Look at the years they were abducted…every other year one turns up missing…odd years, none in even years. How fast you think that thing can get us info on the last fifty or sixty years?"

"Fifty or sixty years?" Wilson asked incredulously. "It'll take a bit, but not as long as last night. Why so far back?"

"Just a hunch I guess. We've been lucky with this thing so far. Let's see what another long shot hunch will bring and see how far we can get."

"You got it. I'll put it in. You do the map right quick." She pounded on the key board and he did the map thing. After a few moments, he got up and went to their wall map of the USA and began poking in tacks, beginning with Cheyenne; then Wellington, Colorado; Idaho Falls, Idaho; Grand Forks, North Dakota; and finally Las Vegas, New Mexico. Then he replaced those tacks with pins with little flags denoting the years of abduction. All on odd years, every other year, beginning with the current year and going backwards.

"Don't know where this is taking us, but I got the feeling we're on to something big…and ugly," Sam noted. "Really big, and I think it'll be beyond us in the wash. Depending on what we get with what you're asking that thing now, we may need to usher this up to the top floor real quick."

"I agree. This should be printing out soon. So, it looks like they're all in the central states, and every location can be driven to within a day or so of each other. That's too much of a coincidence, don't you think?"

"Sure do. That it?" Sam asked as the printer suddenly came to life again.

"Uh, yep, sure is. Make some more of those little flags and let's see what we get."

After more than an hour they were very sure they were on to something very big indeed. It was most likely a serial abductor, possibly serial killer of two year old girls. Counting little Wanda's, there were thirty-three little white flags now on the map. All with abduction dates in odd years, all taken on a Wednesday, in the latter part of April, and all the little girls had birth dates on or just before the 19th of April. And all the flags were in the central, western United States, all within a day's drive or so of each other. Not all had blonde hair and blue eyes; some brunette, and some had black or red hair and some had brown eyes and one had green. Most every race was represented – African American, American Indian, Caucasian, and Oriental American. But the constants remained – all born and abducted in April, on a Wednesday, and all were only two years old when taken; all disappeared without a trace; the families never contacted and the child was never heard of or from again, nor was one ever located; over thirty unsolved cases; over thirty missing and in all likely hood forever.

Thirty-three little girls taken from their families, and only heaven knew what had, or was happening to them. One major question Wilson and Sam had was why hadn't someone picked up on this long before they had? Obviously they were on to something. They figured, and rightly so, that they should keep this as quiet as possible as to not let the abductor know they were on to him…or her…or them.

"Look at this," she said. "We've had two here in Cheyenne…uh…1993 and now. Let's get the case file from the other one and compare them."

"I'll get it," he said, getting up and going to the cold-case file room. He pulled the case, signed it out, and ran back upstairs to their office. "Here we go."

The two read both, each, and the files were almost identical.

"We gotta get this upstairs," Sam told Wilson.

"You think we have everything we can give them?" she asked.

"Probably not, but we have to get what we have up to the Chief. Write this down. Presume first abduction in 1965, Pocatello, Idaho, the latest right here in River City, and every other year after 1965 in a nine state area. All were taken along the I-25 and I-80 corridors except for North and South Dakota. They were all female. All age two. All were born in April, prior to the twentieth. All abducted after their second birthday, with the earliest abduction date being April twentieth, and the latest being April twenty-sixth. There are an unknown number of participants but more than likely two or more, based on evidence found in the two Cheyenne cases. Wyoming, and Colorado have had five abductions; Nebraska and New Mexico four each, Idaho, Montana, North and South Dakota, and Utah three each. No regularity to state chosen can be found; neither can locations within the states. The only constants are the birthdays and ages of the girls and when they're abducted. No set pattern of child's physical attributes either as there have been blondes, red heads, black hair, and brunettes, brown, green, and blue eyes, and every race we have in the US of A. OK, you think that'll cover what we have so far and get the chief's attention?"

"Absolutely, make the call now."

Sam sat at his desk and dialed the Chief's number. After two rings, the Chief's secretary answered, "Good morning, this is Chief of Police Webster's office, I'm Frances, and how may I help you?"

"Frances, this is Sam Bishop. Anita and I have to see the Chief right now."

"Well, let me…"

"Frances …no…not later, NOW! This is real important. Anita and I have stumbled on to something and we need to see the Chief NOW! You tell him we're coming right over with some evidence that'll tear his guts out. You tell him we're on our way."

"OK, Sam, I'll tell him," Frances said and immediately heard the phone being slammed down on the other end. Frances jerked the phone away from her ear and just looked at the receiver for a moment, surprise, and shock written on her face. She had never heard Sam speak like that before. Never! She could tell he was upset and so she buzzed the Chief. "Chief, Sam, and Anita are on their way over. They have something very hot for you to look at. Chief, I've never heard Sam like this before. He was real insistent and even slammed the phone in my ear. You're going to have to see them."

"Frances, you need to schedule them in some time later. I've very busy right now…"

"Chief! Please…sorry to interrupt, but I'm really concerned by what and how Sam said what he did. They're not waiting anyway they're on their way over right now. Please, Chief, something big has happened. I've never heard him like this…ever. Sam said what he and Anita had to show you will tear your guts out. And that's a quote. You have to see them, Jon."

"You've never called me Jon before, Frances. Okay, I've always trusted your intuition. You really think they have something that important to show me that I need to drop what I'm doing?"

"Yes, sir, I do."

"You never call me sir, either, unless other brass is around. Okay, as soon as they get here show them in."

Chief Jonathan Webster hung up his phone and sat back in his chair, rotated and looked out the window of his fourth story office, slowly rocking back and forth. They'll be here any minute, he thought to himself, and God only knows what they've found.

It took only ten minutes before they entered dragging their division captain with them, having literally pulled him out of his office, scaring the dickens out of his secretary, Amanda, without preamble and shoving him screaming curses into their squad car.

Anita began, "Chief and Captain, we've stumbled onto something horrifying. You know that Pierce case we've been working on, Chief?"

"The missing little girl?" the chief questioned.

"Yes, sir, that's the one," Anita answered. "Well, we've been stonewalled from the beginning. No clues to speak of and no breaks in the case either. Sam here said he knew of a similar case down in Colorado – Wellington - so he call an acquaintance down there and the similarities were way too numerous to be coincidental. So, I requested a listing from the national data base and we've come up with something terrible."

Sam took over, "Chief, we're pretty sure there's a serial abductor going around, and he or she or they have been around since at least 1965."

"What do you mean 1965?" the captain interrupted with a stern yet surprised gape.

"Just that," Sam answered. "We have evidence that supports our theory that someone has been specifically abducting two year old girls in a nine state region in the west-central United States every odd year since 1965."

The Chief leaned forwarded in his chair and put his elbows on his desk and asked, "Can you prove this?"

Anita answered, "We're fairly certain we can, sir. We're not saying it's the same perpetrator every time, but the MO is almost identical in all thirty-three cases and the data will prove something is going on. Let me explain. Every year since 1965 - we've not gone any earlier than that yet - there has been a little girl abducted. She was born in April; not after the nineteenth; she was abducted after her second birthday, between the twentieth and the twenty-sixth of April and always on a Wednesday. And that adds up to thirty-three, and it's all here, chief, all of them. Look at this map…Wyoming and Colorado have had five abductions; Nebraska and New Mexico, four each; Idaho and Montana three each, all within a day's drive or so of each other, predominantly along the I-25 and I-80 corridors."

"Here, Chief, we wrote it all down for you," Sam said as he handed copies of their earlier findings to both the chief and the captain. "We're fairly certain Wanda Pierce was number thirty-three. Based on what we've found we feel these need to go national, at least to the FBI and the other eight states affected. We figure we've got just under two years to prepare for the next abduction. Maybe with what we've found we can prevent another one, and maybe nail the bad guy or guys as well."

"My God, I never thought you'd be bringing me something like this," the chief said with an amazed yet concerned look on his face. The captain sat speechless now knowing why he was dragged out of his office.

"Chief, here's the printouts and everything else we've worked up. We have to get this out of here quick," Wilson added.

"Yes, yes, you're both right. Frances, get in here!" the chief shouted.

Frances came bursting in with wide eyes and a look of shock and fear on her face, the chief never yelling like he did.

"I want you to make copies of all this stuff. Make at least…um, let me see, FBI, nine states, uh, twelve copies of each; the map, too. Then give the originals back to Sam or Anita. And Frances, on your word of honor, nothing of what you're about to see or hear leaves your lips. It could mean some child's life," the chief told her looking into her eyes.

"Yes, sir, Chief," she said gathering up the paperwork, then straightened up and looked at her boss.

"Move it girl. Get this done now. I want it done as fast as you possibly can. You two pull up chairs and sit down. You're going over this with us step by step."

Frances quietly closed the door and practically ran for the copy room.

"OK, you two, you've sold me, now tell me step by step what led you to this ungodly conclusion."

It took just over an hour with the questions thrown in by both the chief and the captain. They told them how they had played on a simple hunch and turned it into what would probably be the case of the decade, maybe for the entire nation. The chief stood behind his desk and paced as they talked he and the captain through their actions over the last three weeks and especially the last forty-eight spectacular hours.

Frances didn't even knock on the door to deliver the copies. After she gave the originals back to Wilson, the chief told her to package up the remaining dozen copies and send one each to the governors of the eight other states involved and the FBI. "Give me a copy also. Add a cover letter expounding to the others on the expertise of our detectives here and make it for the Governor's signature," the chief told her. "I'll take it over myself along with his package and these two," pointing at the pair of detectives, "if you don't mind captain."

He didn't.

"Get what's his name on the phone, the chief of the governor's security detail and tell him we're on our way over," the chief commanded. "And don't take no for an answer. Tell 'em even if we have to fly wherever he is we'll be on our way. Now get on out there, lady, and do your stuff."

The chief sat back down at his desk. He didn't say anything for a bit, just sat there thinking.

The captain just smiled at his good fortune at having these two detectives in his division. He was thinking about his future when the chief interrupted his train of thought.

"You two have done...I...I don't know what to say. It's amazing is all; just on a hunch you came up with the case of the decade, maybe even of the century. I'm sure you're going to get commendations from just about everyone on the planet for this. I know that's not what you want, but you take them all anyway. You really deserve it. And if we catch these creeps...well, if we catch these creeps there'll probably be the first lynching around here since the 1800's. Maybe with what you've discovered we can prevent another kidnapping somewhere. Maybe save little Wanda and get the people responsible. We're not sure what we'll find, so get the authorization from her parents for DNA samples so we'll have it on hand."

Again, the chief looked down at his desk and just sat there thinking. He looked up, stood up and walked around his desk, thanked them shaking their hands. Then he told the three they could return to their office. "I'll let you know when I'm going to see the governor and you can drop by and pick me up."

As they left they could hear the chief muttering, "Amazing, just amazing…a miracle…"

None of them said a word on the way to their car. Sam drove. Anita just sat silent as did the captain riding shotgun.

Sam finally broke the silence with, "Anita, you believe what just happened?"

"No…no…uh, no I don't," she whispered shaking her head. I don't know how I feel now either. I don't know if I'm happy, mad, concerned or what."

"Yeah, all those things; I feel the same way. Kinda feel like yelling, or smacking a wall, or going out for an all-night binder. Hard to know what our next step is. Is that all or are we still on the case?"

"You're still on it as far as I'm concerned," Captain Daryl Carlisle told them. "Drop me off at the front door, then go and brief the lieutenant and thanks."

"Yes, sir," Sam answered, pulling the car over in front of the building.

"Boy," Wilson said after the captain had left the car and jumped into the shotgun seat, "I wouldn't have counted on that from him, saying we're still on the case."

"No kidding, lady," Sam agreed.

"I guess we just need to go back to the office and wait until we hear from the chief."

"Sounds good to me, if we haven't heard anything by five, I vote we go out for some dinner and wine…I'll splurge."

Wilson turned to look at Sam and said with a grin, "Sure, Sam, I'd like that very much." She turned her head back to the window and slowly the smile began to spread even wider across her face as the case just took a back seat to a night out with Sam.

Chapter Two

Cheyenne, Wyoming, Detective Division, CPD

Captain Daryl Carlisle's Office

The three, Captain Carlisle, Detective First Class Anita Wilson, and Detective First Class Samuel 'Bish' Bishop, were not talking. The conversation had dwindled down and the three were looking at each other, searching for more ideas before the two detectives had to go get the Cheyenne Chief of Police and together, go see the Governor at nine o'clock.

"If either of you two thinks of anything to help us with this case, act on it, then let me know," the captain told them. "You're investigators – investigate. You've already thought outside of the box, so do it some more. Shoot, just throw the box away. Now, get outta here and go get the Chief; come see me when you get back," he told them with a wave of his hand.

They had been going over the events of the days prior, thinking about ways they might get more evidence or information that might lead them to someone responsible for over thirty abductions of two year old girls.

After the brown-noosing show with the governor, photographs, and all, Anita and Bish, after dropping the Chief at his office first. After meeting briefly with the Captain, they returned to their office and both went straight to the coffee pot with Bish pouring, filled their mugs. Both took healthy sips of the black oil-looking fluid and looked at each other.

"Let's get everything we have on the big table and give it all a good going over," Wilson said. "Maybe we missed something."

"We didn't miss nuthin'," Bish retorted.

"Come on fella, we're human, too," Wilson told him with a smile.

"We didn't miss nuthin'," he said again with conviction.

Together they gathered all the paper they'd collected over the past three weeks or so. Everything they had on the current investigation into Wanda Pierce's abduction and the rest. They viewed all the photos first, those for the two abductions in Cheyenne. Bish got up and got his magnifying glass out of his desk and Wilson said to get hers also. They closely studied the photos for over an hour and saw nothing new.

Next they went over their own notes from the Pierce family scene and interviews - again, nothing new.

Now for the printouts of all the data they collected from the national crime data base, stacks of paper, hundreds of pages deep.

"Here, you take, uh, 1965 to 1995 and I'll take the rest," Anita told Bish.

"Okay," he said. "What if anything do you want to specifically look for or just irregularities?"

"Yes to all of it I suppose," she answered him. "Just go over everything…read every word…everything…"

The pair of detectives bent to the task at hand. Lunch was ordered in – a large meat lovers pizza with more coffee. Dinner was delivered also – Chinese – sesame chicken for Anita, and kung pau beef and shrimp for Bish, and a fresh pot of coffee.

Midnight came and Wilson sat back in her chair to stretch and yawned, and noted Bish writing furiously on a small pad of paper. "What'd you find?"

"Nutin' yet," he mumbled, continuing to write. He shuffled pages and wrote more went back to shuffling pages, stopped, and wrote more.

"That ain't nutin' – what'd you find?" she persisted.

"Vans," he answered.

"What?"

"Vans…panel vans or trucks," he said while writing. "I see vans and panel trucks witnesses have seen. Mostly black or white and every time with what appeared to be Wyoming plates; only number was a two, but those seen had blue – Wyoming plates. Wyoming is the only state with blue plates depicting a bronco rider. Nevada is close and so was Arizona, but Wyoming fits as the only number given began with a two and that's Laramie County," he said with conviction looking up at Wilson.

"I'll check my stack," she said and bent to the task.

At two o'clock in the morning, he was head down on the desk asleep. She had finished her search and found that every mention of a witness seeing a suspicious vehicle, it had had blue plates but no numbers noted. She looked up to tell Bish and seeing him asleep, chose not to wake him. She went to the ladies room and to her locker, got her pillow and blanket she kept in the division, and curled up next to her desk. She was out in just a moment.

Next morning found both in the rest rooms brushing their teeth and washing their faces. Back in the Criminal Investigation – Detectives (CID) room, they compared notes and found they had reports of seven vans, all white, and five panel trucks, all black, all with bluish plates. The only one with numbers was the black panel van with a plate number that began '2'.

"I suppose we could run all Wyoming plates beginning with '2' on black panel trucks and see how many we get," Bish supposed aloud.

"I'm thinkin' white vans, too, because they may be the only plate used," Wilson said.

"So you think whoever this is might be using the same plate over and over?"

"Could be; I think, too, that we should do a run on presumed lost or stolen plates since 1965. We just might get lucky."

"I don't think luck is the word I'd use," Bish said, looking at her. "I think we're doing all that we can and doing it well. I think our detective abilities are great and getting better every day. It seems like we learn something new on a daily basis."

She looked up at him and smiled, saying, "Perhaps you're right."

"Yep."

"Come on, then, let's get to those plates." she said, turning for her desk and computer. She entered her passcode and credential numbers and began entering the information she wanted. After about fifteen minutes of dancing her fingers over the keyboard, she hit enter, sat back, and said, "Okay, should take this a while. I've asked it to run a listing of all plates stolen or lost since 1965, from our state, and only those beginning with a duce. It may take a while."

"I'm thinking a bagel and some fresh coffee – you're buying," Bish told her.

"Me…? Why me?" she asked.

"Your turn, toots," he answered.

"You using that 'toots' term is going to get you into trouble someday," she grumpily said, but got up and headed for the door.

"Sesame seed for me, please," Bish called after her.

"Yeah, yeah, yeah…and honey butter."

The two were sipping coffee and nibbling on their bagels when the printer across the room began doing its thing, causing their heads to pop up. Several pages zipped out and then the thing went quiet. The pair looked at each other and he said, "Doesn't seem like much…outta paper maybe?"

"I fed it this morning," Wilson told him, then got up and went to retrieve the pages the laser printer had spit out - six pages worth of information. She counted and said while sitting at her desk, "Twenty-eight plates in fifty-eight years. Okay, partner, we have our work cut out for us. Here," she handed him the first three pages, "let's get started."

"Why do I get fifteen?" he complained. "That means you only get thirteen."

"You made me buy bagels and coffee," she retorted.

"I didn't make you do anything, ditz."

"Short memory."

"What?"

"You have a short memory – I have a gun," she told him with an evil grin.

He gave her a 'don't even think about it' look and bent to his task.

The six pages contained all the information the Department of Motor Vehicles had on each plate. It included the owner's name, last known address, and phone number, how long they had had the plates, and circumstances surrounding the disappearance of the plates. The two detectives began calling the numbers on the list.

Four hours later, the pair left the CID room going for something to eat. The bagels had not lasted long, nor had the coffee.

"Ya want Chinese, Mexican, Italian, or a Happy Meal?" Bish asked as they entered the elevator.

"Give me a minute," Wilson asked.

"Yes, oh nurturing one," Bish said hitting the button for the parking garage.

She gave him 'the' glance and he cracked a wan smile.

"How 'bout going to Wendy's and getting a burger and some of that ice cream stuff they have?" she said.

"I'm in," he answered.

"You're buying."

He smiled.

They added fries. He had a *Bourbon Bacon Burger*. She had a *Junior Burger*. Both had a *Vanilla Frosty*. Bish celebrated with a resounding belch as they walked back to their cruiser.

"You're so crude," Wilson remarked.

"Cave man, baby, cave man," he said with a sly smile.

"Gonna start calling you Grog," she mumbled.

"I like that – Grog Bishop – has a nice ring to it, don't you think?" he commented while climbing into the driver's seat.

"No."

"Why so grumpy?" he asked giving her a sideward glance.

"I'm frustrated."

"'Bout what?"

"We're not getting anywhere with the list we ran this morning."

"Hey, we're trying. We're doing everything we think of. What…what do you want to do?"

She sat thinking while he drove. From time-to-time he'd glance at her, but for the most part kept quiet and his eyes on the road. He began to hum.

"Beatles, released 1967, *When I'm Sixty Four,* written by Paul McCartney," Wilson blurted out while Bish hummed the tune.

"You're full of useless information, huh…" he said.

"Just drive."

They'd been driving around thinking for almost an hour when her head popped up and her hands went to the dashboard.

He looked at her, surprised, and asked, "What?"

"We need to go see each of those people on the list," she answered.

"Wait…what…all of them?" he returned, disbelievingly.

"Yeah; we just might get a break by having a face-to-face with them. Interview the lot. People always say things differently when you're sitting across from them. The phone is so impersonal…we can't see the emotion in their faces. We just might hit on something important. Come on, head for the office. We gotta see the Captain and get the okay for this," she ended with purpose in her tone.

Bish shrugged his shoulders and turned right to head back to the CPD building. Once the Vic was parked, they took the elevator to the Captain's floor and without preamble, walked right into his office. The door was open after all.

"Cap, we gotta request for you," Wilson opened with as the two detectives strolled in and closed the door.

"Will it fit in the budget," Captain Daryl Carlisle asked rhetorically.

"Probably not, but you know us, we'll do it anyway," she answered.

He gave her a stern look, but asked dejectedly, "What have you got?"

She gave him the particulars, explaining their idea to run the listing for the plates beginning with '2', and gave him her thinking on why they needed to see these people face-to-face.

Captain Carlisle looked at Bish, who gave a quick shrug of his shoulders and a slight head tilt, but offered no comment…yet.

"Let me get this straight," the Captain began. "You want me to authorize you to go around the county at tax payer's expense I might add, to interview – how many did you say?"

"Twenty eight," Bish answered quickly.

"…And see if by chance you can get some kind of indication or information on how to pursue the case further…is that right?" the Captain asked looking directly at Wilson.

"That about sums it up, Cap," she answered with a slight smile.

The Captain looked at Bish again and got the same movements as before.

"You're just along for the ride?" the Captain asked Bish.

"Sure…Cap," Bish meekly answered. "I think it's a good plan, Cap. And we can start right here in River City, since nine of 'em are here anyway. Shoot, that's a third of the list and we just might get something concrete without going outta town."

The Captain sat back in his executive chair and looked from one detective to the other, several times, before speaking, then said, "Okay, I'll authorize the ones in town only. ONLY! Got it?"

A pair of 'yes Caps' spilled out from the two detectives.

"Now git; I got work to do," he ordered the pair.

They jumped up and, Bish opening the door, scooted out of the Captain's office, waiving to his secretary as they sped by.

They went to the CID, got their gear, including their extra magazines and combat vests, and were heading out the door when a fellow detective asked what was up.

Bish answered by yelling, "ROAD TRIP!" as they bolted out the door.

They put their gear in the Crown Vic, and with Bish driving again, pulled out of the station house garage and headed to the first customer's home – they didn't want to use the word suspect as yet.

Nine hours later, Bish drove Wilson home and drove to his place to crash. They had garnered nothing new from the first six on the list of nine in the Cheyenne area. Tomorrow they would see the last three, one on the south side on Rawhide Ridge Road, just off Highway 85, and the other two on the northwest side near Western Hills Park off Interstate 25.

Wilson was driving on this round. She'd chosen the southern contact first, and from where they'd filled up the Vic, she got on I-25 south, exited on the I-80 interchange, and turned left, or east. She exited on the Highway 85, or South Greeley Highway. They passed the speedway then turned right onto a dirt two-track into the subdivision. Sadly, no one was home.

The two got back in the Vic and pulled up to park in the shade of two huge elm trees, and waited…and waited…and waited. At twelve thirty, they pulled out, got back on Highway 85, and went north, going through a Sonic drive through. Bish had a crispy chicken sandwich and Wilson had a three piece crispy chicken dinner. Both had fries and a coke. They drove back to the shade of the elm trees to eat and watch.

"We'll give them another hour then head north, "Wilson said. "Wonder if they're on vacation or something."

"I wondered the same thing," Bish agreed. "Want me to go ask a neighbor?"

"Nah, they might give the bad guys a call and tell 'em to stay away, you know, give them a heads up or something?" she answered.

"I suppose," he conceded.

"They're here," she said in a spooky voice and pointing. Sure enough, a white panel van was pulling into the driveway in front of the home's garage. The two detectives looked at each other with surprised looks. A white panel van was one of the two vehicles described by witnesses to the abductions. They looked back at the van and watched as a rather large, grossly obese man climbed out. He waddled into the house having a hard time climbing the stairs.

"Makes me wanna go on a diet right now," Bish said with a chuckle.

"Man, he's a whopper, huh," Wilson observed.

"Yeah, but I'd throw him back," he deadpanned.

Wilson exploded in laughter. She just couldn't help it as the comment caught her off guard. Once she'd calmed down, Bish asked, "What 'cha wanna do?"

"Come on, let's go talk to the guy," she answered and opened her door.

As they were walking up to the driveway, Bish stopped and pointed at the license plate on the van…it began with '2'. Both froze and looked at the house, especially the windows. Wilson motioned to return to the Vic and together they backed up to the sidewalk and rushed to the Crown Victoria.

Getting in, Bish was the driver as he had the better skills. She would be the first to admit that. He started the beast and slowly pulled away down the block and parked under a stand of cottonwood trees shading the street.

Wilson was already on the radio wanting to talk to the Captain. He came over the net a moment later and asked what was up.

"You know that license plate…on a white panel van?" she asked.

"Yeah, what about it?" he answered.

"We're looking at it."

Silence.

"Cap…you there?" she asked. "Cap…?"

"Yeah, hang on a sec," he told her. After a moment longer he said, "You really have eyes on it?"

"Yes, sir, just down the block from us on the left," she answered. "It's on a white panel van of all things," she repeated.

"Holy…where are you?" he asked.

"We're at the address down south off Highway 85, in that housing area south of the speedway. We saw one man get out of the van and go into the house. I have no clue how many others might be inside the place."

"Okay, standby there and just watch. Don't do anything rash unless they start something, understand?"

"Will do Cap - you sending the backup out to us?"

"Already on their way; you keep watch, out."

The pair sat and did just that, watched the house. The big guy came out again, and went to the passenger side of the van. They heard the sliding door open and could see his feet moving around on the other side. They watched as the guy set plastic bags of something on the ground. It looked as if he was cleaning the back of the van.

"Wonder what he's really doing?" Bish said. "Doesn't look like groceries, does it?"

"Nah, looks like cleaning stuff and bags of trash to me," Anita said.

They continued watching and after several more minutes, saw the guy's motions closing the door and picking up the left over bags of trash and cleaning materials. As he came around the van, they could see a pink blanket with bears on it.

"That's Wanda's blanket over his arm," Bish said.

"Oh, Lord in Heaven," Anita said. "Call it in and we'll go in after that. Gotta take this guy down…he's gonna be a handful, huh."

"'Fraid so, sugar," Bish agreed. "Got all your mags ready?"

"Need to put them on my belt is all…you?"

"I'm good to go. Want me to get the shotgun?"

"What do you think? We're just going in to ask about the plate…right?"

"That sounds good. Let's do it." He had called in the fact that they were going to go take a look. That hadn't gone over well with the Captain.

They walked up to the driveway, and took a look in the van. It was clean as a whistle. Bish went up the front steps first, Wilson following, her hand on her weapon's grip.

Bish looked at her and she gave a nod and he knocked on the door, "Police, we need to ask you a few questions about a missing license plate?" No answer.

He knocked again and heard and felt the big man coming to the door saying, "Hold your horses…I'm coming, I'mmm coming." It was just a moment later the big man, smiling, opened the door and said, "Oh, hello officer." Bish was holding his creds out. "What can I do for you and your friend?"

"We're investigating lost or stolen license plates and you had reported one missing several years ago, right?"

"Yes, golly that was a few years ago. It was on my last van, a black one. I got new plates though, they're on the new van over there," he said pointing.

"Yes, sir, we know that. What we're wondering is if you by chance had seen anything unusual or out of place the day the plates were taken."

"Hang on and let me think…that was a while ago and my brain ain't what it used to be…my waist line, too," he said with a chuckle. I don't recall anything out of the ordinary that day. She was looking at the van wondering if it was new."

"Who was?" Anita asked.

"Helen from next door," he said, pointing to the south. "She saw the van had no plates and wondered if it was new. I came out with the baby as she was about to come up to the door and she asked. I told her no, it was the same one I always had and she said the plates were gone. I went and looked and they were gone, just like she said. I just figured they maybe had fallen off – ain't never had that happen - but saw someone had put the screws back in the holes. That's when I went inside and called the cops…er…police."

"But you didn't see anything before you noticed the screws," Bish commented.

"No, not at all, sorry," the man said.

"May we come in and get you to sign another statement for our reports? Our captain would want that, please," Wilson asked.

"Sure, come on in," he said and backed into the house. "I gotta get out of the way so you two can get in. I'm a bit big you know."

"Makes sense," Bish agreed. Wilson was doing all she could not to bust a gut. They followed the man into his home and found themselves in a small living room with a couch, an easy chair, coffee table and a television, wood floors and no air conditioning.

"Y'all can have a seat if you want, I'll be right back…my meds are working on me and I need to take another leak. Sorry," he apologized.

"No problem, sir, we understand," Wilson said, then, "We'll get the paperwork ready for you to sign."

"Sure, be back in a minute," and he turned and went down a hallway to their left. They were looking towards the back of the house where there was a small dining room and a kitchen.

Bish got Wilson's attention and pointed to the baby blanket on the arm of the couch. He used his phone and took a photo of it. She looked at it for a moment, then, looked up at the hallway, and had the look on her face, the one saying they were in a situation and she meant business. Bish slowly placed his hand on his weapon as he knew the look and got ready for anything. But, they heard the toilet flush and a few moments later, heard the man coming down the hall.

"Whew…that was close," the fat man said coming back into the front room. "Now, what can I tell you officers that I haven't told the police before?"

"Sir, exactly when did you notice the plates missing?" Bish quickly asked.

"I didn't, actually, like I said, a neighbor thought I'd gotten a new truck since it didn't have a plate so she came over and asked me about it," the fat man answered.

"How did you have the plates attached to the vehicle?" Wilson asked.

"You know, those screws or bolts…it was whatever came on the truck," he answered. "I think there were two of them."

"So the plates could have fallen off then?" Bish inquired.

"Nah, I don't think so," the fat man said, rubbing his unshaven chin. "Those hold pretty well and I ain't never had one fall off before. Anyway, if it had fallen off, why were the screws still there?"

Wilson smiled at the guy and pointing at the blanket, asked, "You have a baby?"

"Nah, I was watching Helen's three-year-old yesterday – Helen lives next door – she's the one who noticed the plate actually. Anyway, the little tyke, Shirley, left her blanket in the truck when we got back from McDonald's. She likes the ice cream cups. Anyway, when we got back, I took her to her mom last night and she'd left the blanky. She's done that before…toys, too."

Bish noticeably relaxed Wilson saw and she did as well.

"You babysit often for her?" Wilson asked.

"Yeah; Helen's a waitress and when she has the nightshift I sometimes watch the little one. Usually it's her boyfriend Daniel, but if they're both working, I get the nod. She's a sweet little kid. She cries sometimes when she misses her mum, but good little kid overall."

"Okay, sir, I think that's all we need on the plates," Bish said holding out his hand to shake the fat man's. "Would you sign this, please? If we think of anything else, may we call?"

"Sure thing, come back anytime you like," the big man said as Bish held the papers for the man to sign.

Bish turned and held the door open for Wilson, who said her goodbye's as she stepped out. Back at their cruiser, they looked at each other and she said, "What are the odds that a man with a van with lost plates has a next door neighbor with a three-year-old baby girl, and that baby has the same exact blanket as Wanda Pierce?"

"About ten-zillion gazillion to one I'm thinkin'," Bish answered quietly looking back at the house. "It don't add up, do it?"

"No, it don't, partner," Wilson agreed. "I'll call it in and we'll run his prints off the paperwork tonight when we get back. Let's make tracks."

Wilson called the captain and said, "Not our guy, close, but no cigar, Cap. He was on the up-and-up and everything's cool, well, almost everything, checked out so go ahead and recall the backup."

"What do you mean, 'almost'?" the captain asked.

"We didn't talk to the mother of the baby, Cap, she lives next door."

"Go talk to the neighbor…now. Did he give you a name?"

"Yes, Cap; Helen."

"Go talk to Helen, now," and he hung up the phone.

"Dad-gum, he sounded a bit miffed, don't you think?" Bish said as he pulled into another driveway to turn around.

"He did sound like it," Wilson agreed. "Was she home?"

"I think so. Looked over there and saw a car. We'll see," he answered as he pulled into the driveway behind the car, a white Chevy coup.

They went to the door, knocked, and a pleasant strawberry-blond woman with blue eyes, slender, and holding a baby in her arms answered the door. "Yes, may I help you?"

"Sorry to bother you and the baby, ma'am, but we're officers from the Cheyenne Police Department. I'm Detective First Class Anita Wilson, and this is my partner, Detective Sam Bishop. Are you Helen?"

"Yes, what's going on?" Helen asked, looking past the pair trying to see if something was wrong.

We're investigating lost or stolen license plates, and your neighbor," she said pointing next door, "lost his a while back. Actually we believe they were stolen. He says you were the one who noticed his plates were missing. Do you remember that day?"

"Oh, yes, I had gone over to pick up Shirley after work and noticed no plates on the van and wondered if it was a new one."

"Nice to have a babysitter right next door, huh," Bish said.

"Yes, he's such a nice man, and loves the baby," she added.

"Where do you work, ma'am?" Bish asked.

"I'm a waitress at the Bent Horseshoe Cafe, off 85 up north, about twenty blocks from here. Good food if you're hungry," she said with a smile, giving the place a plug.

"Just might take you up on that," Bish said with a smile of his own.

"Ma'am, is your husband home today?" Wilson asked.

"No – actually we're not married – he's an apprentice electrician and works some funny hours…depends on the job. Right now, Dan's wiring a hew hotel being built up near Frontier Park, just off Interstate Twenty-five. He probably won't get home until late. I can have him call you if you want."

"No, that's fine, I was just curious," Wilson said. "We'll be leaving now, thank you very much for the information."

"Yes, ma'am, thank you," Bish added. The two detectives went back to their cruiser and pulled out before speaking to one another.

"Well, she confirmed everything the big guy said," Bish commented, turning out on Highway 85 and going to the Bent Horseshoe Cafe for dinner.

"I guess we miss-read that one," Wilson commented. "I can't believe we found a guy with a van and the baby with the same blanket as Wanda Pierce. Just blows all the averages outta the window. Where to?"

"No kidding to answer the first question," Bish agreed. "The Bent Horseshoe Cafe…I'm hungry."

"And you're buying."

"Figures."

"That's for the way you've treated me today."

"Me! What'd I do?"

She just pointed and he drove.

The cafe was a nice place, with what appeared to be homemade plywood tables, tastefully made and stained, then covered with several layers of poly. The chairs were high-backed affairs with seat and back cushions. The walls were made to give the impression one was entering a warm, library-type environment. Lighting was subdued but adequate. Nostalgic western music was playing in the background.

"Nice place," Bish observed out loud as they were seated by a host wearing jeans, a snap-button western shirt, a bandanna, and cowboy boots.

"Yes it is," the host told the pair. "I enjoy working here. The atmosphere is superb. What may I get you to drink today?"

"Iced tea," Wilson said, smiling.

"Coffee…black…strong," Bish said with a scowl, still stewing over Wilson's treatment of him over the last hour or so.

"Very well, I'll return in a moment," the young man said. "Here's your menus; if I may, the Irish Stew is the special today, and is the best and what I recommend."

"That's what I'll have," Bish said, handing the menu back to the youngster.

"I'd like to review the menu," Wilson said with a grin.

"I'll return shortly then," and the host turned and left the two alone.

"You're right, nice place," Wilson agreed with Bish's earlier observation.

"I'd like my man-cave to look like this when I retire," Bish said.

"Where would you build something like this?" Wilson asked.

"I'm thinkin' northern Arkansas, somewhere in the Ozarks," he answered.

"How big will the house be?"

"The one I've designed will be about forty-five hundred square feet or so, maybe a little more. It'll have five bedrooms, three full baths, the basement will be a full basement and will have two of the bed rooms and one bathroom, and that's where my man-cave may be. That's not firm yet as I may have a second floor just as large and put the cave up there. It'll depend on the scenery I'll see around my home site."

"Sounds too big; you gonna clean it?"

"Nah, I'll have someone do it."

"That takes money."

"By then it won't be a problem."

"Wow, you hit the lotto or something? You can't afford something like that on a cop's salary."

He looked at her and said in a deadpanned voice, "You'd be surprised what's in my portfolio."

The host was back with their drinks and asked, "Have you chosen, ma'am?"

"Yes, I'll have the Caesar salad and garlic toast please," Wilson answered.

"Very good, I'll place your orders now and I hope your dinner with us will be memorable," he said and turned away.

Bish watched him leave, and once out of ear shot said, "I'll have a real nice nest-egg when I retire from the force. It should cost me three-fifty or so to build and with the extras I'll add, when I'm totally through with the build, it'll probably be marketable at five or five-fifty, and with the land, maybe closer to a million."

"Gee-whiz, what kind of extras you putting in that place?" Wilson asked.

"They'll be a gun room; not your usual kind, but it'll also be a safe room, one capable of making it through a tornado, and secret enough a burglar won't be able to find it. I'll have my guns, ammo, and reloading equipment in there, all in one place.

It'll have its own power supply, own phone line, and lighting, separate from the main house supply. It'll also have room enough for emergency supplies and they'll be a rack for tools, like pry-bars, an axe, shovel…that kind of stuff."

"Sounds more like a Fort Knox to me," Wilson said with a surprised look on her face.

"Yeah, I guess. If I have enough extra cash, I'll put in a hundred-yard underground shooting range - a two-lane deal with a good air filtration system."

"Oh my gosh…you're kidding…"

"Nope. That's what I've designed."

"Are you adding a family to that equation?"

"Don't know yet. I haven't decided on that, not to mention I haven't found the right gal yet, one that'll like what I've designed and how I want to live."

"That brings up another question: how do you want to live?"

"You know, quiet; peaceful; in a nice environment with trees, maybe near or on a lake if there's one up in the mountains. I don't want to live in the flats, like here. I don't want to live near a big city either. The town I'll live near will have less than thirty-thousand folks, probably less. And my closest neighbor will be a mile or two away. I want to be able to sit out on my back deck or patio and listen to nature without hearing a train going by or an interstate or major highway nearby. I want to be able to look out my library/man cave and get inspiration for what I'll be writing at the time. I want to be able to sit outside and sip a nice scotch and do what it says in Psalm forty-six, verse ten, where it says, "Be still and know that I am God." Me and God got a lot to talk about."

"Wow, I never figured you on being a Grizzly Adams type. But, it does sound nice. I like the peacefulness just listening to what you're describing. I could live in a place like that, too," Wilson said, looking at her tea.

"You know, I've been a cop for a long time and seen a lot of ugly stuff. When I retire, I don't want to see that or even think about it too much…you know?"

"Yeah, I think I do."

He noticed the server coming with their dinner and motioned for Wilson to take note. She moved her tea out of the way and the server asked who had the Cesare salad, and she lifted her hand. The server placed her salad in front of her and set her garlic bread to the side, and served Bish his large bowl of Irish Stew, and set more bread to the side for him.

"Thank you," they both said in unison.

"You're welcome, and please enjoy your dinner. If you need anything, just let us know," the youngster said and left them to eat.

Bish used the spoon they'd given him and took a mouthful of his stew. "Wow, this is great, here, you should try this," he said sliding his bowl towards Wilson. "I just might order another batch to go."

She took her spoon and lifted a small portion to her mouth. "Mmm, that is good. Maybe I'll have that next time."

"How's the Caesar?"

"Very good; I'm surprised. They're usually dry to me, but this one is moist and fresh - seems like they just made it from scratch."

"Beg your pardon, ma'am, I overheard, but they do make it from scratch every time," a passing waiter told her.

"Wow, thank you," Wilson said. "This is good." The guy smiled as he walked away.

"This stuff is good," Bish reiterated. "I'm gonna put this place on my list of places to frequent."

"I think I am as well, partner," Wilson agreed.

Bish wiped his mouth with his napkin and looking at Wilson afterwards, asked, "So, what's our next step, oh detective extraordinaire?"

"We go take a look at the others and clear them...or maybe find the culprit doing this. I still feel sick when I think about what someone might be doing to that child, not to mention the others that are still missing."

"Yeah, makes me want to break someone in half when I catch 'em."

"Positive thinking…I like that."

Bish grunted and asked, "What's positive?"

"That you're gonna catch them. That's positive, right?"

"Yeah, but I'm gonna break 'em up when I get 'em."

"Glad you're on my side," Wilson said under her breath.

The host brought their check and Bish grabbed it, added a healthy tip for the host and the server and told the host they would most certainly be back and to compliment the chef on the meal.

They got up and left the place with Bish driving once again. They turned north and went back to the CID, did a follow up with the Captain, did their paperwork and left for the day.

Chapter Three

el Jefe

As always, the new kid screamed for her mommy, incessantly. She cried. Refused to eat, but did take a bottle. It was understandably strange that the kidnapper placed the child in a room decked out for a little girl. Copious amounts of toys, blankets, and nice clothes. Two-year-old Wanda didn't know about that, however. All she wanted was her mother.

One wall of her room was a huge mirror. Behind it sat a woman and the kidnapper. The woman was a nurse maid, Isabella, Issy for short and very strict in her manner and care of the children. She was the teacher. Everything the children learned came from her. They never saw anyone else their entire existence until the day of days as the man put it.

They were sitting in easy chairs for the purpose of watching and viewing their captives. Yes, plural, captives. There were ten rooms in the complex, and each held a captive. Each captive stayed in a room two years and then *graduated* to the next level. Therefore, Wanda would be moving to another room when she turned four, six, and so on.

Each room was furnished and stocked for the age of the child. As the child became older, more educational information was added. The captives even had an open courtyard that Salinas called the terrarium, which they visited twice a week. It held a swing, a small wading pool the younger children could splash around in, and a multitude of outdoor toys for their use. The older children more often selected books to read while outside. There were small trees, grass, a sandy stretch of ground, and a small waterfall fixture that fed the wading pool. Turtles and rabbits acted as the pets for the children. It was a beautiful biosphere for his captives.

What the captives didn't know was the entire complex was underground. Skylights furnished their day and nights. Each room was sound-proofed, so while Wanda screamed and cried for her mommy, the other occupants would not be disturbed.

The new children always reacted like little Wanda. They would scream and cry for several weeks, then slowly begin to calm…and to forget. By the six month they only had fleeting memories of their fathers. By a year or so, even their mothers became momentary glimpses of memory. By the second year, they began to call the nurse maid mother, since she was the only other adult they had contact with.

"She'll make a good specimen Enrique," the woman caretaker said to the master of the house. "She will be a beauty when I finish with her. She will want you with a fervor I promise," she said, eyes wide with the thought of what the man or his son would do with the child in eighteen years or so.

"Yes, Isabella, she'll be a fine one, I agree," Enrique Salinas approved. He, too, eyed the little one with a faraway look, knowing what she would become in almost two decades. He rose from his easy chair he frequently sat in to view his prizes and said a final word to the caretaker, "Issy, you have done well once again."

"Thank you, el Jefe," Isabella replied almost reverently.

"I'll be in the gym if you need anything," Enrique said and turned for the stairwell.

"Yes, el Jefe," Isabella answered.

Enrique Salinas, a well-educated and wealthy business man, was accustomed to getting his way. His staff, as noted by Isabella, called him el Jefe, The Boss. His businesses included trucking and shipping, information technology, several cleaning businesses, and four restaurants in and around the Denver, Colorado area. The cleaning and restaurant dealings were for the most part fronts for illegal alien transfer. His trucking interests brought the illegals into the area, and through his businesses, they were trained and shipped out, or in other words, sold or auctioned off to others for slave labor or worse. Once they were out of his area of operations, he forgot about them - no longer his problems.

Salinas was an illegal himself, but was able to get viable papers showing citizenship, of course illegally. He was smart and excelled in schools, even college. He'd earned a Master's in Business Administration. He paid for his schooling with the proceeds from his criminal activities. After graduating from college, his interest was piqued by passing conversation with a criminal acquaintance regarding human trafficking. Much money could be had in that very lucrative yet dangerous business, and he studied the in's and out's enough to begin operations near Denver, branching into Wyoming and other nearby states.

Several years and a bank full of money, he was sitting on the terrace of his home near Cheyenne, Wyoming, when he had the idea. He didn't want to be married, tied down that is, but wanted an heir or two. His idea was to capture a suitable young lady and train her to become his, what he called his receptor - the mother of his child. If she didn't work out, oh well, there were many others to choose from. Over time, he improved upon his idea, finally settling on the process of acquiring a young female and raising her to possibly be the mother of a child of his.

He would need a facility to house the child – no – children. He would select several and house and train them. When they became of age, he would attempt to father a child with them. Failures would be sold or disposed of. He had many byers since the market was ripe. Still, the facility needed to be hidden. Underground was the likely place for something like he was designing in his mind. It would need to be completely self-sufficient. Each room would have to be a small home unto itself. He needed a designer, an architect…

Salinas was twenty-four when he began that project. He was forty-seven now, and had one son that he considered his heir and kept. Other children he'd fathered and found to be unsuitable were disposed of along with their mothers. Others, both child and mother, were sold, discarded like a company's product should be. That was the sociopathic thought process of Enrique

Salinas. The women were, when he was ready to discard them, sold to buyers out of the country, or disposed of outside of the United States usually in Mexico. He didn't risk having an American-born female discarded in-country. Although he did have a method of disposing of those that worked for him and did not set well with him. A large concrete pad to the northeast of the home proper was a cover of sorts. He would dispose of bodies there using a heavy lift earth mover when necessary.

Occupants ranged from two to twenty years of age. At age twenty, they were 'used' by Salinas. If impregnated, they would be cared for during their pregnancy by the nurse maid. If medical issues arose, the subject was terminated and usually disposed of off the coast of Mexico in an area known for its abundant population of Dungeness crabs, and lesser known population of Great White sharks. These creatures rarely left scraps.

The facility itself stretched for over two-hundred meters, almost 630 feet, all underground. It enclosed ten self-contained small suites, complete with a bedroom befitting the age of the occupant, a bathroom, and a great room, also befitting the age of the occupant. There was the open terrarium on the south side of the complex. It held grass, trees, boulders, a small creek and pond, replete with fish, and was an open-air affair where the captives, under supervision of the caretaker of course, were able to spend time in an outside environment.

The captives were educated…to a certain degree. Most of their education focused on basic educational levels. It was enough to keep their minds engaged while growing up in a method which lead to one thing and one thing only - to be a mother of Salinas' child. They were taught they were special.

Educated from early on that they were unique, thus the reasoning behind their special living arrangements. They knew they were being raised for one purpose, and they were treated like royalty during their time in captivity. By the time they were fifteen years old, they knew what they were being raised for, and welcomed it! They were trained in the pleasures of a man and woman, and knew what was coming for them on their twentieth birthdays. And they were excited about it, more than willing to be what they were being trained for. By the time they were in their late teens, they were boiling with anticipation. Their willingness assured by their training from Isabella, hours and hours of training for one thing and one thing only. At age twenty, the captives were so primed, that it was in their thoughts every waking moment until the day of the event.

Salinas finished his workout, and eased his tired body into his hot tub. He activated the jets, and relaxed. He let the soothing, foaming heat wash over him. He soaked for a half-hour, then got out and stepped into his sauna, which was a sizzling one-hundred twenty-five degrees. Before he sat on the bench, he ladled two full scoops of water onto the peridotite rocks which immediately gave off a hissing steam cloud. He took a deep breath of the hot steam and sat back on a spot on the bench which he'd covered with a folded towel.

He picked up a paperback book he was reading, *Conan the Barbarian*, by Robert E. Howard, and began where he'd left off. He enjoyed reading while taking a sauna. It was no time at all when he began sweating profusely. He used another hand towel to wipe the sweat from his face from time-to-time. After about twenty minutes, he stepped out of the sauna and took a medium heat shower that lasted more than fifteen minutes.

Feeling thoroughly refreshed, he dressed in a pair of old jeans, a flannel shirt, donned his work boots and hat, then left the gym and went out into his back yard to do the day's yardwork he'd planned. He enjoyed the simple pleasure of mowing or trimming a lawn and the hedges surrounding the space.

Promptly at six in the early evening, he was approached by his valet. "Yes, Sims, time for dinner?"

"Yes, el Jefe," Sims answered.

"What is the menu this evening?" Enrique Salinas asked his attendant.

"Ribeye steak in a dry wine sauce, twice-baked potato with cheddar cheese and fresh bacon bits, Batavia and leaf lettuce with carrot spears, tomato, cucumber and toasted Cremini mushroom flakes. Would your palate care for a bottle of wine with dinner this evening Jefe?"

Salinas thought a moment, then said, "Yes, a bottle of chilled Shiraz from Australia would do nicely I think."

"Very good, senior," Sims said turning for the kitchen.

Salinas took off his work gloves and hat, and went to his master suite, took a quick shower and dressed in khaki trousers, a light silk shirt, and Nisolo Huarache sandals. He left his suite and strolled through his home to the dining room.

Sims stood behind Salinas' seat, and as el Jefe entered the dining room, pulled the chair out for the boss.

"Thank you, Sims," Enrique said sitting down.

Sims handed the evening paper to Enrique and asked, "When would you like to be served, sir?"

"Give me fifteen minutes, please, but go ahead and bring me a glass of wine."

"Very well, sir, right away," Sims answered and turned for the chilled wine. He popped the cork and let the wine breath for a few moments, then poured a sip into a crystal Bordeaux glass. He stepped over to el Jefe, handing him the cork, which the man smelled. Salinas set the cork on the table after an approving nod, then Sims handed him the glass. Salinas spun the wine in the glass and smelled the aroma, keeping his mouth open during the inhale. Nodding his approval again, he took a small sip of the wine and savored both the taste and the aroma.

"This will do nicely, thank you, Sims," he said with approval.

"Very good, sir, I'll serve dinner in nine minutes," Sims said while pouring five or six ounces of the wine in the crystal glass, then sat the bottle back into the ice and left for the kitchen.

Salinas scanned the paper and noted the mentioning of the Amber Alert for the missing child, Wanda Pierce. He smiled and thought to himself, *They have nothing to worry about; she'll be well taken care of.* The sociopath in him smiled and turned the pages to the comic section, a section he jokingly called the educational page.

Nine minutes later, Sims rolled in the serving tray and served el Jefe's dinner. Everything was cooked to perfection. The salad was crisp and flavorful. The steak melted in his mouth, the potato, hardy and dripping with melted butter. And the sips of wine interspaced throughout the meal were spot on.

After finishing his repast, Sims cleared the used dishes and utensils, refilled the wine glass, and left the dining room, leaving el Jefe to his wine and paper. After ten minutes or so, Salinas pulled a cell phone out and called the private school where his son, Roberto, was being educated, and spoke with the boy for almost an hour. This he did almost every evening. They talked about sports, namely European football, and who had the best opportunity of winning the cup, and what was going on in each other's lives.

This week, the boy had begun guitar lessons along with a new art class, and a new math class that he especially enjoyed. Enrique was happy his son understood and enjoyed mathematics. It would do him well in his future as the el Jefe when Salinas retired.

Enrique told the boy about the new friend he'd brought home for him. This excited the boy as he was allowed to play with the younger captives in the terrarium. Enrique enjoyed sitting behind the great slab of mirrored glass watching as the children played together and explored the terrarium.

"Father, when am I be able to come home for a visit," the youngster asked his father.

"Soon, young one, soon," Enrique answered.

"I will be excited to see the new child. What color hair does this one have, father?" the boy asked.

"She is blonde, with blue eyes," was the answer.

"Ah, she'll be a real beauty to be in the future, yes?"

"Yes, my son," Salinas answered. "I have to go now. I'll call again tomorrow. Goodnight."

"Goodnight father."

Salinas ended the call, then took the phone, bent it in half on the table's edge and pulled the pieces apart. The top enclosure and screen assembly he set aside. The circuit board, he bent it back and forth until it separated in the middle. The battery and bottom enclosure he sat aside with the other pieces got up and threw the circuit board pieces into the fire burning in the fireplace. He watched as it disintegrated. He would use a new phone tomorrow night. He chuckled while watching the flames burning a burner phone. He turned and went into his den and worked until eleven, then went to bed.

Chapter Four

Cheyenne, Wyoming

Wyoming is well known for its crimson, golden, and red-orange sunrises and sunsets. But the old naval adage, "Red sky in morning, sailor take warning, red sky at night, sailor's delight," didn't apply to Wyoming. Rarely did a red sky at dawn, such as the one this day, bring a foreboding for the day's weather. Bish stood on his back porch, which faced east, and admired the brilliant sunrise, and sipped his coffee.

"Only God can paint like that," he said aloud. "Thank you, Lord, for another perfect sunrise." He shook his head and turned to go back inside. He threw some bread into the toaster, and some frozen sausage patties into the microwave. Both would be done about the same time. He topped off his coffee from the pot, and waited. The toast popped so he pulled it and put a light coat of margarine over the slice. The microwave beep about then and he opened it and placed the two pieces of sausage on the toast. Breakfast in less than four minutes - beat that Mac.

He sat with his breakfast, coffee, and morning paper, took a healthy bite of his make-shift breakfast sandwich, and opened the paper. The headline was the same old stuff – politics – nothing that really interested him. He pulled the sports page and noted the Rockies had won again. They just may go to the series this season. There was always hope. He liked the Rockies and went to a game in Denver once in a while. He'd attended a few Broncho's games also, but liked baseball much more. Professional football was getting cost prohibitive anyway.

Turning to the funnies, he chuckled a few times while finishing his meal and coffee.

Dumping his paper towel and plate into the trashcan, he went upstairs and shaved, brushed his teeth, and jumped into the shower for a hot one. He stood under the stream, hands on the wall, letting the water cascade over his shoulders and down his back. The shower lasted twenty minutes. He dried, got dressed, checked his weapons, and headed to work.

Anita was already there, coffee made, and a computer printout in her hands. "Whus at?" he asked as he strode into the shop.

"Yeah, I feel fine and slept well, how about you?" Wilson shot back.

"Like a log as usual," he smugly answered.

"I fine-tuned the listing of the April kidnappings," she explained about the printout. "I added hair and eye color, place taken, and ethnic background. Odd, there are no Hispanics at all - Blacks, Caucasians, American Indians, and Orientals, but no Hispanics taken."

"Wonder if the kidnappers are Hispanic then?" Bish asked.

"Yep, wondering the same thing, buster," she answered. "I sorted the data by each and nothing unusual came up. Black hair, blonde, red heads, brunettes doesn't seem to matter, just the when – the kid's birth month and birthday are all that appear to be of importance. I wonder why?"

"Yeah, if we could answer that, perhaps we could solve this whole unsavory mess," Bish agreed. "The other known is this person has never taken a Hispanic. Does that mean he or she is a Hispanic or just doesn't like Hispanics? Maybe has a prejudice against them or something like that?"

"Or, considering *Occam's Razor*, whoever this is, probably a Hispanic, doesn't want to take from his or her own race," Wilson said, assuming the easiest answer was the best one to look at.

"Yeah, ol' *Occam's* philosophy is correct more often than not," Bish commented.

"I say we can assume, and I really hate to do that, assume that is, but I think we can assume the kidnapper is a Hispanic person, sex unknown right now but in all likelihood male, probably around twenty-five to thirty-five years old," Wilson presumed.

"Probably male, but could well be a disgruntled mother, possibly a woman that lost a child and is taking others to make up for it or something."

"That is a real possibility," Wilson agreed looking up at him and nodding.

"We need to write all this stuff down and share it with the gang. I'll get a pad and start taking notes," Bish said, bending down and digging in a drawer for a legal pad. He took out several pencils also, and taking one with a good point, began writing: probably male; mid-twenties to late thirties; possibility a Hispanic since no Hispanics taken; remote possibility a disgruntled woman; all abductees taken in April, between dates of twentieth and twenty-sixth; always on a Wednesday, unknown reason why.

"We need to list cities and states again?" Bish asked.

"Nah already got that on a list somewhere in here," Wilson answered waving a dismissive hand over their stack of paper.

"Too many unanswered questions…" Bish mumbled.

"Enough to bring on a massive headache," Wilson said.

"Don't want one."

"Me neither."

"I need a beer."

"Will coffee do?"

"Yep."

"Back in a minute."

Bish looked up as Wilson got up and left the room to go get fresh coffee. He watched her hip action as she left the room. He shook his head and went back to his notes, thought better on that and got up, stood next to the window and gazed outside. He wasn't really focusing on anything, just looking. He quickly got that thousand yard stare, his mind racing with all the information that didn't really lead to anywhere or anything concrete. The license plates and that number two, Laramie County, Wyoming, meant something. The black and white vans did also. But all their information together just brought on more questions and not enough answers.

Anita came in right then and handed Bish a steaming Styrofoam cup of black coffee. He said thanks, then took a healthy swig of the blistering brew, then poured the fluid into his travel mug.

"Stuff's hotter than the black top in July," Bish commented.

"Fresh, just came out of a fresh-brewed pot I made," Wilson muttered. "You see anything new in the mix from your standpoint?"

"Nah, just more confusion's all. Lot of answers but all to the wrong questions, you know what I mean?"

"Yeah, I know. We need to keep digging…maybe we'll find something that'll open this thing up some."

"We need them to make a mistake."

"No, we can't take that chance since we'd have to wait so long for the next grab if we're right about the timeframe. We gotta sink our teeth into this and dig. We got everything from everyone else who's had one of these abductions?"

"Yep, everything we've asked for."

"Okay, go back and contact 'em all again and ask for their guesses, what they think they saw and their gut feelings. Talk to all of the investigators also and ask them the same questions. Tell 'em all to put it in writing and get it to us as soon as they can – email, fax - whatever. Maybe from all of that…I don't know, but maybe we'll get something. I'm gonna go see the Captain and see if he'll let me have another team. Perhaps four of us can make something of all this. Get to it," Wilson directed.

Bish nodded his understanding and turned for his desk. She watched as he moved heavily to his desk and plopped down in his chair. His head hung low, chin almost on his chest then, she saw him take a great breath, hold it for a moment then let it out slowly. He grabbed the phone and a stack of note paper and started punching numbers. She shook her head at his determination and turned for the Captain's office.

Captain Carlisle was sitting at his desk reading a report when he heard the knock on his office door. He looked up, saw Anita, and waved her in. "Howdy, kid, have a seat – what's up?" he asked her as she sat down.

"Bish and I need help," she began. After almost thirty minutes of explaining, the captain continued staring at her.

"What do you need?" he asked.

"Just some help, a fresh set, or two of eyes to look at what we have and see if we're missing something," Wilson answered.

Carlisle sat there thinking for a few minutes, looked at the report on his desk and said, "Here's what I'll do," he said looking at her. "Donaldson and Hicks just got done with a case and are free for the moment. I'll have them join you on this. But, it's only temporary. If something comes up, I'll pull them."

"That's fair enough, Cap, thanks," Wilson said, standing.

"Whoa, there detective," Carlisle said, holding up a hand. "Have you coordinated everything with the feds?"

"Every scrap we get goes to them, you know that," Wilson responded. "Have they said anything to you? Have they come up with anything at all?"

"Answers 'no' to both," he answered. "I'll give them another call and see if they've got anything new. I'll let you know."

She nodded and turned for the door.

"Anita," the Captain called out, "you guys are doing a great job. I hope you get this or these guys."

"Thanks, Cap," Anita said and left his office.

Captain Daryl Carlisle shook his head, lifted his phone receiver and punched in Hicks' extension number, filled him in on his and Davidson's new temporary assignment and hung up. He knew the two would be over with Wilson's team in a heartbeat.

Detective Michael Hicks was waiting as Detective First Class Anita Wilson reached the top of the stairs to her office.

"Hey, Anita, Cap said Pete and I are to join you on a temporary assignment…what's up?"

"That abduction case - Wanda Pierce - we've discovered a bunch of strange things and need some more eyes to look at what we've got and see if we're missing something. I think a couple sets of new eyes on the material we've got might see something we've missed."

"I'm in," Mike said. "Pete'll be here shortly. Where do you want us?"

"Come on in," Anita said with a smile. She opened the door and seeing Bish look up said, "We got Mike and Pete for a while. Temporarily that is."

Bish stood as Mike entered and said, "That's great. Glad to have them to help out." He shook Mike's hand.

"Pete'll be here in a bit," Detective Michael Hicks told Bish.

"I'm here," the speech came from the door as Detective Peter Donaldson walked in. "Got your message Mike, what's up?"

"We've been temporarily assigned to Anita and Bish," Mike answered. "They need some new eyes on the information they've collected…right?" he finished looking questioningly at Anita.

"Yep, we feel we may have missed something in all of this (pointing to the piles of paperwork) and think a few new sets of eyes just might come up with something we missed. Maybe even think of a better way to approach the investigation."

"Shouldn't this be a Fed investigation?" Pete asked.

"It is, but we're continuing from our side with the Chief's approval," Anita answered. "We're sharing everything we have with the Feds, and believe it or not, they're sharing also."

"I don't believe that," Mike commented sarcastically.

"Well, they are," Bish commented.

"I still don't believe it," Mike said again. Looking at Anita he asked, "Okay, lady, where do you want us and what do we start with?"

Three days later, Anita walked into the office with fresh coffee from City Brew Coffee, and a bag full of breakfast burritos from Taco John's. "I cooked," she said as she entered.

Peter looked up and said, "Bless you, lady," and took a cup of joe and three burritos.

Mike took coffee, saying thank you, and sat back down.

"No burritos this morning?" Bish asked him.

"Nah, stomach feels like a quart jug of motor oils rolling around in there," Mike groaned. "If I eat, it might not be nice around here in an hour or so."

"Yuk," Anita said with a grimace. "I have some Pepto in my desk if you want some, might settle things down some."

"Nah, I can't stomach that stuff," Mike answered, which brought laughter from the other three team members. "Hey, that ain't fair."

Anita grabbed a cup and a burrito, Bish a cup and two burritos. They sat at the big table the captain had brought in for them and she asked, "Okay, anything new?"

Bish chimed in answering, "I'm still getting information from the other parents and neighbor witnesses. Some of what we've received is bunk. Some of it gives me the creeps. And some actually makes sense. We'll have to take a close look at those."

"How many are you talking about?" Anita asked.

"Eight so far look promising," Bish answered.

"What kind of information is it?" Peter asked.

"Mostly has to do with the license plates, the partials that is," he answered. "In every instance they began with a two, and that means Laramie County; the plates – or plate - all came from Laramie County. Whoever this creep is must be one of two things: first, stealing the plates from here, or is from here and stealing or using their own plates."

"Okay, anything else?" Wilson asked the other two, which brought shakes of their heads. "Then I think we should concentrate on the plates. Mike...Pete...you two go out and look at all the areas near by and see if there were any cameras in the areas that may have picked up something. Bish…keep on what you're doing. I'm going to see the Captain and give him an update. When I get back, we'll go out and take a look for that black van down south." She took another bite of burrito then mumbled with her mouth full, "Right after breakfast."

After Detective First Class Anita Wilson explained everything to Captain Daryl Carlisle, he gave a disappointing tilt of his head, sighed, and turned in his chair to gaze out of his office window. Wilson had seen him do this on several other occasions and knew he was running a variety of information through his head all at once. She sat back in her seat and waited, patiently.

"How many plates again?" the captain asked.

"Seven all together," she answered.

He continued staring out the window.

"All started with the Laramie County duce?" he asked.

"Yes, sir," she answered.

"You've already run every van and panel truck with Laramie County plates?"

"Yes sir."

It was another several minutes before the captain made another sound, but he turned in his seat, looked at Wilson and said, "Either go or send someone to interview each of the seven witnesses to the plates and see if they have missed anything. Grill 'em…sweat 'em…but get me some answers."

"Already doing that, sir; I told Bish, Donaldson, and Hicks to do that very thing before I left. Donaldson and Hicks should already be on the road. Bish and I'll leave as soon as I get back," Wilson explained.

After a pregnant pause, "Why are you still here?" the captain asked rhetorically.

Wilson got up and headed back to the office. Bish was waiting with her jacket and a stack of papers. She walked in, grabbed her jacket and the pair headed for the underground garage and their cruiser.

"He's a sanctimonious jerk sometimes, you know it?" she almost yelled at Bish.

"I suppose," he hesitantly answered.

She gave him a glaring look while taking in a huge breath, but slowly let it out instead of saying what she wanted. She glared at him for another long moment then turned to the front and pointed.

Bish put the cruiser into gear and pulled out onto Thomes Avenue, then left onto West 19th Street. He remained silent as they turned right on Warren Avenue and headed south over the viaduct. He looked at a locomotive sitting in the Union Pacific Railroad yard, probably awaiting maintenance of some sort. They passed underneath Interstate Eighty continuing south on the CanAm Highway, otherwise known as the South Greeley Highway, on their way to the southernmost housing development in Cheyenne. They would be checking out another lead on a black van.

"Once you pull in, take the second right," Anita directed. "Once you make the turn, go slow since it's a dirt track. Keeps the dust down and gives us an excuse to move through slowly."

"Okay, boss," Bish answered.

He turned into the housing area and took the second right. The road, almost a mile in length, had almost thirty small five-acre ranchetts along its route. They would look for black vans along the way.

"Lot of garages and out-buildings that might be holding a van or two," Bish observed after almost a half mile.

"Yeah, I noticed," Wilson commented. "Makes one wonder doesn't it?"

"Yeah," Bish said, nodding.

"Take the next two lefts and we'll head towards the east exit," she directed.

He took the two lefts and heading east, passed another fifteen or twenty small home sites, looking all the while for a black van.

Nothing, no vans at all along the whole route they took.

"Everyone has garages and outbuildings," Bish commented. "That van could be anywhere out here."

"Yeah; I wonder if we're chasing a fairy tale," Wilson said almost mumbling. "Head back into town and we'll take a look at the big guy's place again."

"That baby sitter guy?" Bish asked looking at her.

"Yeah, I still have a gut feeling on him. And that woman with the baby, Helen, she wasn't… right. There was something wrong with both of them. He was way too friendly. She was just…well, too nice, too prim, and proper. Something wasn't right and I can't put my finger on it."

Bish turned around and headed south to do a drive-by of the man and woman's homes. Once they turned on the dirt track, they drove by slowly. The panel van was gone, but the woman's car was in the driveway and a Harley was parked next to the front door. The boyfriend must have been home.

"Want to stop and talk to the boyfriend?" Bish asked.

"No, keep driving," Anita answered almost in a whisper while writing down the motorcycle plate number. She kept an eye on the house as Bish drove on. He took a right and headed back out to Highway 85, turned left and headed north back to Cheyenne proper and the station.

Back in the CID, they both sat at their desks and didn't say a thing. Bish brought up his computer and began typing his report for the day's activities, including a plug for the Bent Horseshoe Café.

Anita brought her computer up and began her report. She included driving by the man and woman's places and seeing the Harley, and choosing not to stop. She added that she had a gut feeling about the pair, but couldn't put her finger on why the strong suspicious feelings persisted. She finished and prepared to send her report to the Captain.

"Bish, you ready to send?" she asked.

He hit a key on his keyboard and said, "On its way."

She hit her send key and looking at Bish said, "I'm gonna run those plates then I'm outta here. See you tomorrow."

"Okie-dokie, boss," Bish said to her. He watched as she left the CID. He sat at his desk reflecting on the suspicious feelings Anita had about the big man and the woman. He had no such feelings or uncertainties. But, he had been wrong before. He shrugged his shoulders, stood, grabbed his coat, and headed for the door.

The next morning, Bish handed a cup of her favorite coffee to Anita. "Thanks," she said to him with a smile. Her phone rang. "Detective Wilson," she answered. "Okay, Captain, on my way," she said and hung up. "The Captain wants to see us."

She led the way and the pair headed up to the Captain's office, where they found the door open and his secretary waving them on in. Inside, Captain Carlisle pointed to chairs while speaking on the phone, and remained standing until his call was finished.

"That was Chief Webster," he began looking at the two. "He wants, as do I, for the two of you to concentrate on the man and woman you have misgivings over," he explained, looking at Anita. "You," he said pointing at Bish, "keep her outta trouble. Did either of you notice any homes for sale near their places?"

Both detectives nodded negatively.

"Why would you ask that?" Anita questioned.

"The Chief wants them under surveillance," the Captain answered. "I think it's a good idea, too. Maybe someone will let us borrow a garage or an outbuilding for a while so we can set up and keep watch on those two."

"Three," Bish interjected.

"What?" the Captain asked.

"Three...the boyfriend of Helen," Bish answered. "He drives a Harley."

"Okay, then, three. But we need eyes on them. They could be linked to this, but we keep our eyes on them. If we can't find a house or building to set up in, we'll need to look at options."

"Such as…?" Bish questioned.

"Maybe setting up some remote cameras on telephone poles or something," Carlisle said.

"Nope, everything is underground out there," Anita said. "I noted no poles or any above-ground wires at all. A few yard lights on poles, but that's it."

"Huh," Carlisle. "Maybe something else - a tree or bush or something like that. I don't know, but we'll have to find something or some other way to keep an eye on them."

"Maybe on those elm and cottonwood trees we parked under," Anita said. "We'd have to make some excuse to spread around the neighborhood so we can work on the trees. Maybe taking dangerous limbs down or something, even getting the city on board and use their electrical guys to help out. You know, clearing limbs from powerlines running to those lights or something."

"That'll work," Carlisle said sitting up to his desk and getting his rolodex. "I'll make the calls and get it arranged for as soon as possible. You two get ready to help and to monitor the cameras. Now get. I'll call you with the arrangements."

Chapter 5

Cheyenne, Wyoming

Bish loved trees but hated climbing them. But he was thirty feet off the ground installing a satellite camera on a branch that would give them a great view for filming the area. On the test, Anita was in the comm-van, they were able to see both homes and most of the block to the east. Bish had already mounted another camera to the east that was facing west with as good a view as this one.

"A bit to the north, Bish…there, that's great," Anita said. Bish could hear her in his ear-bud, but not respond. He finished mounting the camera, cut a limb off the tree just to make it look good, and climbed down.

"Glad I didn't fall," he complained when he got back into the van.

"Just think of the disability benefits you would've had," Wilson retorted.

"That's not comforting when I think of all the pain I could have gone through," Bish snapped.

"A little pain for lots of gain, as the saying goes," she said and chortled.

"You're climbing the rest. I ain't gonna do it no more," Bish grumbled.

"Big wuss," she said, smiling. "You gonna drive out?"

"Yeah, I guess…gotta do everything else around here," he complained while getting out of the back of the city utility van and going to the cab. He clicked his seatbelt and started the van, then pulled out to the east. The other men from the city environmental office waved as he went by. They would finish running the limbs Bish had cut through the wood-chipper and complete the cleanup of the area.

Bish turned north on South Greeley Highway, heading back to the underground garage where the van would be parked. The camera feed would be seen in the CID on a laptop computer. The four, Detectives Donaldson and Hicks, Bishop and Wilson, would now be on shift work watching the feed twenty-four-seven. Chief Webster had already assured Captain Carlisle, he would have more personnel within the week for added surveillance coverage.

Wilson and Bish would have the first shift and go to seven that first night. Pete and Mike would come in at seven and take over, being relieved by Anita and Bish at seven in them morning. It would in all likelihood be a boring and tedious task watching a seven by twelve inch screen for hours on end. Back in their office, the pair pulled their chairs together and brought up the laptop. Nothing was moving on the screen.

"Probably won't see any movement until work ends, around five or so," Bish commented.

"Yeah, this is already getting old," Anita said.

"Maybe we can put another computer on the desk and watch a movie and this thing," Bish suggested.

"I could go for that," Anita agreed. "We could get some of that white cheddar popcorn I like, a can of honey roasted peanuts, and some peanut M&Ms."

"Gotta be peanut M&Ms or almond," Bish said. "I like those and the new caramel ones, too."

"I could use a Happy Meal or two, myself," Wilson said looking at Bish.

"Yeah, a couple of Big Macs would go good about now – I'll fly," he said looking at her.

She opened her desk drawer and pulling her purse out, dug around in there, and handed him a fifty. "I'll buy, you fly…right?"

"Deal," Bishop agreed and got up to get his coat and keys. "Walmart on Dell Range has a McDonalds; I'll go there and get everything we need - back in a bit."

She waved and went back to viewing the screen. She knew Bish would drop by his place and get his laptop and a stack of movies to bring back. He'd for sure get guy movies and would probably leave the works for Pete and Mike on the night shift. They would appreciate it. She thought about bringing in a few chick-flicks then thought better of it as she didn't want to be crying in front of Bish, the big lug. He'd never let her hear the end of it.

Bish was back in an hour and a half, coming into the office with six Walmart bags stuffed to overflowing, a large McDonald's bag, another book bag that looked to hold sodas, and a bag holding his laptop and movies.

"Need help?" Anita asked.

"Nah, I'll dump it all on the big table," he answered. "Soups hot…come and get it."

Wilson got up and went to the table and got her Happy Meals. He'd gotten her one with a burger and the other with chicken nuggets. Both had fries. She sat back down in front of the laptop and ate the burger first.

Bish sat next to her with his two Big Macs and a large fry tub. He pulled out a bottle of ketchup and held it out to her first, always the gentleman. She squirted a small dabble on her burger wrapper and handed it back to him. He squirted a large dollop on a paper plate then dumped his fries on it. He un-wrapped both Macs, placed them on the paper plate, and dug in.

"You always eat like that?" Anita asked.

"You know I don't…we been out together before to eat," Bish answered. "I'm hungry. Let me be."

"I'll keep my hands outta your way, too," she said with conviction.

"Better," Bish mumbled his reply, agreeing with her.

They ate in silence from then on, keeping watch on the small screen of the laptop. They watched as several cars and trucks drove through the area they surveyed, but nothing moved at the two homes being watched.

Bish picked up his laptop case and unloaded the thing along with his movie selection. Titles included the *Crocodile Dundee* series, both films, *San Andreas, Wyatt Earp, Inside Man, Ghost,* and *I Can Only Imagine.*

"You choose," he said to Wilson. She selected *Wyatt Earp* out of the pile and handed it to him. "I like that one, too," he told her. He put the DVD into his laptop and began the show, and then sat back in his chair to watch both screens and sip on a 7Up he'd opened.

At seven, Pete and Mike showed up. Anita briefed them and Bish told them about the movies and snacks and told them to help themselves. They, too, had brought several bags of groceries in with them in several large bags and told Bish and Anita they could help themselves also. They said their goodnights and Anita and Bish left.

The next morning, Mike briefed that they'd seen nothing of interest and the pair of night duty detectives left. Bish went and made a fresh batch of coffee, Anita on the screen once again.

This quickly became routine and boring to say the least. Just as Wilson was about to complain to the Captain, he came into their office and told them they would be getting two more bodies, and to go to eight hour shifts beginning the next day. He introduced Patrolmen Andrew Nelson and Constance Dominguez, both only out of the academy for less than a month. Wilson briefed the two and told them to review the data and documents on their shift that night. They would be working ten PM to six AM shift. Wilson and Bish would relieve them. They were told if anything happened at either of the two homes, all four detectives would be called and all six would respond.

"Gonna be nice with two more on the team," Bish commented.

"You know it," Anita agreed. "I just hope those rookies keep awake and keep watch."

"They will," Bish assured her. "I told them how to load the DVDs and to enjoy the snacks. They said thanks and that they would bring in a bunch of stuff tomorrow."

"I'm bringing in cop food," Anita said as they went downstairs.

Bish reached into his pocket, brought out a ten, and handed it to her, saying, "Get some holes, too."

"This is enough for ten dozen, you know," she said, putting the ten in her purse.

"That should do me."

"Then you go by Starbucks and get me the usual, please."

"That, I can do. Want me to make it a double?"

"That'll work. See you in the morning."

"Night," Bish answered stepping out of the stairwell and turning for his car.

The rookies were wide-eyed and bushy-tailed when the pair returned the next morning. They were disappointed that nothing had happened all night. No movement, no cars, no motorcycles, no nothing. Their report was quick to say the least - "Didn't see a thing."

Anita opened the donut box and told them to take their pick of the cop food. Both indulged, taking glazed old fashion donuts which were her favorites. They said their thanks and left the office. Bish was already into the first boxes of holes she saw as she turned for her desk.

"You're already at it I see," she said, almost disgustedly.

"I'm hungry and this is cop food after all," he retorted. "Sit and have some. It's not bad."

She shook her head and sat next to him, got herself a glazed old fashioned and looked at the screen. They could see several cars and one truck pulling out for work; about the same vehicles at the same time as the other workday mornings. There was nothing new moving at the moment. The motorcycle in front of the woman's house hadn't moved in three days and she wondered if the guy was on a break or maybe this was his weekend. She made an entry in their logbook, sat back and took a bite of her cop food.

"You goin' ta see the captain this morning?" Bish asked.

"I suppose I should go and give him a report," she responded, taking another bite and a sip of her coffee.

"How can you do that?" Bish asked distastefully.

She looked at him like a child caught with her hand in the cookie jar and with her mouth still full, mumbled, "Whaf?"

"That," he said, "putting donut and coffee in at the same time…YUK!"

She almost choked, placing her hand over her mouth so as to not spray the room. She bent over in her chair trying not to laugh, holding her mouth for all she was worth. Bish couldn't help it and began to laugh as he slid the trashcan over to her.

After she'd sprayed the can, she looked up at him, laughing, and yelled, "I hate you sometimes!"

"Yeah, right you do," Bish agreed still chuckling.

"I almost choked to death, you cretin," she choked out. "Good grief. I'm probably covered with donut and coffee. Here, look me over and see if you see anything before I go to the captain's office."

"Sure thing," Bish responded with a demur look on his face.

She gave him a severe look and sternly said, "Never mind." She got up and stormed off to the ladies room to check in the mirror. She took a few damp paper towels and wiped some spots of donut that had splashed back on her blouse. It only took a few moments and she was on her way to the captain's office to give her report.

Amanda, the captain's secretary, held up a hand as Wilson approached and said, "He's got someone in there with him, and it'll be a few minutes."

"That's cool; how ya doin', there Amanda?" Wilson asked.

"I'm doing great. How's Bish?" Amanda returned.

"He's as big a lug as he was last time you asked; he's doing great himself," Wilson answered, smiling.

"I bet he is," Amanda answered, looking down at her desk.

The captain's door opened just then and a radio show host from FM 103, The Range, stepped out of the captain's office. He, too, was smiling and nodded at both Amanda and Wilson as he went by.

"Get in here, Wilson," the captain yelled.

She gave Amanda, a look and a shrug then turned for the door. "Mornin', boss," she began. "Want an update?"

"Yeah, give to me, lady," he answered.

She closed the door and sitting down in his one guest chair, said, "Nothing new, really, and nothing moving out that way. The motorcycle guy has come and gone a few times, most likely to and from work. The woman's gone to work and left the baby with the big guy. He hasn't gone anywhere in two weeks of watching. Hermit-like I guess. I don't think we need the rookies anymore. Bish figured out a way of doing twenty-four hour recording onto a thumb-drive. Next day we can view the tape, as-it-were, and look for movement or anything of interest."

"I talked with the feds," the captain began, "They don't have anything new either. They got nothing - no ransom request, no contact, nothing at all. You think whoever took the kid just sold it right away and that's it?"

"Could be boss, or worse," Anita mused, sadly.

"I don't wanna think about 'or worse' myself," the captain said. "Okay, do the thumb-drive thing and let the two rookies go back to the squads. You still want Mike and Pete for a while longer?"

"Why, you got something new for them to do?" she shot back.

"No, just thinking out loud, really," the captain said miserably.

"They're still pouring over all the data we've amassed over the last two months. Those two really know how to dig. I'll keep 'em as long as you let me."

"Okay. I wish something would break either from our efforts or the feds."

"Me too, boss, me too."

Chapter 6

Cheyenne, Wyoming

Bish was standing at the office's only window looking at nothing when Anita returned. She stopped in the doorway when she saw him. She glanced at Pete and he held his finger up to his mouth indicating to be quiet then, gave a nod of his head for her to look to her left. She saw the imprint of Bish's fist in the wall. Anita looked back at Pete and he was watching Bish, so she, too, turned and looked at the big man standing at the window. She slowly shook her head, looked down at the floor then, taking a deep breath, said, "Okay, fellers, we're taking the rest of the day off. We're all beat mentally and need some time off. I applaud your efforts, but I feel we're not being as effective as we should. Not because we're not trying. We need some time off. Today's Thursday, and I don't want to see any of you in here before Monday unless I call. Clean up your areas and head on out."

She went over to her desk and began putting things away. Mike and Pete were quick and silent, putting their paperwork away, gathering their jackets, and heading for the door. Both just waived as they passed Wilson.

Bish was still standing at the window, having ignored Wilson's order. "Bish," she called out to him. "Bish," she said again, commandingly louder.

He turned his head in her direction and without looking at her questioned, "What?"

"Get outta here and take some time off," she urged. "Get a Mexican dinner or something, take a load off, and get some rest.

I need you at your peak on this and not dropping into a deep, dark, funk.”

“Yeah, got it,” he mumbled. He turned the other way, went to his desk, got his weapon out of the drawer, put on his coat, and left without another word. Nor did he clean up his desk.

Detective First Class Anita Wilson stood by her desk and watched the quiet show as Bish left the office. After he was gone, she shook her head, went over, and put all the paperwork on his desktop into his top drawer. She finished policing up the office and after getting her weapon and jacket, left the building.

The next morning Anita’s cell phone rang. It was Bish. “Hey, boss, I’m taking some time off and I’ll be going on a little trip. I’ll see you Monday, week,” he told her.

“You okay?” she asked.

“Yeah, just gotta get away and veg for a while, you know?” he meekly stated.

“Did you eat last night?” she asked, motherly.

“Yeah, went to the Tortilla Factory and got a super burrito, the full order, with an extra quart of their hot green chili sauce. It hit the spot. Afterwards, I got my Bible out and read Matthew, chapter six again you know where Jesus talks about not worrying, to let him have our problems?”

“Yeah, I know it well,” Anita confessed.

“Yeah, well, I figured I needed to give it up for a while, the case that is, and go chill out somewhere so I’ll be heading out here in a few minutes. That is, if you’re okay with me taking off for a while.”

“I’ll sign you out, just tell me you’ll be okay, and not do something stupid.”

“No worries there, boss. I’ll be fine.”

“In that case, I’ll sign you out as soon as I get to the shop this morning.”

“Thanks, boss. See you later,” and he hung up not wanting to hear anymore from her. He’d already packed and grabbed his full-to-bursting Kelty backpack, his weapons of choice, a

Bennelli M4 twelve-gauge shotgun, a Ruger SR-9E, and a Ruger M&P 15, in caliber .223. The latter two having each seven magazines he'd already loaded. The two gun bags and the Kelty weighed in at a hefty ninety-seven pounds, but he threw them over his shoulder and headed for the door like they were nothing. He went down to the garage and put the bags into his midnight-blue Jeep Wrangler Apex, pulling the SR-9E out and clipping it to his belt. He had already put in food and some extra water.

Satisfied, he nodded to himself and got in, pulled out and headed for Happy Jack Highway, otherwise known as Wyoming Highway 210, and turned west. Almost twenty years earlier, he'd bought a forty acre tract of land adjacent to National Forrest property, near Albany, Wyoming. In the years following, he'd built a small cabin on his property, a one-room affair. It was nothing fancy, but served the purpose for him, which was solitude.

Driving over, he listened to a Bible app, which at the moment was pouring forth the book of James. Right then, it was reading from chapter three, which was a chapter dedicated to taming the tongue and said, quoting verse six, "The tongue also is a fire, a world of evil among the parts of the body."

Bish smiled and said out loud, "Boy, do I know that."

He pulled into Laramie, Wyoming, around eleven and as he pulled off of I-80 west, he turned onto Wyoming Highway 130 and pulled into a McDonald's, going through the drive through and getting three Big Macs with fries and a large drink. Lunch and dinner were now taken care of.

The drive on Highway 130 was uneventful and he turned left onto Wyoming Highway 11 for Albany, Wyoming. After a fifteen minute drive, he turned off to the south on the dirt two-track he'd made, that lead to his property. The land was almost entirely covered with trees, the cabin being in a small meadow that from the sky resembled a handgun, with the grip pointing to the northeast and the barrel to the southeast. He had a creek that for the most part was dry, but this time of year it had just above a trickle of water flowing down the east side of his place.

He backed into a heavily treed area where he'd cut a carport-like opening for his jeep, got out and unloaded his gear into the cabin. The carport-like area was completely covered by heavy pine boughs so the jeep could not be seen from the sky. Back at the jeep, he grabbed his McDonald's fare, closed and locked his vehicle and returned to the cabin. First thing he did was light a fire and once it was going, placed an eight-gallon stewing pot filled with water on the holding rack. The stew pot had a faucet Bish had installed. This would be his hot water tank while he stayed in the cabin, refilling it as needed. He then started a pot of coffee.

Next, he unfurled his sleeping mat and bag and an additional wool army blanket he picked up at an Army surplus store in Fort Collins, and fluffed up his pillow. He picked up his long-gun case and set it upon his bunk, opened it, taking out his Ruger M&P 15, inserted a twenty-round magazine and charged the weapon and leaned it next to the front door. Above the door on a rack especially made for it, he placed his fully loaded Benelli. He considered it his bear gun.

Since his Ruger SR-9E was always loaded, his grandfather once told him an unloaded handgun was nothing more than an expensive rock, he didn't bother with it as it was already on his hip.

Finally, he pulled out his camp chair, unfolded it, and sat on his front porch listening to the birds and other sounds of his palace in the popple, waiting for his coffee to finish perking. A Meadowlark, Wyoming's state bird, settled on a branch of a tree to his front and began calling for its mate. Bish loved the sound of the birds singing. He smiled and thought he would run into town the next morning and get a big bag of bird seed and give the gaggle of critters a treat.

Finally smelling the coffee, he went inside, poured himself a steaming mug full of the hot fluid and sat back on the front porch and began to think. He sipped his brew and thought about the abduction of the little girls. Who in their right-mind would do such a thing? Why would they? Why? That was a good place to start so he began jotting down reasons and after an hour of thinking had written down: to sell; to sexually abuse then dispose of; to ease the pain of losing one's own child; custody battles between divorcing parents; ransom; forced labor/slavery; illegal adoption; extortion; child prostitution. He figured there just might be more reasons, but felt he had covered most of the basics.

He could scratch a few of the reasons as the trail they were on was too organized, always in April, only on odd numbered years, child is always right at two years old, and never Hispanic. His anger began to rise once again, so he got up, took the last sip of his coffee, set his mug on the porch rail, and went for a walk around his place. As he neared the creek, he could hear the trickle of the water flowing, a soothing sound, and along with the birds, settled him down some. He knelt by the flow, scooped a palm-full of the clear liquid, and took a healthy swig. Fresh and cold; he did not fear drinking the water in the creek as it flowed right out of the mountain his property was upon. He knew where it left the rock and had tracked the flow to the end of his property line, so knew that other than the odd animal that might urinate or defecate in the water he was safe to drink it.

As he eased down into an area he called his bottom land, he came face-to-face with a young bull moose. The two looked at each other. Bish waved and moved more to his left as to not disturb the massive creature's grazing. The moose kept a wary eye on the human moving away. Bish smiled and thought seeing the big critter was a good sign. He had seen mule deer and elk on his place, but this was the first moose.

He came to the cliff that bordered the eastern side of his bottom land. It rose close to one hundred-fifty feet at a sixty to seventy degree slope. He looked for new landslides, but saw none. Bish liked looking at the stones in the cliff face and had taken a couple and put on the window ledge in the cabin. Today, he didn't find anything worth taking back.

Back down to earth, he turned for the cabin and another mug of coffee. Sitting on the front porch again, he thought about the team they had working the abduction case. All were good detectives and had things well under control with the information they did have. It was nice the febs were allowing them to continue to investigate and share information. It was clear they were just as perplexed as the CPD team. He continued to think.

Chapter 7

el Jefe

Sims looked in on el Jefe. He was reclining on his leather recliner looking out his huge picture window. It was the only seat in the room and was positioned so that the person could observe the view of the Rocky Mountain Front Range unobstructed. The view was impressive indeed, and Sims often took advantage of the seat when the boss was not around.

Today, the range was snow-covered and looking magnificent with the early morning sun shining on the mountains. Enrique Salinas, el Jefe, squinted just a bit while viewing the picturesque scene. He pressed a button on the arm of his leather-covered recliner.

Sims heard the chime and intentionally made a three count in her head before entering the room. He quietly approached the recliner and said, "Yes, Jefe?"

"Coffee, black, strong…and a pastry," he told him.

"Yes, Jefe," he answered and quickly left to do his bidding.

Enrique was taking a holiday of sorts and was staying in his Colorado home for a while. He also had some business to take care of while he was in the Centennial State. The business would be pleasurable for Enrique, but not so pleasurable for the few he would be dealing with. He smiled at the thought.

This man was a true sociopath. He hungered for power, dominance, and influence. He was ruthless in his pursuits, and manipulated those he had control over, often becoming angered when he didn't get his way. And that usually meant someone was in very deep trouble and in most cases meant a cheap thrill for Enrique.

The closest relationship he had was his son and that only because el Jefe knew he needed a successor. The boy was being groomed, and the youngster knew the reasons why. Enrique had slowly been enlightening the boy as to his future duties and life style. The young one did not know all of his future as yet. He would be tutored by a trusted associate, Issy, on love making and the ways of making a woman enjoy the encounter. He would begin his sexuality lessons on his next birthday, his fourteenth. Enrique smiled at the thought of the boy's first encounter. He would be well trained by Issy.

Enrique felt he was entitled to everything he had and did. His conscience knew no bounds when it came to dealing with others. Even his son was the recipient of his ire from time-to-time. Enrique was smart enough to know not to make mistakes. He kept his anger and irritation at others in check, and would deal with them later if he thought it necessary. He would use his aggression in private settings and let his underlings clean up the mess he left behind in most cases, using his favorite dumping ground in Colorado, a place just north of his home in Boulder, Colorado.

The next morning, Enrique prepared for his day. He had a cup of strong coffee in his viewing room, while sitting in his leather-covered recliner. The snow had melted somewhat, leaving dark blemished areas on the east side of the mountains. He was dressed in heavy duty, black cargo pants, a black, heavy duty, button-up, long-sleeved shirt, and heavy duty, water proof hiking boots. He knew he would be getting messy this day.

He took in a great breath and bellowed, "Sims!"

Very quickly, Sims came into the room and simply said, "Sir?"

"Have my Hummer brought around," he instructed.

"Right away, Jefe," Sims said, and turned to do his duty.

Ten minutes later, Salinas was driving north along a dirt track on the back side of his property. The two-track lead him to a pole barn that sat on the northwest corner of his property, well away from neighbors and those that might hear. There were no hiking or biking trails within miles. It was a relatively remote environment for the business at hand.

As he neared the structure, he noted two other vehicles, both he knew well, a truck, and a jeep. He gave an audible harrumph as he pulled his Hummer in next to the jeep. He got out and took a deep breath of fresh mountain air, looked around the place, both to take in the scenery and to ensure no one was around, then turned for the door.

Inside he found his men with the two prisoners in the middle of the barn. The prisoners were bound to poles and had triple-thick hoods pulled over their heads. The three men Enrique employed to handle such people, were standing by near a table. They were sipping hot coffee when he entered.

"Want a cup, Jefe," one of them asked.

Enrique answered with a nod of his head. The man quickly brought el Jefe a steaming cup of the brew, and received a nod for his effort. He sipped the liquid for several moments, contemplating what he would be doing this day. He slowly walked over to the two bound prisoners and poked one in the ribs with a finger. The man jumped in his bindings and moaned. Enrique knew the man was gagged, most likely with a knotted hemp rope with two knots in his mouth. No one could speak through that.

These two men were caught skimming cash from two of el Jefe's organizations, one a gambling establishment and the other a drug operation. Enrique walked around both men and finally motioned for the other three to take the one he'd pointed to and tie him to a chair.

Once this was done, Enrique had them move the seated man in front of the other man tied to a pole. When this had been done, Enrique had one of the men pull the hood from the seated man's head. The man blinked at the sudden blinding light. Once his eyes had adjusted, his eyes were wide, where one could see the whites all the way around the iris. He was petrified, and that's the way el Jefe wanted him.

"You know, Phillip, that we check and double check receipts of all my businesses?" el Jefe asked.

The man looked up at el Jefe, appeared to shrink some, and nodded his head vigorously.

"Then why did you think it was appropriate to skim money from me; to steal from me?" el Jefe more commented than asked.

The man seemed to shrink even more and began to shake uncontrollably.

"Phillip, why did you do this?" el Jefe asked, almost fatherly.

Phillip was sweating profusely looking up into el Jefe's eyes and shrugged his shoulders.

"You thought you could get away with something like this? Don't I pay you handsomely for your services? Don't you get a very nice vacation twice a year for you and your lovely wife?"

Phillip nodded vigorously.

"But still you stole from me, didn't you," el Jefe asked again in a fatherly fashion.

El Jefe paced around the two men once again, coming to a stop beside Phillip. He looked at the man tied to the chair, slowly shook his head, and turned to the men, pointing to the small table with a tool bag on it. Two of the men quickly carried the small table to their boss and set it down on the seated man's left.

Enrique paced around the men again, coming to a stop next to the table. "Do you know what we do with people that steal from me, Phillip?" he asked.

Phillip vigorously shook his head positively in answer.

Enrique looked at him and slowly opened the tool bag on the table. He took out a Phillips screwdriver, a hammer, a pair of needle-nosed pliers, a pair of regular pliers, a vise-grip, an electric soldering iron which he had one of his men plug into an extension cord, and a Hawk-billed, curved carpet knife, with a blade what was as sharp as a razor. He laid them all out on the table for Phillip to see, then, Enrique walked around the tied prisoners a few more times.

He finally stopped next to the small table again, looked at Phillip and shook his head, then, turned to the man tied to the pole and yanked the hood from his head. The man blinked rapidly in the light, finally looking at Phillip, then at el Jefe. His eyes got wide in recognition.

"Yes, Daniel, you've been listening and know what you're here for, don't you?" el Jefe said with a sinister smile.

The man didn't make a move. He didn't shake nor did he indicate with his eyes any recognition of what el Jefe had just said.

"So, you'll be the strong one, then," el Jefe said to the man tied to the pole. This too, elicited no response. Enrique gave a small flick of his eyes and looking down at the table, selected the carpet knife. He looked once more at Daniel, then, looked down at Phillip, and asked, "Phillip, have you ever felt how hot another's blood is?"

Phillip gave a slow nod of his head to the negative, and a look that was obviously dreading what was to come.

Enrique gave a small smile to Phillip and with his right hand, took the curved-bladed knife, and slowly drew it along Daniel's throat. Daniel's blood shot from the wound with each remaining heartbeat, directly onto the seated Phillip, who cringed and whimpered in fear.

Enrique took two steps back so as to not be drenched in the blood raining from Daniel's throat. He looked on as if he saw such things daily. It was nothing more than what he would think of a leaf falling from a tree. Taking a life was not a big deal to Enrique Salazar.

Daniel finally expired; the blood quit pouring from his wound. His last breath escaped in a bubbly froth from both the wound in his neck and from his mouth and nose. His head and body came to a sagging rest, hanging lifeless and limp in the bonds.

Phillip began to shake even more. He was whimpering and taking great gulps of air between sobs, knowing what was to come. He looked with pleading eyes at el Jefe.

"Phillip, you are the lucky one today as I'm not in the mood to play," Enrique bending down to look him in the eyes, said almost nonchalantly. "So," and with that he drew the knife rapidly across Phillips throat, and stepped away. He turned towards his men and said, "When he's gone, get rid of those in the usual place. I'm going back home," he told his men and turned to leave.

Chapter 8

Cheyenne, Wyoming

The large man pulled the black panel van out of the pole barn and watched as the garage door closed properly. He drove around the barn and turned towards his home. In the driveway, he turned off the engine, got out and went to the sliding door on the passenger side and opened it. Inside, the van appeared clean to the big man so he gave a snort, closed the door, and went inside the house.

Inside, he turned to the left, down the hallway to the bedrooms, going to the last bedroom on the right. There, he found the room just as he'd left it, barren, and with a large hole in the far corner. This he went to and climbed down a ladder into a subterranean facility. Not a basement, but a much enlarged crawl space. It now held several rooms replete with doors, and walls. One, an office, had windows on two sides. He went into the office and brought up a laptop computer that was sitting on a small desk. He sat down and patiently waited while the computer went through its security procedures before allowing access.

The machine finally ended the process and left a prompt window on the screen wanting someone or something to enter a password. This he entered from memory, a fourteen-digit affair which had upper and lowercase letters, numbers, and special characters. It was a very strong password and would require someone wanting to break into the system days of time consuming effort to decode.

Once he hit enter, the computer still took a moment to process the command and bring up the operating programs he wanted. He did a rapid triple-click on one of the icons and an encrypted communication program popped up. Once again, he entered another fourteen-digit password, different from the first, and waited for the program to come up. Once it did, he opened an untitled-notepad page and began typing.

The big man's keyboard skills were excellent as his fingers rapidly danced over the keys. The request was for information regarding his next assignment as he knew his associates and himself would be soon tasked with finding and abducting another subject for the boss. He knew he needed the information sooner rather than later as they would need it to properly do the surveillance of the victim. They needed to know the families routine and have it down to memory. They could not afford mistakes in their business, the business of abduction, especially children.

The big man hit enter and the encrypted message disappeared from his screen. He logged out of the message program, then, logged out of the computer shutting it down. He got up and stretched as he left the office and turned to the right, pausing and giving a quick shake of the chills as he had an aversion to small, enclosed spaces. He took a deep breath and continued.

This was a hallway that turned into a tunnel as it passed through the foundation wall of the home. The tunnel stretched before him and from where he entered, he could not see the ending. The passageway was lit by a long strand of string lights, which cast a dull-yellow glow on the walls. He walked for almost ten minutes before he came to a shaft with a ladder. He stopped, tilting his head, listening carefully before going up the ladder.

At the top, he once again paused, listening. Hearing nothing, he unlocked the hatch cover and looked out, taking in a deep breath of fresh air as he did so. He looked around the room of the house and seeing nothing out of the ordinary, closed and locked the hatch and climbed back to the tunnel. He walked along until finally reaching the end of the long passageway, coming to another shaft with a ladder, which he climbed, stopping at the top and listening. Hearing nothing, he unlocked the hatch and climbed out into the pole barn he'd left earlier with the black panel van.

He walked over and squirmed into a blue, 2019, Toyota Prius, and started the engine. He used the remote to open the garage door and pulled out, closing the door as he left. He drove out to Highway 85 and turned north. After about four miles, he turned left into the Diamond Horseshoe Cafe, and parked. It took him a moment to wriggle his way out of the small car, and once out, smoothed his clothes, breathing hard.

Inside, he chose a barstool at the counter and sat down. The lady behind the bar walked up and he said, "Hey, Marg, how's it goin'?"

"Slow today for some reason; how ya doin'?" she asked.

"'Bout the same, just gettin' by and gettin' bigger every day," he boringly answered. "Can't hardly get in an outta that car anymore I'm gettin' so big."

"You telling me you want a salad and a glass of water?" she skeptically asked.

"Nah, the usual should do," he said with a grin.

"Double bacon burger with cheese, double order of fries, a little on the crispy side, and extra pickles…and a diet Coke, right," she rattled off by heart.

"That'll do I recon," he said.

"Diet Coke coming up," she said turning for the fountain head.

He pulled out his phone and began playing a game of solitaire while waiting for his lunch.

Bish had just sat down and brought up his computer when he almost leapt out of his chair, seeing the black panel van parked at the big man's house. "Hey, the van is there!" he yelled to no one in particular.

Anita got up and moved to look over his shoulder. Sure enough, the van was there and she asked, "When did it pull in?"

"Don't know, didn't get that far yet," Bish told her. "I'll run it back and see and see who got out."

"I'll watch," she said, remaining by his shoulder as Pete sauntered up.

"Me, three," Pete said with a smile. "What are we looking at, anyway?"

"The black van showed up at the big guy's house," Bish told him while hitting the enter key to start the film again. He'd run it back twelve hours and as the video began, he sped up the show to save time. Ten hours' worth of time flew by when they saw the van pull up. Bish slowed the film and they watched together as the big man got out, sauntered around the van, opened the sliding door on the passenger side, closed it, and then, went inside the house.

"Well, that was a real thrill," Pete commented, sarcastically.

Ignoring the comment, Bish said, "I'll keep watch."

Anita went back to her desk and Pete headed for the coffee pot. "Me, too, please," Bish said holding his empty cup up.

Pete said, "Sure; Anita, you want some, too?"

She lifted her cup and Pete took the three empties to fill.

Eight hours later, the van had not moved and Bish was fed up with watching. He had done some paperwork while watching, but was fed up nonetheless. He stood up, stretched, and said, "I'm outta here. I got it on record. The van never moved nor did the fat guy leave the house. He's probably in there watching cartoons on the tube or something. See ya tomorrow," and with that he left.

Anita waived as he went by and Pete just grunted. Pete would be next to leave and left silently. Anita continued paperwork for another hour, then left. The video continued to silently record.

The big man pulled the Toyota into the pole barn and closed the door. He had four bags of groceries to take back to the house so loaded them into a collapsible utility wagon. He turned on the lights to the tunnel and began the long trek he despised back to the house.

He was putting the groceries away when he heard a knock at the door. Cursing to himself, he left the kitchen and looked to see who it was.

It was Helen from next door. "Hey, what are you up to?" she asked him as he opened the door.

"Putting groceries way's all," he answered. "Wanna come in?"

"Got any coffee?"

"Yeah, Keurig okay?"

"Sure nuff."

"Come on in, then, sugar," he said stepping out of the way so she could get in.

"Can I talk to you about sumptin?" she meekly asked.

"Yeah…anything, you know that," he answered.

She sat heavily at the small kitchen table and with a heavy sigh, said, "I think we're being watched. I…I got a feeling I'm being watched all the time lately. Don't see anybody…no unusual cars or trucks or nuthin', just got a feeling s'all."

"Well, I hope you're wrong, sugar," the big man said as he fixed her a cup of coffee. "I can't say I have the same feelings or nuthin'. I watched those dudes the other day cuttin' limbs off the trees around the neighborhood, but didn't see them do anything weird."

"I watched 'em, too," she said. "Didn't see a thing, but I still have a feelin' that we're bein' watched."

"Daniel coming home tonight?"

"Yeah, should be here around six or so; why?"

"Call him and ask him to drive around the hood before he comes in. Take a look around the place and see if he sees anything out of place. He might see something."

"Okay, I can do that. Has el Jefe called yet?"

"No, and that bothers me. Usually he's already called by now so we can scope out the next target which should be in Utah, Idaho, or one of the Dakotas this time. We'll see. I'll give you a call as soon as I hear from him."

Taking a last sip of her coffee and standing, she said, "Okay, I'll go call Daniel. See you later," she said ending the conversation, going to and out the door, and then turning for her place next door.

He watched as she left – he liked watching her hips move – and slowly closed the door, going back to putting the groceries away. He placed his box of Kellogg's Frosted Flakes in the pantry and closed the door – that's when the throwaway phone claxon sounded. He rushed over and answered it with, "Good evening, el Jefe, I am ready," meaning he had paper and pencil ready to write.

The boss gave him a first name, last name, hair color, eye color, race, state of residence, address, and the date the abduction should take place then abruptly hung up.

The big man had been writing furiously and when the line went dead, he immediately destroyed the burner phone and put the pieces in several different trash cans around the house. He sat at his small desk and pulled out a Rand McNally road atlas and turned to the map of Idaho, found the target community and began laying out routes of travel, both to the place and escape routes. He would go to Google Earth and take a detailed look at the community in question. In the atlas, he saw the little town was right off the east side of Interstate Highway Fifteen.

His part of the operation was now in full swing. He was in charge of planning the abductions and driving the selected vehicle to and from the community in question, then to the pickup point. He called Helen and told her it was on and that he wanted to have a meeting with she, and Daniel as soon as possible, to iron out details. She said as soon as she could tell Daniel and get him home, they would be over.

The big man got up and gathered maps, paper, pencils, and fired up his computer to log onto Google Earth. While he waited, he got up and made himself a sandwich and grabbed a family-sized bag of Ruffles to go with it and a Diet Coke. He sat at his work table and began eating and going over the maps he had available.

Interstate Fifteen ran north to south very close to the little town targeted. He looked closely at the map and decided their primary route home would be south on I-15, turning east on Idaho Highway 33, north on Highway 20, then east again on thirty-three. They would travel on it until it ran into Wyoming. It would become Wyoming Highway 22 then, and they would take it to Jackson, probably staying the night there.

The next day, he decided, they would take Highway 1961 north to Moran, then east on Highway 26 all the way to Casper, Wyoming, then, I-25 south to the drop off point. They would be home that night with a lot of money in their pockets.

As he'd studied the maps, he wrote the primary route down on his pad of paper. Now for their backup route, deciding to head due east on the A-2 Clark County Road all the way to Boondocks, Idaho, and stay the night. The next day would be a long drive to Wyoming, over some very rough roads winding through the mountains, eventually ending up in Riverton, Wyoming, and staying the night there. The following day they would drive to the pickup point, collect their money, and head home.

The secondary route would be arduous at best, because it would be all the back roads they would have to traverse. Some of those would be dirt two-tracks in the mountains and if they ran into either rain or snow, which it was apt to do in the spring at high altitudes, they would have a lot of difficulty. His biggest concern is if the authorities completely closed the routes.

He began making a listing of the additional supplies and equipment they would need…just in case. High-lift jack, two shovels, rope, snow chains for rear tires, sand bags for stability and possibly traction, extra food and water… The list went on and on. He made an additional listing of clothing they would need and possibly need, which included heavy, waterproof winter boots. They could be used in any weather conditions for the time they would be traveling.

By the time he felt he had good routes planned out, lists of equipment and clothing made, he'd finished the family bag of

Ruffles and was on his third Diet Coke. He heard the knock on his door and knew Helen and Daniel had arrived.

"Come on in!" he yelled.

The duo from next door came in all smiles and ready to discuss the mission. They sat at the table and he offered Diet Cokes and sandwiches, which they declined. He opened his fourth Diet Coke and began telling them what and where their mission was and began going over the lists with them. They agreed on almost everything, with Helen adding additional items their victim might need on the trip back. They definitely had to keep the kid healthy and happy.

The big man said, "I got a funny feelin' 'bout this un. I'm gonna get some more shotgun shells to take along. You guys get additional ammo for your handguns. I'll do the same."

"What makes you feel funny?" Helen asked him.

"Those cops coming by when they did and now you guys feelin' like you're bein' watched, s'all," was his mumbled reply.

"They were just following up on those plates," Helen said in a reassuring voice. "They're probably busy and that's why it took so long for them to come by and ask. I don't think we need to worry any."

He looked at her and said, "Still, get that ammo. We need to be ready for anything. And Daniel, see if you can pick up another couple of shotguns, good ones."

Daniel finally broke in and hurriedly said, "Okay, man, we'll get the ammo and the shotguns. Let's finish this up. When and who is going to do the recon of the kid's place in Idaho?"

"Being taken care of," the big guy answered. "They'll be sending me videos and stills so we can do some more planning. I gotta figure out a third departure route just to be safe. I got the primary and secondary routes planned. Secondary will be a booger if there's weather, but I think we can safely do it. Longer, but, you know. Soon as I get the mail with the videos we'll get together again and watch 'em."

"Fine," Daniel said.

"Okay with me," Helen agreed.

"Alrighty then, I'll see you guys later," the big man said, ending the meeting. "Give Shirley a hug for me," he asked as Helen and Daniel got up and left.

The video continued to recording back in Cheyenne, documenting Helen, and Daniel going into the house and departing about an hour later. It would be worth the team viewing the next morning.

Chapter 9

Cheyenne, Wyoming

Oh-four-thirty is when Bish showed up in the office. Anita would have said it was, 'oh my word it's early'. That would have been many laughs for Bish. As it was, he started the thirty cup coffee pot and stood there watching while it perked enough so he could get the first cup. It would curl one's hair it was so strong.

It took seven minutes. He smiled, put his cup under the spigot, pulled the handle, and let the very black, steaming liquid fill his mug. He stood there, taking a tentative sip, and gave a resounding ahh. The smile remained.

He went over to his desk, set his mug down, took off his coat, draping it over the backrest, and began to pull his chair out to sit when he remembered the computer that taped the surveillance of the big man's home. He went over to it, turned on the monitor, and waited for it to light up.

Bish ran the time stamp back to just before they left the department the previous evening and hit enter. Twenty minutes later he almost dumped his mug of coffee as he grabbed the phone to call Wilson, Donaldson, and Hicks to tell them all to get in fast.

He went back to the computer, flipped back to the time stamp, froze the image there, and waited for the rest of the team to come in. He wondered about calling in Dominguez and Nelson, the rookies, but deferred to Wilson's leadership on that.

Seventeen minutes later, Wilson, moving fast, came into the office and threw her coat towards her desk, grabbed her mug and filled it from the pot of coffee Bish had made. "So why the rush?" she asked him, taking a sip afterwards.

He quickly explained and told her his thoughts on Dominguez and Nelson.

"Call 'em in. I'll take the hit from the Captain," she instructed.

Bish quickly called the rookies and got whoops of joy from both. They had never been called in before.

In the meantime, Wilson went over to the surveillance computer and hit enter and watched. She, too, stopped it after about fifteen minutes and backed it up to the timestamp. By then, Pete and Mike were in and getting coffee. Another ten minutes and the rookies were in.

"Everyone grab a chair and pull it up over here around the computer," Wilson told everyone. "Connie…Andy…get a cup of coffee if you want and join in," she told the rookies.

Once everyone was gathered around, seated and sipping on their coffee, Anita began with, "Okay, we've got movement on the video. Helen and her boyfriend, Daniel, went into the big man's home and when I last viewed it, were still in there. We do not know what they're doing, but with the van out there and the three of them together, somethings up. Let's watch. I want all eyes on the screen and if you see something interesting, write the time stamp down and we'll get to it when we finish. We'll go back to those points afterwards," she said and began the video.

Almost two hours later, they watched as Daniel and Helen left the big man's home, with Daniel appearing to be arguing with Helen about something due to his arm gyrations. Three times, he pointed to the west, and all the officers wanted to or tried to look that way to see what he was pointing at.

Wilson stopped the video, sat down, and asked what they all had, "Bish, you start."

"For those of you who don't know, when Daniel was doing all the pointing, that was to the west," he said. "He was pretty upset it appeared. My questions are one, what were they doing at the big guy's house, and two, what happened to upset Daniel so much?"

"Yeah, I agree," Pete agreed with Bish. "Do we have authorization to check calls going in and out? My question is what prompted everything? Was it a phone call or something…maybe an email or a text message?"

"No, we do not have authorization to tap or watch phone usage," Wilson answered. "Maybe the feds do…I'll give them a call shortly after I brief the captain; anyone else?"

The officers looked at each other and Connie said, "My questions are the same as theirs," and left it at that.

"Me, too," Andy agreed.

Wilson looked at Mike, who was deep in thought, looking at the floor. "Mike?" she asked.

He slowly looked up and said, "Maybe the big guy made a pass at Helen and that's why Daniel boy was upset. Maybe he was pointing back to the house and wondering if she and the big guy had been messing around while he was at work. Maybe the dinner was a bust and that's why they left," he said for an ending, giving a shrug of his shoulders.

Wilson looked at the team and said, "Okay, I'll go brief the captain, get his input and if he approves, I'll give the feds a call about the phones; anything else?"

"Ask him if he wants us to go live on the surveillance…does he want us out there watching," Bish asked. "It's January; if they're gonna grab another kid, we know it'll be the end of this coming April. Maybe the feds'll wanna do the watching. Be warmer for us."

Anita looked down as she was smiling. "Okay, I'll ask him. Someone make some more coffee while I'm gone."

The rookies jumped up to do that as Wilson left the office. "Wow, aren't we the lucky ones, huh?" Connie asked Mike.

"Yes indeed, we are," Hicks agreed, dumping the used coffee grounds in the trash and reloading the filter and new grounds into the hamper.

The coffee started, the pair of rookies sat back down near Bish's desk and kept quiet, taking in all the excited activities of the Detectives. Both silently wondered how the three of them could be so enthusiastic over things they had already investigated. They watched as all three detectives appeared to gather and stack paperwork into different mounds of disarrayed papers, computer printouts and heaven only knew what else.

"NELSON!" Detective Hicks yelled. "Get over here."

The poor kid almost jumped out of his skin and would wear the coffee stain for the rest of the shift, but got up quickly and almost ran to the detective's side. "Yes, sir," he reported.

Hicks looked up at the kid and said, "Get your chair and come back. I want you to sift through this and look for anything we might be missing about a next target. Look for trends in locations, times and dates of abductions verses where and so on," he instructed then went back to doing something else.

Nelson did as told, getting his chair and a slight chuckle from Connie as he did so, and sat down to look at the chart the detectives had made on the abductions and other paperwork with witness statements and evidence. After ten minutes, he gathered the stack of correspondence relating to the dates and places, and moved over to an empty desk with a computer. He brought up the system, opened Excel, and began inputting data.

The first thing he noticed was only nine states had abductions…why? Next, he noticed the only town or city that had a second abduction was right there in Cheyenne, Wyoming…why? Once he had all the data input, he began messing with the data using the *Sort* function. He found they were all very near Interstate Highways. They were all within a hundred mile distance of a major interstate. That led to him bringing up Google Earth and looking at the towns and marking the each place of abduction. It took him a while to find all the small towns, but when he was finished, he had a rough-looking cross of sorts. He looked at the marks again and suddenly, they looked like a big 'X'…and Cheyenne was where the lines intersected.

Nelson looked up quickly with the revelation. He looked at all the others in the room, working at their own pieces of this puzzle, and as the rookie, felt he needn't speak up just then. He'd wait.

He went back to messing with the data and saw the number of abductions in each state, what Detectives First Class Wilson and Bishop had already figured out. He thought about that for a few minutes and thought about the dates. Maybe that would be something, but after sorting the data by date, all it gave him was a time-line order of dates. He didn't feel this was the way to go.

After looking at and sorting the data for almost an hour, he felt there was no rhyme or reason to the madness at hand. He thought he would be onto something by now and felt insecure after banging all that data around in his head and on the computer.

Then he remembered that guy in the video, Daniel, pointing to the west. What was to the west? Map! He grabbed the map and looked and figured out the only two states where previous abductions had taken place were Idaho and Utah, both west of Wyoming. The more he thought about it, the more he knew the next crime would take place in one of those two states.

He went back to the data in the computer and saw that both Utah and Idaho had had only three abductions each. The Dakota's and Montana were the only other states with three abductions, but they were all north and east of Wyoming. He thought about it for another ten minutes and saw Detective Wilson come back into the office.

"Okay, everyone, listen up," she said, hands on hips. "The captain is on our side and wants us to put an eye on the house. He's going to try and arrange for us to get that rental property down the street for an observation point. He's going to go to the judge and see if we can get a wiretap and the okay to add more cameras around the property. He's going to brief the feds and see if, or what, they might want to do."

She looked around the room at the expectant faces and followed up with, "You folks get anything while I was out?"

Rookie Patrolman Andrew Nelson slowly raised his right hand, with his finger pointing up, and had a fearful look on his face. When Wilson saw his hand going up tentatively, she said, "What Nelson…you have something?"

"Uh…I…uh…" he stammered.

"Come on Andy, spit it out," Wilson directed.

"Well, I created a spreadsheet in Excel and crunched all the data…a lot," he slowly began with. "Anyway, I sorted the data in many different ways and really didn't get anything from it directly. But I remembered the video we watched. That guy, Daniel, was pointing to the west several times. Well, I, and I think we, assumed he was pointing back at the big guy's house…right?"

Nods from everyone.

"Well, I looked at the data and figured the only two states that were west of us were Utah and Idaho, and looking at the data, there were five states that had only three abductions. Utah and Idaho are on that list, so I'm thinking that maybe the next abduction will be in one of those two states."

He had been looking at the paperwork in his hands and as he finished speaking, he looked up and every face was staring at him. The room was dead quiet. Andy, the rookie, suddenly felt like he was under the scrutiny of God Himself. He looked at Detective Wilson with what most would be described as huge puppy dog eyes, pleading.

"Let me see your data," Wilson told him and moved over to the desk he'd pulled up to. The rest of the team did likewise, surrounding the kid and his computer.

Andy showed them his spreadsheet and did a few data sorts to show his thinking process. When he was done explaining how he came to his conclusion about Utah and Idaho, he looked up at Wilson and could see her in deep thought.

She suddenly reached for the phone on his desk and he nearly flipped out of the chair. As it was, he moved back some and she looked at him, smiled, and said, "Don't worry, kid, you've sold me. Amanda, hi, its Anita again…I need to talk to the captain now. We think we've had a bit of a breakthrough on the abduction case. Okay, Patrolman Nelson, and I will be right up."

She hung up the phone and said to Nelson, "Gather your stuff, kid; we're going to see the captain.

Nelson sat there looking at her. A rookie cop in the captain's office wasn't a good thing, and it showed on his face.

"Move it, Nelson…we gotta go on this," Wilson directed. That got him moving. He dumped the spreadsheet information onto a thumb-drive and gathered the loose paperwork, got up and followed Wilson out of the office.

"The kid's scared outta his mind," Pete said with a chuckle.

"Captain's gonna melt that kid," Mike agreed. Everyone in the office, save rookie Connie, broke into laughter. Bish got another cup of coffee and sat at his desk.

Amanda showed the pair right into the captain's office. "Both of you sit down, I'll be with you in a minute," Captain Carlisle said. The pair chose seats and waited as the captain finished a phone call. "So, what now?" he asked Wilson.

"Patrolman Nelson here has come up with something you need to see and hear," she began. "He has a theory about where the next abduction is going to take place and I agree with him. Andy…" she said motioning to the rookie.

Nelson stood and said, "Good morning, captain…uh…may I please put this in your computer?" he asked, holding up the thumb-drive. The captain just nodded and pointed.

Nelson put the drive in and, with the captain's permission, brought up the Excel spreadsheet he'd made and began explaining his theory. After he was finished talking, he looked at Wilson and sat down. The captain was deep in thought. Both officers sat quietly while the *boss* thought the kid's theory through.

After what seemed to be an hour to Nelson, the captain finally sat up in his chair and said, "I agree with you, kid. Anita, I want you to have your team contact every law enforcement agency in both states and give them a heads up. I'll notify the feds and see if they want to do something. Without knowing which state or what town, all we can do here is keep a close eye on that van. Once it moves…" He paused for a moment, thinking once again, and then, looking at Wilson, said, "I'm gonna give you two more rookies to help out with watching those places. If that van moves I want somebody on it every second. Even if it means crossing county or state lines! Got it?"

"Yes, sir," Wilson quickly answered with a surprised look. Going over county and state lines was a huge no-no. Their jurisdiction would end at the Laramie County line.

The captain caught the two off guard and stood up quickly. Both hurriedly did likewise and the captain asked, "Anything else?"

"No, sir," Wilson answered.

"Then get to it. And Nelson…good work," the captain complimented the kid.

"Thank you, sir," Nelson replied.

With a wave of his arm, the captain dismissed the pair and they left the room, leaving the thumb-drive behind.

Back in the CID, Anita called the team together, explained what the captain wanted, and assigned who she wanted to make the calls to Utah and Idaho, then, looking directly at Nelson, said, "And Patrolman Nelson got an atta boy from the skipper. The others began to clap for the kid, and Bish reached over and slapped him on the back. Andy promptly turned red with embarrassment.

Bish leaned over to Andy and said, "Don't be embarrassed, kid. Ya done good. Be proud of what you've discovered. You just might have saved a kid's life." Andy hadn't thought about that and the surprise showed on his face. Bish smiled at him and gave him a positive nod.

"Okay everyone, let's get to it," Anita ordered. Everyone got up first and congratulated Andy on a good job. Connie gave him a wink and he pinked up again with embarrassment again.

Pete and Mike sat at their desks, looking up numbers and calling Utah and Idaho law enforcement agencies, explaining what was happening. A few wanted the FBI's Special Agent in Charge's (SAC) number for verification, even though the detectives had given them badge numbers and the captain's number - anything to cooperate with another agency. Maybe one or the other state's LEA's would get lucky and catch these jerks.

Nelson and Dominguez went over and stood at Wilson's desk and awaited orders. "You two will begin the surveillance on the two homes. The captain is working on a place right now. As soon as we get the okay to move in, I want you (pointing at Dominguez) to get over there right away. The captain's secretary will give you the information on who to see for a key. You (pointing at Nelson) will take over at seven this evening. Both of you get outta here and get changed into civilian clothes. Don't forget your side arms and extra magazines. Pack your over-night kits and bag some groceries for yourselves." She opened a drawer, pulled out a cash box which she unlocked, and gave each of them fifty bucks and said, "This is for you to buy food and necessities. Don't forget toilet paper…probably won't be any at the place. Now get. I'll call you Connie, when I get the information."

The two turned to leave, grabbing their coats and heading for the door. "Don't forget to write," Bish yelled as they left. Looking back at his desk, he chuckled as did Mike and Pete.

"You three get busy," Wilson ordered. It got quiet quickly. She waited impatiently for the call from Amanda, with the information about the home for the surveillance detail, and with who the two rookies would be with. In the meantime, she decided to go over Nelson's data for herself. She took special notice of the map he'd used to mark all the towns and cities where the abductions had taken place. She looked at the red marks and understood why the kid said it looked like a strange kind of 'X'. She wanted to call it more of a rough-looking cross, and Cheyenne was indeed the center. Maybe Cheyenne was the headquarters for this operation of serial kidnappers.

"Bish," she said.

"Yeah," he answered.

"I want you out there tomorrow morning with Connie," she directed. "If that van moves, don't let it outta your sight. Captain's already given authorization to cross county and state lines on this. Just make sure you have a full tank before going out there."

Bish's eyes got big at that announcement, but he said, "Got it, Anita," in a straight forward voice. "Anita…," she looked up at him, "…you don't need to worry about this. If they move, we'll be on 'em like stink. Ain't no way they'll get by us, I promise." He shut down his computer, put his coat on, looked at Pete and Mike, giving them a determined expression and left to get his kit and probably a bucket of KFC.

Pete got up and went over to Anita's desk and stared. Mike soon followed.

"What?" she said after a minute, trying to ignore them, but not being successful.

"What do you want us to do now?" Pete asked. "Utah and Idaho know. We wanna be part of this in the worst way."

"Yep," Mike added somberly, "worst way."

"I s'pect we'll need to go prepare, huh?" Pete asked her. "And we'll fill the tank."

She smiled and gave a snicker. "Both of you get out of here and get ready. I'll be in touch. I'll probably assign you each one of the rookies. Help them out. Train 'em right. This is not one to get good-humored on. Give it to 'em straight and don't pull any punches. This one is gonna be ugly. Watch yourselves and the rookies. I don't want to do any death notifications or the mountain of paperwork involved with one, you hear? Now, the two of you get."

The two nodded their heads, got their coats and left, leaving Detective First Class Anita Wilson alone in the office. She sat looking at the door with a sour look. She felt this was finally going somewhere…somewhere that wasn't going to be good. She suddenly got a chill, and knew beyond doubt that someone was going to get hurt on this case. She feared it would be someone on her team.

A meek knock on the door brought her out of her melancholy thinking. She looked up and saw two uniforms standing in the doorway, looking at her with frightened looks.

"Detective Wilson?" the taller of the two asked.

"Yes, come on in," she said. "What can I do for you?"

"Captain Carlisle told us to report to you for extended duty," the tall one answered. "He said we would be working for you indefinitely. Is that true?" the young man asked rather sheepishly.

"Yes, it is," she said. "Tell me your names and I'll give you your assignments." The two looked at each other and the shorter gave the tall one the nod to go first.

He stood up taller and said, "I'm officer Clint James. I've been on the force a few months. I graduated Douglas with Connie…I mean Patrolman Dominguez."

"I'm Patrolman Tom Alton, er Thomas, ma'am," the shorter of the two said. "I graduated Douglas with Patrolman Nelson. Glad to meet you," he ended, holding his hand out to shake hers.

She stood and took his hand, giving him a firm handshake. She shook Clint's hand also. "First thing I want to know is are you two really ready for this?" Both said 'yes ma'am'. "I'm afraid, gentlemen, that this is going to get dirty. You two need to get into a frame of mind that anything, and I mean anything, might happen on this case. How much did the captain tell you men?"

Clint spoke up saying, "He told us pretty much everything and said that Andy had come up with something good and that's why we're being assigned to your team."

"Good," Wilson said. She stood there for a moment looking back and forth at them, and then sat in her chair. She let out a deep sigh and said, "Okay, men, first thing is go home, change into civilian clothes – something comfortable – pack an overnight bag, stop somewhere and get some groceries for yourselves and then get back here. Don't forget your side arms and extra magazines. By the time you two get back, the others will be here and we'll begin." She reached into her desk, got her lock-box back out and gave each of them fifty bucks and said, "That should get you started. So get on outta here and I'll see you in a bit."

"Thank you, ma'am," the two said in unison and left.

Anita sat there in the quiet for a few moments thinking. After a few moments of silence, she opened her bottom desk drawer, the big one, and in back of all the paperwork and folders, dug out her additional magazine holder. It held two magazines. She checked they were fully loaded, the placed the thing in her purse. She now had five full magazines of ammunition. She got her coffee cup and filled it, sat back down at her desk and enjoyed the moment of quiet. She felt this was the quiet before the storm, the stillness before chaos. She sat with her coffee cup just in front of her lips, both hands holding the steaming mug, closed her eyes, and prayed.

The next morning Bish met Connie at the Burger King and splurged for some biscuits and eggs. They left the kid's car at Burger King after telling the manager, and drove south of town to the surveillance house. Nelson was happy to see them and said he had been bored outta his mind all night. He told them nothing had moved all night and he didn't see anyone come or go from either place.

The two of them went up to the second story where the camera and video equipment were set up. Bish used the binoculars to look around the neighborhood and not seeing anything out of the ordinary, sat down next to the monitor. Connie was already watching.

"You been on many stake-outs?" she asked him.

"Not really," he answered. "A few and they're all like this; boring until something happens and usually it's nothing much."

"I should have brought a book or something," she said.

"Yeah, all we have is time to watch while we're out here and a good book comes in handy. I got my Bible in the bag and a Tom Clancy novel, *The Hunt for Red October*. This'll be the fourth time I've read it. It's a good book."

"You read the Bible?"

"Every day if I can. Even if it's just a few passages, I try. Not always successful with life such as it is."

"I haven't read it much. Mom and Dad used to take my brother and me to church, but I wasn't really into that stuff much. Why do you read it, and do you go to church?"

"I do go to a little church over by Albertson's when I can. It's a small church – about a hundred folks or so and that's why I like it. There are always these two guys at the front door greeting everybody, shaking everyone's hands and giving the ladies hugs. It feels kind of like home in some respects. And the pastor really tells it like it is. Preaches directly from the Bible, and he tells us every time, that the only thing good he has to offer us is God's Word. He was being honest…"

Bish got quiet then and Connie stayed quiet also. He picked up the binoculars and began scanning the area again, watching. It was going to be a long day.

At nine fifteen that morning, the big man exited his house. Connie was quick and seeing the guy outside, got Bish's attention and pointed. They watched as the guy got into the van and backed out.

"That's our que, kid," Bish said getting up. "Let's go." He practically ran down the stairs after grabbing his bag. Connie did likewise and the two slammed the car doors and pulled out just in time to see the van make a left to go north on Highway eighty-five.

Bish got his radio out and notified Wilson of the movement. She told him not to lose the guy and that she would alert everyone else, and to give her an update every five minutes or so.

They stayed back, not saying anything, keeping an eye on the van. They followed him underneath I-80 and over the viaduct going over the railroad yard, and continued on Warren Avenue. The guy took a right on East Pershing Boulevard, then a left on Evans Avenue. He then pulled into the Cheyenne Regional Airport terminal and parked.

Bish was on the radio quickly, "Hey, he's pulled into the airport and parked, going inside now. We'll wait in the parking lot and watch," he told Anita.

"Okay, let me know what he's doing. Might want to send Connie in to watch and see if he gets on a flight. We'll need to get on it fast. Let me know as soon as you can."

Connie quickly got the other hand-held radio, got out and went into the terminal. She saw the big guy at the National Car Rental desk and he was filling out paperwork. She went around a corner and radioed Bish and told him.

"Keep an eye on him," Bish told her. "If he leaves, get back to the car quickly."

It was not too long when the big guy shook the clerk's hand and smiling, left the counter heading for the door. Connie followed him out and watched as he got back into the van. She hurried to the car and got in.

"He's pulling out," she told Bish. "He got an envelope from the guy at the counter and left with a smile on his face. I couldn't see what was in the envelope, sorry."

"Don't be sorry, it was probably impossible to see anyway," Bish told her. "I've rented cars there a couple of times and they put the contract and the keys in it. That's probably what it was. You have to drive over to the other terminal over on Airport Parkway to get the car out of their lot. Next question is why did he rent a car?"

"I guess we'll see, huh?" Connie stated.

"Yeah, I'll call it in." Bish called Wilson and told her what was going on and said as soon as they knew make and model of the vehicle, he'd let her know.

It wasn't long for them to find out as a newer looking black Cadillac Escalade came out of the parking area. They could clearly see the big guy behind the wheel. He turned left on the parkway and then took a right again on East Pershing Boulevard.

Bish called it in, ending with they were heading west on Pershing. Wilson told him she had the team gathered and they were listening in, and then told him to keep a running dialog going on telling the big guy's actions. If necessary, she would send another unit to back them up in a tag-team operation.

Bish keyed the radio again, "Okay, were turning south on I-25."

"You got a full tank, right?" Wilson asked.

"Roger," Bish said with a chuckle.

"Follow him everywhere he goes," Wilson ordered.

"We got 'em," Bish answered. "We're turning west onto I-80 now."

Wilson came back on and said, "As soon as you know he's heading towards Laramie, I'll send Pete and one of the rookies on Happy Jack to get in front of you. Let them take over in Laramie. You refill and if they continue on I-80, you follow 'em."

"Got it," Bish answered.

Connie asked, "What if he goes past Laramie?"

"Now you know why Wilson said to pack an overnight bag," he told her with a grin. "This just might be a long drive."

Sure enough, the guy went by the Harriman Exit and that meant that in all likelihood he was heading for Laramie or points beyond. Bish called it in and in a flash Detective Peter Donaldson and Patrolman Clint James, dragging bags and coats, flew out of the office and headed for Happy Jack Highway with lights going. They had to really move it to get to where Happy Jack Highway intersected with I-80. When they arrived, they informed Wilson and Bish and were happy to know they had made it in time to take over the tail.

Bish radioed Wilson and said they would be out of radio range soon as their range was just west of Laramie, and told her he would use his cell phone afterwards. Donaldson did the same. The two Cheyenne unmarked police vehicles were within view of the big guy's Escalade. Bish had told Donaldson that he and Connie would be getting off on the first exit in Laramie, filling up and driving through town and getting back on I-80 if necessary.

That is just what they had to do, as the big guy never slowed down, continuing on his way westward. He had no clue he was dragging two police vehicles along as well.

Bish and Donaldson were very surprised when they crossed the Wyoming border into Utah. Wilson was surprised also, but directed them to continue the tail. She had briefed the captain, and he, taking her along, went and briefed the chief. The chief contacted the FBI task force and told them what was happening. The feds, as usual, thanked them for the information but offered no assistance.

They followed the big guy's Escalade to Interstate Eighty-four, and shortly afterwards, turned north on Interstate Fifteen and quickly crossed into Idaho.

Bish looked at Connie and with a beaming smile said, "The kid was right."

They continued their track letting Wilson know every hour or so, or sooner if necessary. They drove through Idaho Falls, continuing north and were surprised as the big guy pulled off in Dubois, Idaho, a small community of less than a thousand souls. The odd thing about the small town is it is the county seat of Clark County, Idaho. The biggest enterprises in the community were the Phillips 66 gas station and quick mart and the U.S. Postal Office.

That's where the big guy went, the gas station, pulling in to refuel, which was odd, since he'd refilled in Idaho Springs. They watched the man fill the Escalade then, went inside, and came out a few minutes with a large bag of Ruffles and a huge

126

soft drink. He was sucking on the straw as he opened the car door. He started the car and pulled over to the Dubois Rest Area, parking in the shade of a tree.

Bish pulled in on the opposite side of the rest area and went inside to take a whiz. Connie stayed with the car. Donaldson and James stayed at the gas station, with James running in for snacks and drinks.

Two hours later, the big guy pulled out of the rest area and drove to Main Street then, turned north on Poison Street. He went by the rodeo arena and turned right on Second Street North, turning south onto Thomas Avenue.

Bish and Connie were getting the grand tour of the little hamlet. They were watching as he began to slow down. They did also. The big man was looking at something. They watched as he slowly made another turn to the east, soon finding out it was West Second Street South. He made another turn to the south on Reynolds Street and pulled into the Beaver Creek Inn, parked, got out, and went inside.

Bish told Connie to drive and he jumped out and ran down the street in time to see the big guy get back into the Escalade and park in front of a row of rooms. He got out of the SUV with a small bag and unlocking the door, went inside one of the rooms. A dog was barking behind the row of rooms.

Bish motioned for Connie to pick him up and once inside the car, called Wilson and told her what had happened.

"Is there another hotel in the area?" Wilson asked him.

"No clue, but we'll find out," he answered. "I'll call Pete and ask him to look around while we keep an eye on the Escalade."

"That'll work; let me know," she said and hung up.

"Dude, there is no other place to stay in town, the Beaver Creek is it," Donaldson told Bish. "What do you want to do?"

"Go find the sheriff's office, talk with them, and see if they might have a safe-house or something we can borrow for the night," Bish told him. "Connie and I will take the first shift, and we'll eyeball him 'till midnight. You guys take over then. I guess if we have to, we'll sleep in the cars."

"You sure there's a sheriff's office in town?" Pete asked.

"This is the county seat, man, has to have one," Bish answered.

Pete found the sheriff's office in the county building over on Clark County Road. Of the two-man shop, the sheriff was the only one in. His deputy was out on patrol. Pete introduced himself and his rookie partner, and after the sheriff introduced himself, briefed him on what was happening and gave him Wilson's phone number if he wanted collaboration. Pete told him about the big guy getting a room at the Beaver Creek place and told him their dilemma.

Sheriff Donald Clark, that's right, Sheriff Clark of Clark County, confirmed there were no other accommodations in town. Then, "But, I just bet my wife would love to have some visitors tonight, even being bothered at midnight. This is the neatest thing to happen in our neck of the woods since…ever, actually. We'll, maybe the night ol' Jim Blevins got drunk and run his truck into the Forest Service building front door." That brought a chuckle from everyone. The sheriff picked up the phone, called his wife, and told her what was going on and that they would be putting up four folks for the night. She was indeed, elated, even going so far as to say she would be making her special chicken enchilada casserole for the visitors to eat.

"You boys are a hit with the wife if she's going to go through the motions of fixing that casserole," the sheriff said. "I'm really glad you're here for that," he said with a beaming smile. Apparently his wife's chicken enchilada casserole was a real hit. "You boys go right on over." He gave them his address and they thanked him and departed.

Pete called Bish and gave him the address and said the sheriff was most helpful and they would be having the casserole for dinner. They pulled up to the sheriff's house and his wife was waiting on the front porch. She was a portly woman with sagging jowls and flat, tired blonde hair. She was dressed in a robe, sweat pants, and slippers that looked like the pink Hostess Snowballs, but furry. She was all smiles and greeted the two as if they were old friends.

"Come on in, boys," Missus Dorothy Clark said in welcome. "Y'all come on in and make yourselves at home. Take a nap and I'll have the casserole ready when you get up, say about ten tonight?"

"Nice to meet you, ma'am, I'm Detective Donaldson and this is Patrolman Clint James," Pete said as introduction. "And ten will be just fine. Actually, ma'am, you don't need to go through all the trouble for us. We can just have a sandwich."

"No, no, no, no, no, that won't do, no sir-ree, Don won't have that," she argued. "If I didn't fix something special for visiting LE's from another county to eat, why I don't know, he'd probably have a conniption or sumptin."

"Well, ma'am, we'll be happy with whatever you fix for us and we thank you very much for your hospitality," Pete said.

"Yes, ma'am, we're very appreciative," Clint agreed.

"You boys come on in and take a load off. If you want to sack out, there's two bedrooms down the hall on the right, you just go ahead and get comfortable. I know about stake outs and such and know they're trying, so y'all just get comfortable. I'll wake you about ten and you can take a shower and clean up. Now go on…get," she ended with a flip of her hand.

As they were walking towards the bedrooms, Clint asked Pete, "Are all sheriffs' offices like this one?"

"Couldn't tell you, kid," Pete answered. "I'll see you about ten, night."

"Yeah, night, sir."

Chapter 10

Dubois, Idaho

Morning brought a magnificent sunrise. Reds, oranges, yellows, and purples adorned the eastern sky. Bish and Connie stood silently, taking in the artwork that only God could do so well. Even a Van Gough painting couldn't do this justice. A flock of geese heading south topped off the vision.

"That was the best thing I've ever seen," Connie whispered almost to herself.

"It sure is, little sister," Bish agreed almost as silently.

Their revelry broke when Pete came over the radio saying, "Hey, did you guys see the sunrise?"

Bish and Connie looked at each other and laughed, climbed into the car and Bish, picking up his radio, said, "We did indeed, knucklehead."

"Why are you being so mean this morning?" Pete questioned. "I ain't a knucklehead…what's up with that?"

"You are when you interrupt us looking at a magnificent sunrise like that one," Bish answered.

"Oh, sorry, it was beautiful, huh," Pete said.

"Indeed. Has he moved yet?" Bish asked.

"He hasn't come out, but the lights came on about a half-hour ago," Detective Donaldson told him. "We figure he's in the shower getting cleaned up. Might be some action in just a bit, we'll let you know."

"Okay, the sheriff's wife fixed us some sausage and eggs for breakfast. You guys need anything?"

"Nah, we'll get something from the Phillips when we pull out since you're taking first lead."

"Roger that, good buddy, we're 10-8 and 10-76," Bish reported then, started the car.

He was about to pull out when Connie asked, "What were those ten numbers you were saying on the radio to Detective Donaldson?"

"They're the old ten codes we used to use on the radios," he explained. "I was just foolin' around. Pete knows what I said, and by-the-way, it was that we were in service, 10-8, and en-route, 10-76.

"Ah, thanks, we weren't taught those at Douglas," Connie said.

"Yeah, we don't use 'em much anymore. Some of us old timers still spit 'em out once in a while, but not often anymore." He pulled out of the sheriff's driveway and made his way over near the inn. He radioed Pete and told him they were in position.

"Okay, good buddy, to borrow a phrase, he's putting his stuff in the Escalade now. Get ready for action. We're going to the gas station, get something to eat and top off the tank. Talk to you in a bit."

"We'll let you know if he heads to the station so you can move. See you later," Bish ended the conversation. "We have the ball now, kid. Keep an eye out for that Escalade."

Connie just nodded and watched the entrance to the Beaver Creek Inn, and watched as Pete and Clint drove out and by their position. All four waved at each other.

Ten minutes later, the big guy pulled out of the inn and turned north. Bish and Connie slid way down in their seats as he went by, and they watched him turn west on Clark County Road. They waited a minute and followed, turning just in time to see the Escalade turn right onto Thomas Avenue and head north again. As they got to the turn, they could see the vehicle had slowed to almost a crawl again as it went past the houses lining the avenue.

"He's casing a home," Bish said. "I wish we could tell which one. Look closely on your side for a home that might be housing a newborn or very young child. I'll do the same over here."

Connie nodded and got quiet.

The Escalade crept along until it turned left onto West Main Street. Bish sped up to follow and watched as the big guy went by the gas station and turned north on I-15. Bish quickly called Pete on his phone and told him they were going north on the interstate. Pete said they would follow in a few minutes.

Bish and Connie followed along in silence. Both looked at each other when the Escalade pulled off the interstate and turned east onto West Camas Creek Road, otherwise known as Road 006. Bish quickly called Pete and told him about the turn. Bish and Connie were a bit confused.

The road, 006, was a dirt road, well maintained, but dirt nonetheless. Dust got onto everything. They rolled up their windows to keep the dust down inside the vehicle and pressed on, finally turning south onto Denny Hi Road and following it to Miracle Mile Road and then turning east again onto, of all things, Clark County Road. This they followed all the way to where it ended at a junction with Highway Twenty. The big guy turned south on it and drove to Idaho Falls, where he turned east on Highway Twenty-six. He crossed the Wyoming/Idaho border near Alpine Junction and turned south on Highway Eighty-nine, following it to Highway Thirty, to Kemmerer. There, he pulled into a Sinclair station to refuel.

"'Bout time, my bladder's about to burst," Connie stated.

Bish chuckled and said, "Yeah, mine's a bit tight, too. We'll watch until he pulls out then refill and empty tanks; how's that?"

"That will work," she answered.

Bish called Pete and told him what was up. Pete said they would take over as they had filled up back in Cokeville and still had plenty of fuel, and that they were about ten miles behind and should get there before the big guy pulled out. Bish and Connie had pulled into the Port of Entry, flashed their creds, and parked on the south entrance, watching and waiting. It wasn't long and they saw Pete pull into the Port of Entry and stop on the north side to wait. Bish and Clint waved at each other.

"You know Patrolman James?" Bish asked.

"No, not really, met him and that's about all," she answered.

The big guy was pulling out of the Sinclair station and as he went by, Pete and Clint pulled out behind him. Bish quickly drove over to the Sinclair and both piled out and headed for the bathrooms. Afterwards, Bish pulled the car over to the pumps and filled the tank. Connie came out with a bag of chips and two sodas and they continued their journey with Connie driving.

"I bet he's going to Highway 189 and merge with I-80, and head home," Bish speculated out loud.

"You really know this area?" Connie asked incredulously.

"Yeah, had to come get a prisoner in Kemmerer once, and that's the way we went back," he explained.

Just then, Pete came on the phone and told them that is what was happening. Bish laughed and Connie smiled. They drove on.

Once on I-80, Bish called Wilson and filled her in on the morning's events. She told them to follow the Escalade no matter where it went, and to call again when they got to Laramie. She would send another team to the stakeout house to watch. Bish, Pete, Connie, and Clint, were to get a good meal and some rest and to report the next day if indeed the big guy went back home. That was fine with the four of them. Rest was definitely on the menu as they'd just done almost a thousand miles in two days. And with the stress of trying to stay incognito, they were beat.

Bish called Pete and said, "Hey, Wilson's buying, where you want to go to dinner before we hit a sack somewhere?"

"How about Tortilla Factory, it's on the way home after we drop off the big guy, anyway, I'm in the mood for something with a kick, and we'll be off duty, right?" Pete asked.

"Yes, off duty so a stiff margarita will go good, right?"

"Absolutely, partner."

"Then it's a plan. See you there after the break-off."

"Ten-four good buddy."

Bish laughed and hung up. "We're going to Tortilla Factory after the break-off, and yes, margaritas are on the menu."

"That sounds great," Connie said. "I like that place - good food, good atmosphere, nice people – I like their super burritos, the one with pork. My mouth is watering already."

"Mine, too, so hush up about food already," Bish said with a chuckle. "My stomach is rumbling now."

Pete and Clint refueled in Laramie, as did the big guy and Bish. With full tanks all around, they continued eastward on I-80, and once reaching Cheyenne again, turned north on I-25, getting off on Pershing Boulevard to Airport Parkway. The big guy turned in the Escalade and resumed his travels in the van and went directly home.

The four tired officers turned him over to Detective Mike Hicks and Patrolman Andrew Nelson, and promptly drove to the Tortilla Factory for a nice meal and some drinks.

Bish got home about six-thirty, poured a two-finger shot of eighteen year-old Glenfiddich, and parked in front of the television for a movie. He woke at ten-thirty, went to his bedroom and undressed, climbed into the sheets, and promptly fell asleep.

Bish walked in at seven in the morning. Wilson was at her desk and asked, "So, it went well?"

"I guess," Bish replied. "He drove by some homes very slowly, twice, and that was pretty much it. I think the trip outta town to the east was an alternate escape route and he drove it to familiarize himself with the route. At least that's what I'm thinking. But I believe he's our guy and Helen and Daniel are in on it, too. Maybe not the end parties, but definitely in on the action. I believe the big guy, Helen, and Daniel, abduct the kid, and then take her to whomever is funding the action. I suspect the big guy plans the abduction and the routes, and is the driver going and coming.   I suspect Helen and Daniel do the abductions, put the kid in the van and there you have it. They leave. If it's quiet, then they leave by the easy route, in this case that'll be I-15 south to I-84, and finally I-80. Otherwise, they'll use the eastward route we used to come home. The scenic route as it was really beautiful country through there."

"You weren't on a sight-seeing tour; tell me more of what you suspect, even if it's far-fetched."

He looked at her, reached over and slid a chair next to her desk and sat down to think for a moment. "I suspect the buyer or whoever tells the big guy who the target is. Once the big guy has the target name, address, and such, he draws up the plan to include actually driving planned routes to and from the target place. He may even have to make several trips to plan it all. Meanwhile, Helen and Daniel are either sitting back waiting, or just may be preparing for the actual event. Buying supplies, baby stuff, foods for the adults, the materials for the actual abduction once they have the information about the place in question. They may have already begun that process. I'd love to get a look in their garage and that storage shed they have in the back - even the big guy's garage."

"And who the dealer is - I don't have a clue but, there has to be a dealer. Someone who finds the kid, and based on the background information we already have, we know a lot about his or her targets. I should have asked Sheriff Clark if he knew of any pregnant women or those that had babies recently. There couldn't have been that many in a hamlet of around thousand people.   We, or rather the Idaho authorities, could put surveillance on the one or two or three there might be in a small place like that. And we can rule out Hispanics so that might lessen the number.

"The big guy already has his refueling points marked. They won't stop for meals. They may have to stay overnight somewhere. That's a possibility, especially if they have to do a tertiary escape route. You know April in Wyoming, there may still be a lot of snow along that route we took back, and parts of it may be closed until May or June. You need to make the decisions, which if the big guy goes out again like he did, are we going to track him again like we did? Or are we going to do something else? I thought about why he rented a vehicle and wondered if he thought someone had put a tracking device in the van. If so, what will he do for the actual event? Take the van anyway, rent another one, or buy a new one.

"We need to look at tools they might use. I want to get someone that investigates break-ins to brief us on what kinds of tools to look and watch for. We also need someone who's married with kids to come talk to us about what the kidnappers will need to take along just so we know. Shoot, we just might be the ones transporting the child if something happens and we'll need to be prepared for that. Geeze, that scars the crap outta me having to transport a baby."

Wilson looked at Bish and saw him staring into nothingness, his eyes wide as saucers. She looked down at her desk and grinned.

"Anyway," he said after breaking from his trance, "I think we ought to get a round-table discussion going on this as soon as we can. Get everyone together and discuss this. Have lots of legal pads and pencils available and write everything down, even if it seems far-fetched. We just might get something outta a session like that."

"I'll talk to the captain," she said, looking at him. "He'll make it mandatory and I like the idea myself. I also like the idea you have of talking to a married person with a baby, to know what they might need to carry along on a trip. I like your thoughts on the van and the tracking device. That just might be why he got a rental. You've got some good thoughts on this."

"Thanks, boss," he said. "I was looking at that data the kid put together…"

"Yeah…?" Wilson prompted after a moment.

"Yeah, and I'm figuring the next one is going to be Caucasian. Vast majority have been Caucasian. She'll have brown eyes and dark hair most likely. That seems to be the favorite. I'm thinking the dealer, or buyer, is the one we really want. He or she is the one taking these kids after they're abducted." He lowered his head and was quiet for a moment, and then almost in a whisper, "I'm not real sure I want to know what happens then."

Wilson looked up at Bish and saw a look on his face she had never seen before. "Bish…you okay?"

He looked up at her with that gaze and said, "I'm sorry boss, but if we get to this person, I'm afraid they're gonna have ta die." And with that, he got up and left the room.

Wilson sat there staring at the door as it quietly closed. She knew that Bish could most likely chew nails right then and knew she shouldn't go after him. He needed time to cool down, or whatever he was. She sat back in her chair and thought and could not ever remember seeing him with that look before. He'd always said that when it came to kids and animals, he was a person that really wanted to do harm to the ones hurting either.

She remembered the time they'd responded to the ER for a kid that had been burned. When they got there, they found out that the two-year-old had been burned with a cigarette repeatedly by the father, who just happened to be out in the waiting room. It was everything she could do to restrain Bish. The doctor, nurse, and medical assistant all helped to restrain him. Once Wilson had gotten his attention and got him settled down some, she marched him out of the ER the back way and sent him home with orders to take the next day off and settle down.

But this look was different from the ER episode. She shook with the chills and knew that look was not a good one. Bish had already made up his mind – whoever it was taking those kids was going to die. Another cold chill ran down her spine. She was going to have to talk with him, and soon.

She picked up her phone and dialed Sheriff Clark, in Dubois, Idaho, and filled him in on the situation and asked him if he knew of any close to two-year olds on that street. He did and told her he would call in a reserve deputy and begin a watch on the residence. She thanked him and hung up.

Chapter Eleven
el Jefe
Denver, Colorado

Enrique Salinas answered the phone like an impatient CEO might. It was the big man calling to give a report on his travels. "El Jefe, I hope you are doing fine, sir," the big guy began.

"Dispense with the pleasantries and tell me what you have to report," Salinas said, rather impatiently.

"Si, senior, uh, the trip was uneventful, and thank you for the Escalade rental," the big guy said. "I took the direct route and observed the property. It should be nothing for us, very little obstructions around the property. Only two LE's (law enforcement) in the community and should not be an issue. The return trip was taken on the secondary route. Although very scenic, it will add an additional day to the trip. We'll need to plan for that. I do recommend the direct route both going and returning to the drop off point.

"I did look at a tertiary route, but it would be an extreme path to say the least and do not recommend it at all. We'll take the primary there, and depending on circumstances, return the same way. If circumstances dictate, we'll use the secondary route. An advisement on that is the time of the year. There may very well be snow present, and routes may be impassable or closed entirely. A chance we'll have to take. I believe one more trip is called for with my second along for the ride for familiarity reasons, especially the secondary route. We will have to do more planning for that and take appropriate measures for the weather, and take along appropriate materials and equipment to handle possible unsavory road conditions. That is all I have for you sir."

"Very good, make your plans and take action," el Jefe directed. "Call again after your next visit and we'll finalize the plan."

"Si, senior," the big guy said and hung up, knowing el Jefe had already hung up.

That evening, the big guy went down the ladder in the hole in the floor of the bedroom. At the bottom, he turned to his right and followed a tunnel out of the basement that led to his neighbor Helen's home. He climbed the short ladder to the hatchway and knocked several times. It took a moment, but the hatch was lifted by Helen.

"Hey partner, more news from el Jefe?" she asked as the big guy climbed out.

"Yep; Daniel coming home tonight?" he asked.

"Actually he should be here in about a half hour or so," Helen said with a smile, then, "Would you like a glass of sweet tea while you wait?"

"Well, darlin', you already know the answer to that, don't you," he said with a laugh. "Where's the little one?"

"She's probably just now waking from her nap if you'd like to go get her," she answered.

"I'll get the little tyke," he said smiling, turning for the hallway. In her room, he saw she was already sitting up in her crib playing with a small stuffed animal. "Come here, little lady," he said reaching in and picking her up. Shirley was all smiles and pulled at the man's collar.

Back in the kitchen, he sat at the table and sipped his tea as he held Shirley on his knee and bounced her. She giggled and giggled and while the toddler happily played, he and Helen talked about the neighborhood's happenings.

After a few minutes, Helen asked, "Was el Jefe satisfied with the trip report?"

"Yes, and he approved my suggestions so Dan and I will be leaving to make the same trip once again, to get him familiar with the routes in case he has to drive for some reason," he responded. "There'll be a lot of planning to do as the secondary route just may be treacherous that time of year with the weather. The primary route may be just as bad if a blizzard rolls through the area. We'll really have to prepare for this one."

Right then, Daniel walked in, set his helmet down on the couch, and went into the kitchen. First thing he did was reach over and pick up Shirley. "Is that sweet tea I see?" he asked.

"Sure is, sugar, want a glass?" Helen asked.

"Absolutely and thanks," he answered. "How's it going, big guy?"

"Tolerable I recon," the big guy replied. "Talked with el Jefe."

"Yeah, what's he have to say?" Daniel asked.

"I gave him the trip report and he okayed another trip so you and I can go and see the routes," the big guy said. "When are you off for three days again?"

"Next week, Thursday, Friday, and Saturday…wanna go then?"

"Yeah, that'll be fine. Want the Escalade? It was nice."

"Oh yeah, that would be great," Daniel said with a smile and bouncing the baby all the while. "Will we have time for a full recon while we're there?"

"We can make it so, number one," the big guy answered with a chuckle.

"Okay, captain Star Trek, I'll get my camera equipment ready. You have the topo maps or do I need to pick some up? I'm going to Fort Collins tomorrow for the boss at the job-site, and I can pick 'em up then if needed."

"Yeah, we'll need 'em so do that and get anything else you may need," the big guy directed. He reached in his pocket and pulled out a roll of cash and handed it to Daniel, "Here, here's a couple of grand, get what you need."

"Will do and thanks."

"What about me?" Helen asked.

"You need to start a list you think we'll need for the toddler. Everything she might need for an extended trip in rough terrain during sever winter conditions. You gotta plan this one right. If we have to take the secondary route, we'll have to be prepared for any contingency. No kidding around on this one. The weather could be a real factor on us this time. I gotta feeling."

"You always have a feeling about something, but I'll do my best and list everything we'll need. How much time do I have?"

"Well, it's November, so, about a month of planning and gathering supplies and equipment. After that we'll start the dry runs and hash out the weaknesses we find in the operational plans. That do for you?"

"That'll be more than enough time to make the list and pick everything up after we hash it out. I may have to make a trip or two down south to Fort Collins and maybe Loveland…we'll see."

"Okay, you do that and Daniel and I'll make the trip next week. Got it?"

Both said they did and the big guy tipped his iced tea glass back and finished it. "Ahh," he said, "that's good stuff. Thank you."

"You're welcome," Helen answered.

Get in here!" el Jefe yelled.

Sims practically flew into the room saying, "Yes, Jefe."

"Sims, good, you're really fast, you know it? Anyway, call Issy and tell her to speed up the training on the girl. We're about to need another room up north and I don't want anything to go wrong."

"Si, senior, will do," Sims answered. "Will that be all, Jefe?"

"For now, dinner as usual this evening," he replied.

"Very good, senior," and with that, Sims left the room.

Salinas leaned back in his chair and gazed out of his office window. A fresh snow had fallen that morning and he loved to gaze out of the picture window at the front range of the Rocky Mountains after they'd been dusted with a fresh coat of snow. It was pleasing to the eye and very relaxing. Pleasing to the eye…he thought about the young woman in training for his next pleasure-filled outing in Wyoming. He smiled, denoting an evil that most living humans had never seen. Issy had seen it, but of course she would have reason to see it and live. He sat there enjoying memories and the scene.

He leaned over to his small dry-sink and poured himself a stiff shot of eighteen-year-old scotch. No ice, just the liquor, neat. He sat back, took a long sip, and relished the fiery liquid along with the view. He settled deeper in his chair and the smile returned after a satisfying ahh.

The phone rang. On the third ring, he picked up the handset and said, "Yes."

It was his accountant with news, "el Jefe, you did well last month, clearing just over one hundred million all told. Less than a million taxable, of course, and the funds dispersed in your usual accounts around the world. The hard copies will be on your desk by noon tomorrow. Do you have any questions for me, sir?"

"Which business did the lion's share?" Salinas asked.

"The channels from Venezuela, through Mexico, to the states, of course, uh, better than seventy million."

"I believe it should have been better, don't you think?"

"It would have been if not for the American president building that fence. Most of the traffic now must be underground, by air, or by sea, not to pun the U.S. Marines, and that makes transport rather difficult in both directions. I have some loss figures if you'd like to hear them…"

"No, I understand and know about the fence. We'll need to be more creative with this new…fence."

"Yes, el Jefe, would you like for me to create a development team to work this issue? I'd be most happy, too."

"That would be appreciated," Salinas said and hung up. He spun in his chair to gaze out the window again, sipping his liquor, and thought about the new development with the fence on the southern border of the United States. It did put a dent in his income of close to thirty million dollars a month. That hurt to him and was not acceptable. He wondered if he might need to make some personnel changes along the pathways from Venezuela on up. Making a few examples out of people usually did the trick and got merchandise flowing smoothly once again.

Chapter Twelve
December
Cheyenne, Wyoming

The first big snowfall of the year was underway. Bish stood at the office window watching the snow falling. Yes, falling! It was one of those very unusual snowfalls in Wyoming, as the snow was coming straight down, not horizontally as was customary. Normally, the winds in Wyoming kept the snow going to the south or east in a very hurried, horizontal manner. This storm, so far, was a quiet, Christmas-like dream snow storm.

Rookie Patrolman Clint James sauntered up and stood beside Bish watching the snow. He was originally from Mesa, Arizona, and commented, "I though the wind blew during snow storms here."

Every detective in the room and two other rookie cops jumped up and yelled at him to keep his mouth shut. "You never use the '*W*' word during a storm like this," Bish explained while holding the rookie by the front of his shirt, toes just barely touching the ground, and Bish's nose a scant millimeter away from the kid's, eyes glaring.

Bish set the wide-eyed kid back firmly on his feet, and gently smoothed his very rumpled shirt. Once he was done with that, he pointed to the rookie's desk and said, gently and quietly, "Sit." He watched as the kid staggered back to his desk while the others still stood and glared. Bish turned around and continued to watch the storm.

Once Clint had settled down, Detective First Class Anita Wilson rolled her chair his way and quietly said, "I should have warned you, but one never uses the '*W*' word around here, especially during a storm like this one. That's real taboo in this neck of the woods. You're very lucky you're not bleeding," and left it at that, moving back to her desk, suppressing a grin.

It was a well-known fact that the wind in Wyoming was indeed a much discussed topic among newly arrived people, those passing through, and vacationers. It was especially commented on if one was traveling west on Interstate Eighty, especially those driving the eighteen-wheelers. The high winds actually had an effect on how high-profile vehicles performed going up to Monument Pass, elevation just under eight-thousand feet above sea-level. Native Wyomingites would comment to those going east on the interstate, that they could go to Omaha, Nebraska, with a sheet and a skate board on a *nice* windy day.

Bish continued to gaze out the window. The snowfall was still coming straight down; the rookie had not jinxed the place with an unwanted wind. Wind in a snowfall such as this one would create impassable drifts, sometimes eight to ten feet in height. He finally left the window, poured himself a mug of coffee, and sat down at his desk thinking it would be a white Christmas after all.

The big guy and Daniel were stranded. They had begun the return trip on the secondary route when the storm hit. They had made it to Highway Twenty, and after speaking with a guy at Elk Creek Station, had made it to a place back in the trees that was closed for the season, but the man at Elk Creek Station knew the owner and had called for the two. The man was kind enough to open a cabin for the two and said they could wait the storm out there. He charged them twenty-five bucks a night saying that was for the utilities while they stayed. He even invited them for dinner that evening with his wife.

Four days they were stranded. The morning of the fifth day, they paid the owner of the cabin fifty extra bucks just for being so nice, and left after cleaning up the cabin. They followed a plow going south on Highway Twenty, and by that evening had made it to St. Anthony, where they found a bed and breakfast with a room still available. The following morning, they changed their route and went to Idaho Falls, catching Interstate Fifteen to Interstate Eighty-four and finally to Interstate Eighty. They stayed the night in Evanston, Wyoming, and drove home the next day.

The big guy called el Jefe as soon as they unpacked, told him about the storm and being stranded, and told him the secondary route would be closed most likely until spring. They would be held to one way in and out.

"This could be a dangerous mission, el Jefe," the big guy said, knowing that there would be no change in the mission parameters.

"Then there will be only one way," Salinas said with finality. "Make sure there are no problems. None – understand?"

"Si, senior," the big guy answered and hung up knowing el Jefe did not hear the 'yes sir'.

He went to the kitchen where Helen and Daniel sat at the table. He poured himself a cup of hot water for hot chocolate, and sat down.

"How did he take it?" Daniel asked.

"Told us to use the primary route and to leave no problems," the big guy muttered. "That means we need to include that additional weaponry just in case."

Helen and Daniel both looked at each other knowing this one could be bad.

Little did the trio realize just how bad it really would get, and sooner than they thought.

"You wanted to see me Captain?" Wilson asked as she walked up to Captain Carlisle's office.

"Yeah, get in here and close the door," the captain replied. "Be right with you," and he continued talking on the phone.

Anita sat down and waited. She looked around the room, stopped her sight on the captain's 'I-love-me-wall' looking at his awards, diplomas and photos. One photo was of him and the mayor, another of the captain and the governor of Wyoming. Big smiles and forced poses.

She heard the phone hang up and looked at the captain, waiting. He was sitting in his chair musing what he'd just heard on the phone.

"That was the FBI," he began. "They got a federal judge to grant them the okay to tap the big guy's phones, cell, and land-line. They're working on the women next door. They're going to give us authorization to listen in. You still have those rookies working the case?"

"Yes, sir," she quickly answered.

"Get them trained on the devices post haste," he directed. "I want to be listening every second. I know that guy and that woman are involved in this. We've got four months to make headway on this. I don't want to see another family destroyed by abduction." He was referring to the fact that Margaret and Bryan Pierce, had divorced over the loss of their daughter's abduction almost two years prior. Both remained quiet for a few moments.

"Anita?" Carlisle gently asked.

"Yes, sir?" she said.

"We can't let another kid wind up with these people," he said in almost a whisper. "We can't." He looked up at her and said, "You need anything at all you let me know. We're gonna move mountains to not let this happen again. Got it?"

"We'll do everything we can, Cap, I promise," Anita assured him.

He nodded and that was the end of that meeting. Anita went back to their office and called everyone in, giving them the briefing on the phone taps and that they would all from that day forward be working exclusively on the abduction case. "Time off for Christmas would be as normal, but after that…just don't expect any time off after that, understood?" she said and for an answer got nods from everyone.

"Bish, take two rookies and go train them on the tap devices," she directed. "Mike, you'll do the same with the other two when Bish is done. Pete, I want you watching those two homes like a hawk…scoot," she ordered and Pete got up to leave. "I'll have some relief out there with you after the training."

"No problem," he said, giving her a thumb up as he grabbed his hat, coat, and gloves.

She watched Bish, as he, Connie, and Andy left to go train. Mike, sat Clint and Tom down and began going over something. She finally got up, poured herself a mug of coffee, and then sat back at her desk. She took a couple of healthy sips of the steaming liquid, sat her cup down, and opened her bottom drawer, the big one. She reached inside and brought out her additional magazines – all six of them. She began taking the rounds out of each magazine, leaving the bullets in a pile next to her phone. After all ninety rounds were out, she took out a cleaning cloth she kept in the same drawer, along with a bottle of Ballistol gun cleaner and lubricant, setting them on her desk.

She dismantled all six magazines, wiped them clean with the cloth, and then placed a small amount of the lubricant on all six. Satisfied, she put the magazines back together, and reloaded all the bullets.

What she didn't realize, was Mike, Clint, and Tom were watching her intently. Mike knew. The rookies wondered.

Wilson placed all six magazines in their pouches, setting them in so that as she withdrew one, it would slide into her firearm with the bullets in the proper direction, thus saving a second or two of time. She looked up seeing the three looking at her.

"Mike, get 'em ready," she ordered. "Full load-outs and get 'em issued an M-4. We're not taking chances. Tell Bish to get the other two ready when they get back," she said getting up and leaving.

When she returned, she had her M-4 and all seven magazines with her. She sat at her desk, stripped the rifle down, and cleaned it. Next, she unloaded and broke down all seven of her twenty-round magazines for the weapon. She preferred the twenty-round mags as they made the rifle easier for her to handle, especially in the prone firing position. She just wasn't that tall, and she had to lift up to fire the rifle with a thirty-round magazine, throwing her sighting off, and in a real fire-fight, she would be exposing her head to gunfire.

After she finished cleaning, lubing, and reloading the magazines, she placed a full one in her rifle and set the lot in her case. She heard a noise and looked up as Mike, Tom, and Clint walked in with rifle cases, a bag full of ammo boxes, and a sack of magazines. Mike steered them to the large conference table and they began the process of stripping and cleaning their weapons.

Anita watched the rookies closely as did Mike. She watched as the two reassembled their thirty-round magazines, remove ammo from the boxes, slide the spoons onto the mags, add the stripper clips with ten rounds each, and zip them into the mags. Three clips to each magazine, seven magazines, two-hundred-ten rounds of lethal .556, green-tipped, armor piercing ammunition. These rounds could conceivably travel completely through a house once fired. Walls in homes these days would not protect anyone in a firefight. She hoped they wouldn't have to use them.

Bish returned with the other two rookies. Mike jumped up and leaning in close to Bish's ear, whispered what Wilson wanted them to do. Bish looked at her and she nodded approvingly. He looked over towards the large conference table and saw the ammo boxes and weapons. He told Connie and Andy to hang up their coats and follow him.

Mike grabbed his coat, weapons and ammo and said, "Let's go you two. We got some training to do," and left the office with the two rookies in tow.

Anita got up, poured herself another mug of coffee, and sat back down.

Bish, Clint, and Tom came in then and began placing their weapons and ammo on the conference table. Bish looked up at Wilson and said, "The armory wants to know if we're going to war. They even called the captain and he told them to give us whatever we wanted." He looked at her for another moment, and then got down to business with his weapons.

"Bish," Wilson said, and when he looked up at her she continued, "I want you to take Clint out to assist Mike. You and Tom relieve them tonight at seven and I'll have Mike and Connie relieve you two in the morning at seven. Tom, you go with him and take your weapons with you. I want everyone fully armed from now until this thing is over with. After you drop off Clint, you two go get something to eat and some shut-eye."

Bish nodded his head and said, "Got it." He continued loading thirty-round magazines.

The office now smelled of cleaning solution, and to most folks that handled firearms on a regular basis, that was like aftershave or perfume. It was a pleasant smell that everyone who had anything to do with firearms liked. It would take a day or two to dissipate.

Bish and Clint finished the job on their weapons, policed up the cleaning supplies and area with Tom's help, and then the two of them left with their loads.

"Tom," Anita said.

"Yes, ma'am," he answered looking at her.

"I'll want you on those tap devices as soon as we get the greenlight," she directed.

He smiled and said confidently, "Yes, ma'am." He sat down at his desk and began reading the daily reports.

Wilson got up with her coffee cup, went over to the window, and watched the snow continue to fall. Her mind raced. So much information going through her, and most of it not leading anywhere except to Cheyenne. They were missing something and whatever *it* was, would tie everything together. She knew they were missing an important piece of the puzzle, and she figured that *it* was the person or persons paying the bills. Maybe they would get lucky on the phone taps.

Right then her phone rang on her desk. She walked over, looked at the ID panel and saw it was the captain, "Yes, sir," she said answering.

"We got it," he said. "Federal judge in Denver gave us full access to tap both homes, their cell phones, and get this, the judge added cell phone tracking so you can keep track on them."

"That's great, captain," she said with relief in her tone. "Sir - if I may ask - when are we to get the authorization to start on the phones?"

"Right now if you have someone available to come up here and get the paperwork," he answered.

"I have Patrolman Alton here…I can send him right up," she responded.

"Send him and I'll give him the authorization…Anita…get these people will you?" he said in a subdued tone.

"He's on his way, sir, and yes, sir, we'll get 'em," she answered and hung up.

"Tom, go to the captain's office and he'll give you the authorizations for the phones to be tapped," she directed him, and he jumped up and headed out of the office with a smile on his face. She saw that he was just as excited to get this case over with as the rest of them. *Now, maybe we can get the rest of the story*, she thought and turned for the window again.

Chapter Thirteen
January
Cheyenne, Wyoming

The knock on the door startled the big guy as he wasn't expecting anyone.

"Just a minute," he yelled reaching down to get his robe and slip it on. He was still in his sleeping shorts and tee shirt. He put the robe on while walking to the door. There, he unlocked the door, unfastened the chain, and opened it.

"el Jefe!" he exclaimed. "I had no idea it was you…please, please come in, senior," he said with a flourish wave of his hand.

Salinas entered the home and stood there for a moment while the big guy, leaning out the door for a second and looking around ensuring no one was about, closed the door.

"To what do I owe this pleasure, senior?" the big guy asked.

"I want to make sure you know there will be no problems next April, correct?" Enrique Salinas intoned.

"Si, senior, no problems at all," the big guy answered. "We have everything under control, Jefe. The plans are complete, equipment and supplies are being listed and bought, and we have a complete inventory made up if you would like to see it."

"Yes, I do," Salinas said, curtly. "Where do I sit?"

"Please, senior, this way," the big guy said and led the way into the dining room, where Salinas sat at the head of the table. The big guy opened a folder and handed a multiple-page Excel spreadsheet to Salinas.

Salinas took it and began to read. He slowly read every word, flipping the pages as he read. He read it three times.

"It does indeed appear you have everything thought out for this mission," Salinas said, handing the spreadsheet back to the big guy.

"Thank you, Jefe; would you care to see the routes?" he stammered.

"Yes," was the curt, one-syllable answer.

The big guy reached back and got the atlas, opening it to Wyoming, and putting a finger in the page for Idaho to mark it. He set the atlas down in front of Salinas and began explaining, using his bulbous finger as a pointer, the routes he'd planned.

"This secondary route is the problem, no?" Salinas asked.

"Si, Jefe, because of the uncertainty of the weather," the big guy explained. "The route, er…here and here is closed due to the storm we just had, and may very well be closed for the rest of the season, according to the Bureau of Land Management and the Wyoming Department of Transportation. They explained that when there is a significant snowfall, they do not clear the roads in the high country because of budgetary constraints. All we can hope for at this point is fair weather for the next few months…hehe, global warming, no?" he chuckled.

Salinas looked at him and shook his head. He wasn't in the mood for jokes. He took the atlas and looked over both routes and said, "Did you consider going north on I-15?"

"Si, senior," the big guy answered quickly. "The problem with going north is it is a main highway and leads to another main highway. If the van is identified, we would be very easy to apprehend on a major highway. Going south, it is only fifty miles or so to Idaho Falls and we can cut eastward on secondary state roads and highways from there. If the roads are impassable due to weather, we believe going south to I-80 would be the best and most direct route."

The big guy stood back up after that as his back was beginning to ache. Salinas continued to look at the atlas.

"You have thought this through, my friend," Salinas complemented. "I will not argue with your logic on the routes, and if the weather closes the highways, then that is an act of God we cannot contend with. When the time comes, make your route according to your best judgment and assessment of the conditions. Above all, protect the niña pequeña, understand?"

"Absolutely, senior."

Salinas looked at the big guy and gave him a half smile. "Do you feel you need more money for the proper equipment for this mission?"

"No, senior, you have provided more than enough."

"Very well, I must be on my way," and el Jefe got up and headed for the door. "If you need anything, contact me as usual."

"Understood, el Jefe, it was a pleasure and an honor to have you in my home," the big guy said with a slight bow.

Salinas left without another word. The big guy stepped out the door with Salinas, and watched as el Jefe got into his white BMW X7, backed out of the drive, and headed east.

The big guy went back inside after waving one last time. He went to the kitchen and poured himself a generous shot of whiskey in a tumbler, went and sat in his recliner, and knocked the shot back in one gulp. He cringed as the fiery liquor went down, and then he took a huge breath. He wiped his forehead, realizing he was sweating profusely, and leaned back into the recliner and tried to relax.

The Jefe had never visited him before and it made him very uncomfortable knowing the man himself had been to see him. This was an extremely unusual event and made the big guy nervous.

The whiskey had settled him down somewhat, and he shut his eyes to attempt to relax even more. He was just about to fall asleep when someone knocked on the door. He jumped up, startled, and with a fearful look on his face. He quickly got up and went to the door, unlocked it again, and opened it.

"Hey," Helen said with and a smile, then after seeing his face and that he was white as a sheet said, "Are you okay?" She stepped into the house, put her arm out to grasp him, and again said, "Hey, are you okay?"

After a sigh of relief, the big guy nodded and uttered, "Uh huh."

She turned him and guided him back to his recliner and said, "Sit, I'll be right back," and she went into the kitchen after making sure he was in the chair. She saw the bottle of whiskey sitting open on the counter, grabbed it and walked back into the living room. She saw his tumbler, picked it up, poured another healthy shot of the liquor, and handed it to him.

"Drink it, now," she directed.

He tossed the liquor back and took another deep breath afterwards - and took another deep breath after that.

"He was here," he blurted suddenly.

"Who…who was here?" Helen asked.

"el Jefe," he answered almost in a whisper.

She lifted straight up and turned to look at the door, her eyes wide and fearful. "He was here?" she asked.

"Yes," he answered weakly.

"What did he want?" she asked.

"He wanted to see our plans…he looked at the equipment and supply lists and then went over the atlas map with me, the primary and alternate routes." He looked up at her and as her eyes met his, he said, "And he approved. He even asked if we needed more money – I told him no."

"This makes me nervous!" she exclaimed.

"YOU!" he screamed. "You weren't here. You didn't see his face. You didn't see the looks he gave me when I answered his questions. It felt like he was skinning me while he looked at me. It was unnerving," and he reached for the whiskey again.

She watched as he poured the tumbler half way with the amber liquid, lifted it, and tossed it back once again. She knew he'd had at least three shots of the whiskey.

"You need to take it easy on that stuff," she said meekly. "We need you with your head clear." She took the bottle back to the kitchen cabinet and got him a pack of crackers thinking that would help soak up some of the booze.

"Did you ask him for the shotguns?" she asked, and then, "You should have said yes to the money. That way we could have gotten the shotguns."

"Look, you don't understand," the big guy mumbled. "I ain't gonna ask that man for nothing. If he wants us to have something, he'll make sure we get it. I want to stay on the side of him that keeps me alive."

"So, how are we going to get the funds for the shotguns we need?" she asked him. "Should I try to call him?"

"NO!" he yelled at her. "Don't call him. Okay, okay, I'll put a message through the usual channels. We should never directly contact him unless it is a dire emergency or unless he's directed it."

"You really are afraid of him, aren't you?" she asked, sarcastically.

He gave her a scathing look and said, "You better believe it, Helen. You need to learn that kind of healthy respect yourself. Don't underestimate el Jefe. If you do, you'll be dead before you know it. He doesn't mess around and neither should we if we want to stay alive."

She looked at him and could see the seriousness in his face, along with the fear. "You really are scared of him."

"Yes, I am," he answered with conviction, head hung low. "He's the only person I've ever been afraid of."

She suddenly got a cold chill that ran up and down her spine, and after a moment asked, "What do you think we should do then…about the shotguns that is?"

"Well, we can't be seen buying shotguns so we'll need to have someone do it for us or maybe steal them from somewhere," he answered.

"Let me think on this and we'll talk later," she said, heading for the door.

Bish and Tom had relieved Pete and Clint at the observation post and were watching as Helen left the big guy's house.

"She was in there an awful long time," Tom said. "Think they're…"

"No, I don't," Bish interrupted. "You've got a dirty mind, you know it?"

"I guess," he said. "What do you think they were doing?"

"Don't really know, but I bet it has something to do with that guy that visited earlier. I wonder if those photos we took can be matched with someone in our data base," Bish wondered aloud.

"Want me to give Detective Wilson a call and ask?"

"No, she's busy enough. We don't need to be bothering her needlessly. I'd never seen that guy before. I wonder if he was selling insurance or something."

"I don't think so. I could read the surprise on the big guy's face from here when he opened that door and saw that guy. He knew him for sure, and I figure he wasn't expecting him by the look on that face. He looked…scared…too."

"Yeah, I kinda got that feeling myself and it makes me wonder if that's the money man or something. I noticed, too, that he didn't touch anything as he went in so no prints. He used his knuckles when he knocked on the door."

"And the big guy looked all around before he closed the door, did you see that?"

"Yeah, kid. He was in there quite a while, too. I would have loved to have a bug in that house to hear what they were talking about."

"Is that hard to do…uh…get authorization to bug someone's house?"

"Very, and one wants to have the right judge to authorize it, too. I don't trust a few of our honorable judges. Not that they're dirty or anything, it's just they talk too much after work. How do I know that? Visit Uncle Charlie's bar some Friday night after work and you'll see what I mean."

"I had a prime rib sandwich on Saturday at Uncle Charlie's. That was great."

"Yeah, I've had 'em myself and they are good. Makin' my mouth water, you know."

"Sorry, didn't mean to." Bish smiled at the kid and went back to watching.

The rest of the afternoon and early evening went boring as usual. No new traffic or movement at either house. Peter and

Clint showed up just before seven as scheduled. Bish gave them the rundown on the day's events and said that Wilson was running the photos they took, but that they didn't have any word on a match as yet.

Bish and Tom climbed into Bish's old Jeep and headed east. "You hungry?" Bish asked.

"I could eat," Tom answered.

"Ever eaten at Little Bear's?"

"Nah, that place is outta my salary range."

"Well then let's go, my treat."

The big guy had chewed his nails down to the quicks, and a few were even bleeding. After el Jefe had left he'd gotten a very bad feeling about the next mission. If the weather settles in while the operation is underway, they would be in real danger if something happened. And there was always the big unknown, that scary anonymous…whatever…that might pop up and unglue the whole process. He was in full worry mode since the man himself had visited. That had never happened, even when the big guy's old man was running the operations for el Jefe. The only reason the big guy had known the man at the door was el Jefe, was when his ol man retired he'd introduced the two so Jefe knew who would be doing the collections.

He sat back in his chair and thought about his past, growing up in Colorado, not knowing his mother, his father saying she died giving him life. He frequently wondered if that were true. He often thought his father, or the man who said he was his father, had been lying to him all those years. He supposed he'd never know for sure just what his past really had been.

Getting up, he went into the galley kitchen, rinsed his hands, and poured himself a glass of water, drinking it down nonstop. He let out a satisfying belch afterwards and placed the used glass into the sink. He looked around wondering what he could do next, and decided to go to the pole barn as he had some work to do on the Aztec artifacts that had arrived from el Jefe's smuggling operations in South America.

As he pulled himself out of the hatchway, he grunted with the effort and reminded himself he needed to lose some weight and exercise more. It would never happen of course, but he could dream. He pictured himself as doing something like Stallone did in that fighter movie, and dreamed he could be like Balboa, statue and all. He began humming the theme song from the movie and it got him moving.

He turned on the lights and went over to the table where he worked. His job on this project was to clean the pieces, photograph them, and then repack them in the wooden crates for shipment to whoever paid the big dollars for the item or items. He always wondered why people would pay so much money for carved rocks. He could think of many other ways to spend that kind of money, and his mind wandered back to Balboa. If he only had a lot of money, he could pay someone to train him and keep him on track with losing the weight and exercising. Maybe in Barbados or someplace cool like that. Maybe Belize…

He worked for several hours and cleaned up and closed up near six that evening. He slowly trudged his way in the tunnel he hated back to his home and made dinner. He set up his TV tray, turned on his set, placed his dinner on the tray, and sat in his recliner to eat while watching the news.

A knock on the door made his hair stand out. At the second round of knocking, he got up and went to the door.

"Yes?" he asked leaning in to the door.

"Hey, it's me, Daniel…let me in, dude," Daniel from next door said.

The big guy unlocked the door and let him in. "Hey, what's up?"

"Helen told me el Jefe came by today – that right?" Daniel asked.

The big guy shook his head positively and said, "Yeah, he ain't never done that before. Even when my old man was doing this stuff. I really got the creeps from it."

"Oh man, what did he want?" Daniel questioned. "We mess something up?"

"No, at least he didn't say we messed up. He wanted to see everything, all our plans, and stuff. Dude, he read everything. He even said we did good with the planning and stuff. I didn't ask about the shotguns though."

"Yeah, Helen told me. We'll have to do something about that. How much money we got left?"

"A little over four large, why?" the big guy asked.

"Not enough for two shotguns that we need," Daniel answered. "To get what we want, we'll need around six or so, maybe a bit more."

"What're they made of gold or sumptin?"

Daniel chuckled and replied, "No, but we'll need the extras that go with them."

"What do you mean, extras?"

"Well, with the Remington 870, for example, you can get a load extension giving you eight rounds and one in the chamber. Nine rounds of double-ought buckshot is a good tactical advantage. You can also get a pistol grip for it giving you better control."

"What about the other one you were looking at?"

"The Mossberg 590A1 tactical – a mean S.O.B. It can be loaded with nine rounds. It has a pistol grip you can add, and you can add flashlights, red dot scopes, and a sling if you want one, although I feel they get in the way. Especially in our situation, since if we have to use one it'll be from the van or from an urban situation. Those two we can afford. Either of them will do us well and using buckshot, they can't be traced. We just gotta remember to use gloves when we're loading them, that way our finger prints won't be left behind for the PD to get. We'll need one of each or two of one or the other."

"We'll get the money. I don't really know how right now, but we'll get it. What else will we want since the budget is limited now?"

"We'll need ammo, say four boxes of double-ought buckshot. That'll give us a hundred rounds. We have those two M&P 15's in .556 from Ruger and we already have enough mags and ammo for those. Same with those nine-millimeter handguns. Don't need any more ammo for those so say another forty bucks for the buckshot and we'll be good. I'd say we'll need less than seven large to get it all. Might even have some left over maybe, but I think seven will do."

"Seven – okay, I'm on it. You locate the weapons and I'll locate the rest of the money. I can do that."

"I'll do the buckshot, too."

"That'll work. Okay, anything else we need to figure out?"

"Not that I know of, man. I think we've got it under control. Get the guns and ammo and we'll be set. Ready to go. Just gotta get the green light from el Jefe."

"Yeah, but after today, I'm not sure what's gonna happen. I couldn't read him at all."

"What do you mean?"

"I ain't gotta clue why he came here. Nothing. I was blown away when I saw him. Scared the crap outta me, man."

"No clue, huh?"

"None, brother, none."

"Geeze man, that's scary. He didn't say why he was here?"

"All he said is that there would be NO problems. He really emphasized that. Then he wanted to see our plans, equipment and supply listings, then lastly, to review the routes on the maps. I mentioned the weather and what problems it might make for us, but he didn't really seem to care about that. Just that we got the mission completed without problems."

"Dude, I wonder what's going on. I can't believe he came here. Man that worries me, too. I'll talk with Helen. Maybe we can come up with some extra funds."

"No, man, you keep your money for Shirley."

"I'm sure we have enough. I'm making good money with the electrical job. And since I'm getting six or eight hours of overtime every week, it's really good money, so don't worry about us. We're good."

"All the same, man, you take care of that baby. She's special, that little one."

"I will, I promise. I gotta run. Don't get an ulcer over this and I'll try to do the same," Daniel said with a chuckle as he left.

The big guy got up, reheated his dinner in the microwave, sat back down in his recliner, and ate while watching the tall blonde chick turn letters on a wall.

Chapter Fourteen
February
Cheyenne, Wyoming

The weather was horrible. High winds, horizontal snow, mostly going to Nebraska, I-80 closed both ways from Pine Bluffs to Rock Springs. I-25 closed from the southern border to Buffalo, and from there I-90 was closed to the norther border. Three-fourths of Wyoming was being blanketed by a moisture-laden cloud cover, and from it, heavy snow fell. Miserable is what visitors called it. Folks from Wyoming called it tolerable because they knew it would pass. Wyomingites tell outsiders they never have to rake the leaves in the fall as the high winds take them all to Nebraska. So why bother? Some of the snow went to Nebraska also - just some.

The fluffy white stuff had to be cleared from driveways and sidewalks within twenty-four hours of falling. It had been falling for two days now. Daniel had the plow out clearing his and the big guy's driveways and sidewalks of the white stuff. Drifts were already nearing three feet in height in a lot of places, some even deeper than that.

The big guy looked out his front picture window, saw Daniel, and waived. He looked up at the dark gray of the cloud cover and knew they would have snow for at least another day or so. He also knew their secondary route would most likely be closed until June or later. He knew they would have to take the primary route in and out on the mission. They would not have another choice. He was pleased they had been able to get the shotguns, and for much less than then they had thought.

Down the block and across the street, Detective Samuel Bishop and rookie Patrolman Andrew Nelson watched Daniel plowing the snow. "That's always so cool to watch, a plow doing its work," Andy said. "When I have a place of my own, I'll have an ATV with a plow like that one."

"Ya think?" Bish rhetorically said with a smirk.

"You bet," Andy said. "Gotta have one or will have to shovel and I really don't want to waste my day shoveling snow. I'd rather see it pushed aside in style."

Bish chuckled and looked at the kid. "In style? You're nuts, you know it?"

"Why, 'cause I like snow so much?" the kid asked.

"Not only that, but you're enthusiasm about plowing snow is just crazy," Bish said with a smile.

"I suppose so. I am a bit crazy. But, you're my role model."

"What?"

"Yeah, I picked you as my role model for the CPD. Us rookies got together and pulled people out of a sort of lineup and I chose you."

"But I'm not crazy."

The kid almost fell out of his chair he was laughing so hard. Choking back another round of laughing, he said, "You don't really believe that, do you?"

"Nah," Bish said and laughed. "Ya gotta be a little crazy to do the stuff we do."

"Yeah, where else can you carry a gun, drive a really fast car, get into bar fights, legally, and get paid to boot," the kid said beaming.

"Now you're certifiable," Bish said. "I'll have to introduce you to my therapist."

"That'll be a treat. He sticky on that privacy law, or can I get some intel on you from him?"

"She...she is *very* sticky on the privacy laws. And she could take you out in a heartbeat since she's also my sensei. She can hurt you, then treat you and make you feel better about it. So much so, that you'll thank her while writing the check."

"She, huh, what's Detective Wilson think of that?" the kid asked with a sly smile.

The room suddenly became very still and quiet. The kid just found out *that* was a very sticky subject and one not to bring up.

"Sorry, Bish, I didn't mean anything by it," the kid confessed sincerely.

Bish looked at him, smiled, and said, "It's okay, kid, I can't blame you for speaking the truth. I do have feelings for her. But I guess that's a natural thing to happen when two people have to be so close together every day. Just becomes natural I guess."

"Still, I'm sorry I spoke out, I won't do it again," the kid apologized again.

"Don't worry about it, Andy. Maybe I need to watch my own emotions when that subject comes up in a conversation. I tend to over react I guess."

"Honestly, you two do seem to make a great couple. I mean, I guess what I mean is that I hope to find a gal someday and have a great relationship like you and Detective Wilson. You two seem…well, so natural together. It's almost as if you two know what each other are thinking about everything all the time. That takes time to develop together and you two are naturals. You really click, you know?"

"Yeah, kid, I do know. You're right, we do click. It's almost uncanny how the two of us work together sometimes. We just know what to do and who'll do what without saying a word. Sometimes just a look and we know how to act, how to make a certain situation go our way. Just by a look," Bish said almost in a questioning whisper.

Andy kept his mouth shut as he saw the look of almost disbelief on Bish's face. He knew Bish and Anita Wilson had something that most people never have. The two detectives were in tune with each other. They flowed. They mixed. He decided then that he would do everything in his power to become a detective like these two he was fortunate enough to have been assigned with, even temporarily.

"Sir, may I ask you a few questions?" Andy asked Bish.

"Sure, kid, fire away," Bish said, now turning his attention to the young rookie.

"What can I do to help my pursuit of becoming a detective with the CPD?" Andy asked.

"Good question. Let me think a moment. I suppose first would be try to stay outta trouble. Do what's right…every time. Next, take all the training you're offered. Don't hesitate. Say yes to it all. They'll know you're serious by that. You and your peers are going to get some good write-ups from this as you all four are doing great so far. If you tell any of them I said that, you will regret it."

"My lips are sealed."

"That, too, will be something they'll look for - whether you can keep your mouth shut or not. Some things we do are secret and the less that know about it the better. There's just some things we don't let the public know, mostly for security reasons and to protect ourselves. We definitely don't share most of our operations with the public. Some, yes, just to give them some information they, that is the media, can use in their stories.

"This is Wyoming, kid, and if you shake someone's hand in a promise, make sure you keep it. Most if not all of the old-timers around here swear by that and can get a little testy about not fulfilling something you shook on. It's like signing a contract. You bust that and you'll never get ahead in Wyoming.

"And since this is Wyoming, you need to remember a lot about the culture here. It's really different if you haven't already picked up on that. Most folks are friendly, but in a quiet sort of way. They don't make friends very easily here. They need to know you – really know you before they may even consider you a friendly acquaintance. You have to be on the up-and-up with 'em. This place is full of cowboys. If you don't know about cowboys, get some good books and learn. You really need to read books on Wyoming history. Promotion boards will have a county Commissioner on the panel and they'll ask all kinds of questions about Wyoming and how you feel about cattle and sheep, for instance. And you better say beef is tops. You say you like sheep and the shooting will quickly start. Read and learn. If you happen to sit next to an old-timer in a coffee shop or bar, strike up a conversation and ask questions. Learn the culture and the culture will accept you.

"And don't be a bit surprised if they ignore you. Don't take that to heart; it's just one of those things. A lot of 'em don't trust newcomers. You gotta give 'em that. Just give them a smile and say something like you're sorry you bothered them or that you're sorry you broke their train of thought. That's a start."

"Wow, a lot to take in, thanks. If you don't mind, you remember when I told you we selected someone to be a role model and I chose you?"

"Yeah, I do," Bish said, looking the kid in the eye.

"Would you consider being my mentor while I 'grow up'?" the kid said, using his hands to put the quote emphasis on grow up.

"Kid, I'd be honored to be your mentor. I'll help you the best I can. But, you have to do your part. Be quiet, pay attention, and don't screw up. That's my first advice for you. I guess what I'm trying to say is be amenable. Don't take to heart what some folks will do to you as a newcomer around here. But, be open-minded about Wyoming culture. Remember, you'll be dealing with American Indian tribes, too. Read and learn. Before long you'll find yourself changing and becoming more Wyomingite in nature. That's when you'll notice folks opening up to you more often. Be true, be a straight-shooter. Be square-dealing and trustworthy. You do that and the public will accept you and you'll get promoted."

"Wow, you sound like my father," Andy said with his head down.

"Then you dad is a good man," Bish said.

"Was…was a good man, he passed in 2012. Mom went in 2020. I miss 'em."

"I miss mine, too. Where you from, kid?"

"I was born in Bossier City, Louisiana. Dad was in the military and we traveled a lot. He retired in 1980, and we stayed in Iowa. I figure I'm from Iowa because of that. He bought a small place, thirty acres, and grew feed corn and hay for the local ranchers. So that's why I said you sound a lot like him. Where we lived in Iowa you had to be a straight-shooter so-to-speak. So I know where you're coming from. Thanks."

"So you know how to throw hay bales."

"Oh yeah, I do indeed know how to do that," the kid said with a huge smile.

"That's your in around here. When they start haying, ask to lend a hand. You'll rake in the friends then."

"I bet. I'll keep that in mind. Shoot, I can help if anyone around here grows corn, too."

"Nope, no corn," Bish said with a laugh. "Potatoes and sunflowers for the most part up at this altitude. Lots of hay and straw growers. And if you do get an ATV with a plow, offer to help out a neighbor. That'll get you brownie points, too."

"Brownie points," Andy laughed out, "my mom used that term a lot; brings back some memories." Both got a good laugh at that. Bish went back to watching Daniel move snow and Andy hit the head.

Andy was drying his hands on a paper towel as he came out of the head and saw Bish watching Daniel. "The snow still coming down?"

"Boy is it," Bish returned. "I don't think this stuff is gonna quit anytime soon," he added.

"Is this the biggest you've ever seen around here?" Andy asked.

"No, the one in 1985, really had us socked in. The town was closed up for four days on that one. No one could get out. If we had an ambulance run, the medicos would follow a plow to the address, load the patient, and haul it back to the hospital. If we got a call, depending on what it was, we might have gone out on the CAT. That thing'll climb trees."

"Really!"

"Yeah, that thing has an eight-foot plow we could attach and it would just about go anywhere." He laughed and added, "We went way over budget that year."

"Oh, man, I hope this isn't one of those. Can you see us stuck out here with limited supplies and equipment?"

Bish looked at the kid and thought a moment, then got on the radio, "Detective Wilson, you there?"

"Yes, Detective Bishop, go ahead," Wilson answered quickly.

"Patrolman Nelson came up with a good idea and I approve," he told her.

"What's that?" she asked.

"Remember 1985…" and he let that hang for a moment.

"Yes, yes I do, why?"

"Patrolman Nelson thinks that if this storm is close to or as bad as that one we could be in a jam out here with our limited supplies and equipment. That make sense?"

"It does. We'll get the list out and have a team run it out to you after dark. We're on it. Tell Patrolman Nelson good job."

"He heard. And thanks. See you in a while, over."

"Keep warm, out."

Andy looked at Bish and said, "You made it sound as if that was my idea."

"It was in a roundabout way. Your comment sure made sense and after 1985, we made up a contingency plan for just about everything, including stakeouts. They'll bring the works out to us, extra food, water, clothing, sleeping materials, additional winter gear that includes snowshoes and walking staffs. We'll be set when the kit gets here. It even has extra ammo in it."

"Wow, I never figured on that."

"They'll probably bring it with the CAT. That means around back so we might want to go take a look and see if there are any obstacles out there."

"I'll do that," and Andy jumped up, put his coat on and took off.

Kid's gonna be a good one, Bish thought. He turned his attention to Daniel once more and saw the big guy standing on the front porch waving at him. He saw Daniel wave back and turn the plow back towards the big guy's house. *Wonder what's up with this,* Bish thought as he watched Daniel stop the ATV in front of the house, get out, and trudge his way up to and inside the house.

Bish keyed his throat mike and told Andy, "Hey, kid, we got movement, make it quick out there."

"On my way back now," Andy answered.

When Andy got to the observation room, he asked, "What's up?"

Bish told him what had been going on and to watch. They both sat quietly watching, their eyes just above the window seal, the blinds down to just above their eyes, giving them a space of about two inches to view the outside world.

Helen, with a bundled up Shirley, came out of her home and trudged over to the big guy's house. Once she was inside, the two cops looked at each other and sat back.

"Man, whatever it is it's gotta be important," Andy stated. "No one goes out on a day like this unless it's absolutely necessary. Maybe we'll get something on the phone taps."

Bish looked up at him and grabbed his radio again, "Detective Wilson, you on?"

"Here Detective Bishop, go ahead." Anta answered, "What's up?"

"Got movement and wondered if you've picked up anything on the phones, over," Bish told her.

"Standby," Anita said.

The pair waited for almost fifteen minutes, then, "Bish, Wilson, yes, we did get a call. Stand fast, the CAT's outta the bag."

"Got it, out," Bish answered.

"What was all that about?" Andy asked.

"The taps did get something. That comment, the CAT's outta the bag…"

"Yeah."

"That means the CATs on its way here soon and Detective Wilson will probably be on it and give us a briefing on the phone. Can't do that on the radio."

"Ah," Andy said, nodding his head. "Want me to go down and watch for them and help with the stuff they bring?"

"Sure, that'll be fine. They'll appreciate it," Bish said with a smile. *Kids gonna do great.*

Chapter Fifteen
February
Cheyenne, Wyoming

The helicopter settled gently onto the recently plowed landing pad, a small dust storm of snow rising around the noisy contraption. The blades began to slow as the engine spooled down, and once the snow cloud abated, el Jefe, and his son climbed out of the aircraft and scooted over to his Cheyenne, Wyoming, home…it was almost time.

As he neared the home, both Sims and Isabella opened the door and greeted him. He and the boy gave Sims their coats and smiled at Isabella, and Salinas asked, "Everything going smoothly?"

"Yes, el Jefe, everything is splendid," Isabella quickly replied. "She is most expectant, senior."

"Very good," Salinas said. "Sims, dinner at six this evening, and we would like Cornish Game Hens if you please."

"Yes, sir," Sims answered. "Would you care for wine or a mixed drink this evening, senior?"

"I'm thinking a mixed drink; an Old Fashioned would do nicely." The boy would most likely have either Mountain Dew or Dr. Pepper.

"Yes, el Jefe," Sims replied.

"Isabella, let's go downstairs, you run along and have some fun," Salinas said to the boy, and turned for the library and the secret stairwell. He pulled a dictionary off a shelf and pushed a button imbedded in the back wall. An audible click could be heard, signaling the doorway had been unlocked and Salinas replaced the dictionary.

Isabella had been standing near the secret doorway and as the click sounded, she pulled a lever opening the entryway for the boss. He walked over and began the downward climb, Isabella following.

The staircase went downward for three stories, a landing at each level, with no doorways on the first two landings. The third had only one door, and Isabella quickly punched a seven-number code into the number pad, opening the door to the underground facility holding the ten rooms with occupants ranging from age two to twenty. It also held a terrarium, or court yard, where the captives could play or just relax in the sun. There was a small pool and a small creek ran through the facility they could wade in if they so desired.

The captives, all female, were allowed many freedoms while in captivity. The older they got, the more freedoms. They had full liberty beginning at age ten when in the terrarium. They could wear clothing or not as they wished.

At age sixteen, they begin their *training* and *education* for the big day, the day Salinas would have his way with them. By the time they reached the *age*, which is the time Salinas decided he would have them, they were for the most part very ready to cooperate, actually to be at a point of need. There had been only one instance of abject refusal and that young lady was disposed of after a rather painful night with Salinas' and then his ranch hands.

"Would you care for a beverage, el Jefe?" Isabella asked while he got his chair ready for his time in the facility.

"Yes, please, sweet tea with lime if you have it," Salinas replied. "If not, a 7Up would do nicely, thank you."

She bowed to him and turned to meet his wish.

Salinas walked his chair down to where the young lady's room was, the young lady that would be the subject of his desire in a few weeks. This particular female was acquired, as he liked to call it, in April of 2013, from Santa Fe, New Mexico, and would be twenty years old soon. She had flaming red hair and emerald green eyes. He was sure she was of Scottish/Irish ancestry, and he had come to see her several times in the last year. As was his want, none of his captives had ever seen a male, save for his son when they were younger. He wanted himself to be the first they ever saw when the time came.

Salinas sat down in his chair and got comfortable as Isabella came up to him with his beverage. He took it from her, had a sip and smiled approvingly at her, "Thank you, Issy, you may go." He sat back in the chair for a moment while she left, and then, using a remote, opened the curtain revealing a huge ten by eighteen foot see-through glass. He could see through it, but from the other side, one only saw a reflection.

The girl, or rather young woman, happened to be admiring herself in the huge mirror only a few feet from where Salinas sat. She was nude, not having dressed as yet. His desire was noted by his intake of breath as the curtain unveiled the red-headed beauty that stood mere inches away. She was completely unaware she was being watched.

Salinas used this time to view his captives, learning their actions and the way they did things in their rooms. He wanted to know them, their habits, their favorite things, the way they moved. His mood today was one of veneration for the woman on the other side of the glass. She had no clue he was there as she admired herself. She turned and moved to her couch, sat and picked up a thick book she was reading and a glass of sweet tea. She sipped the tea and set it back down, then opened the book and began reading.

Over the next hour, Salinas observed her. He pressed a button on his remote and Isabella quickly came to his side. "Yes el Jefe?"

"What book is she reading?" he asked her.

"*Without Remorse*," she replied.

"Ah, yes, Tom Clancy. A very good selection, thank you, Issy," he said to her, smiling. The captives were all taught to read and were allowed to read fiction only. They were taught to the eighth grade level in most subjects. If they were sold at the end of their times here, they would need to be educated, somewhat. He smiled while watching the girl read.

She finally set the book aside, stood and stretched, moved over to her armoire, selecting jeans and an orange, silk blouse to wear. Once she was dressed, she went back to her tea, sipping it as she walked around her room. Lunch would be served soon, and she looked ready for it.

Salinas watched her for another thirty minutes. Satisfied, he called Isabella once again and told her she had done well once again. He asked if she would be using the terrarium that afternoon, and she replied, "If it is your desire, senior, I will arrange it."

"Yes, please do so," he said, looking at her. She turned to leave and he watched as she left. Once she was gone, he rose and went back to his library and did some work at his desk. It would be a pleasant afternoon he felt.

Sims came in and asked, "Senior, would you care for lunch today?"

"I think not, Sims, but thank you for asking, I'm just not in the mood to eat," Salinas answered.

"Very good, senior, if there is anything you need, please ask," Sims said and turned away.

Salinas went back to what he was doing. After a while, he picked up a burner phone and dialed the big guy's number.

The pickup was almost immediate, "Yes, el Jefe?" the big guy answered.

"Have you checked on the routes and is the secondary passable?" Salinas questioned.

"I have checked, senior, and the secondary has indeed closed for the season and may not be reopened until June or later, they're saying," the big guy quickly answered. "The storm brought unusually heavy snow into that area for this time of year. We will be using the primary for this mission."

"Ahh, disappointing news, but I suppose an act of God cannot be disputed," Salinas said.

A nervous chuckle from the big guy was the return answer.

"Have you and the team completed acquisitions?" Salinas asked.

"Yes, el Jefe, we have. We acquired everything needed for the mission and are very prepared," the big guy stated. "The bebita will be well taken care of, el Jefe. Not to worry, senior."

"Very well," Salinas said and hung up. He destroyed the burner phone after the call and went back to his paperwork.

The big guy looked at the phone knowing the boss had hung up. He quickly destroyed the burner phone and discarded everything but the master card and the battery. Those he would burn later. He shook his head at the way the boss treated he and the others, but the money was very good. He had saved a lot of his money over the past eight years and would be going to Belize or Barbados and spending a month on a beach once this current mission was completed.

Bish suddenly sat up straight. Detective First Class Anita Wilson caught the movement out of the corner of her eye and looked his way, seeing him holding the headsets as tightly to his ears as he could. He snapped his head to look at the recording device, ensuring it was on and continued to listen closely. His head snapped to Wilson as the call he was listening to ended. He waive furiously for her to come over.

Wilson got up as did Peter, Andy, Connie, and Clint, who had also seen Bish's sudden movements.

"What?" Wilson questioned.

Bish looked up at her and smiling hugely, said, "I think we got them on this one. For sure the boss of this group is Hispanic. They call him el Jefe, the boss, and they were talking about a mission that was coming soon. They talked about a bebita, which is Spanish for baby girl, and that the secondary route was closed until at least June due to deep snow." He looked at Peter and said, "That's the trip we took through the mountains coming back from following that big guy I bet."

Peter agreed with, "Yeah."

"That guy, el Jefe, asked about supplies and equipment and wanting to know if everything was ready and the big guy said it was. Guys, this is February. Soon will be another kidnapping unless we figure out how to stop these people. I think these guys are the ones. I think we got enough to move on the big guy's house and maybe even the gal next door, Helen."

Wilson looked at him and said, "I need to listen to that tape…right now."

Bish rewound the tape to the beginning of the conversation and hit play. Everyone leaned in closer to listen.

"I say we bust 'em," Bish said after the short call ended. "They specifically mentioned a mission, a bebita, and about primary and secondary routes, and that the secondary was closed for the season. Since Peter and I followed the big guy that time, and knowing that they've closed that route over the mountains for the season, I checked on the WYDOT page on the internet, I think we have enough to go with." He looked pleadingly at Wilson.

She looked back eye-to-eye, staying quiet, thinking while they stared at each other. It seemed a long time but she finally broke the silence and staring match by saying, "Make a copy of that now," and turned for her desk. She made a call and once the other end answered, said, "Amanda, Wilson here, I need to see him right now."

The team watched her expectantly, and when she hung up, she said, "Bish, Peter, get that tape and follow me." She got up and headed for the door to the office with the two detectives in tow.

At Captain Carlisle's office, Amanda ushered them right in. "Hi, cap, we have a tape you need to hear right now," she said handing him the thumb drive.

"What's this about?" he asked.

"Just play it Daryl, please," she almost demanded.

She never used his first name, so he knew something important was on that drive. He inserted it into his computer, brought up the file, and hit play. Just like back in the office, the three leaned in closer to hear.

Carlisle stared at the screen as the tape played. Once it was done, he played it again, staring at the screen. When it finished, he stopped the program and sat there looking at the screen, thinking.

Finally, after what seemed to be a long time, he picked up his phone and as soon as Amanda answered, said, "Amanda, get me Judge Masterson on the phone, quick." He hung up and sat back, saw the other three leaning in towards him and he said, "What…sit down will ya!"

The three scrambled into the three extra seats in the room and waited. The captain sat in his swivel chair swaying side to side while he waited. They could see he was thinking so didn't interrupt. Five minutes later his phone rang. He quickly answered it.

"Yes, your honor, thank you for getting back to me so quickly," Carlisle said. "We have a development sir…yes sir, that case. I would like to ask you for a search warrant. Yes, sir, we've gotten new information off of the phone taps, may I play it for you sir? Yes sir, here we go," Carlisle said and hit play as he placed the phone near the speaker. Once the tape had played, he got back on and quickly said, "Yes, sir, it's on its way over right now. Detectives Wilson and Bishop will be bringing it. Yes, sir, they on their way," he said, hanging up and pulling the thumb drive and handing it to Wilson. "Get!" he yelled and they practically ran to the car, leaving Peter standing in the captain's office alone. "You get, too!"

Peter went back to the office and informed the team they might be getting a search warrant and to get ready. "Weapons, vests, and ammo everyone, we're probably going in hot," he told them. "When you're ready, get back here and we'll wait for Wilson and Bish. Move it!" Rookies scattered going to their lockers to get their M-4s, Vests, and ammo.

Peter briefed Mike on what the captain did and told him things might get moving quickly now. He looked at his partner and said, "I gotta bad feeling about this one, Mike. We best get the man upstairs on our side," and with that, bowed his head and began to pray silently. Mike did the same.

It was a moment later, when Peter felt a hand on his shoulder, and peeking, saw Clint joining in on the prayer session. He saw Connie, Andy, and Tom creeping over to join in as well. He smiled, closed his eyes, and continued to pray.

Chapter Sixteen
March
Cheyenne, Wyoming

Detective First Class Anita Wilson and Detective First Class Samuel Bishop, walked into the office, carrying their M-4 rifles and additional magazines and ammunition. Bish went to his desk and placing his equipment on the desk top sat down.

Wilson set her equipment on her desk and, still standing, looked around the room at all the expectant faces. Detectives Michael Hicks and Peter Donaldson were attentive, as were Patrolmen Connie Dominquez, Andrew Nelson, Clint James, and Thomas Alton. All were looking at her with wide, expectant eyes. Peter sipped his coffee.

"We have a search warrant for both the big guy's house and Helen's place," Wilson began. "Judge Masterson has ordered that we do this quietly." She saw shoulders sag a bit. Detective Bishop and I will serve the search warrant. I want all of you ready to go at a moment's notice. I want each rookie to be with an experienced Detective. I know about the mentor thing and think that's great so join up with your mentor. Connie, you and Clint tag along with Pete and Mike until you join with us if needed," she saw understanding by the nods of their heads. "Bish and I will be leaving in just a bit. I want all of us to go over equipment first and Bish I want you to give the safety briefing while I'm seeing the captain. I'll be back in fifteen minutes or so." She hesitated then said, "Bish and I prayed together in the car so if you're the praying type, I'd go ahead and do that."

"Anita," Peter interrupted, "we've all already done that."

She smiled at him and said, "That's good." Looking around the room at everyone's faces, she said, "Safety first if you have to go out. Listen to your mentors – it just might save your life. Watch each other's backs. If you do have to go out…well, good luck." She picked up the warrant paperwork and left for the captain's office.

The others looked at each other, not moving. Finally, Bish said, "Okay everyone, get to it. Check those weapons for functionality; check your ammo and other gear. Peter, Mike - make sure the radios are charged and voice mikes work. If we all do have to go into action, I want coms up at all times. Like the lady said, watch each other's backs, and you four," pointing at the rookies, "listen to your mentors. Do what they say when they say and how they say. I don't want anyone to get hurt so watch what you're doing at all times.

He looked at each rookie and asked them, "What does a blue fire call mean?"

Clint quickly raised his hand, and after Bish pointed to him said, "It's a call from an officer that has been involved in a live-fire incident. The call requires an all-out response from every available officer in the vicinity to assist if directed by the dispatcher. It's never used unless it is a dire circumstance."

"Very good," Bish complemented him. "If you hear that call, come in quick and hard, and above all else, be careful. If you're forced to use your weapons, make sure of what is behind your targets before firing. Keep your safeties on unless you have to fire." He was quiet for a moment, then looked at everyone on the team and said, "Equipment check in ten. Get it done."

The seven of them began checking and rechecking firearms, magazines, their communication gear, vests, and everything else they would be taking along if required to respond. In the flurry of activity, no one noticed Detective First Class Wilson reenter the office. She stood by her desk and watched all the activity and was satisfied. She checked her own equipment, knowing full well that Bish had already gone over hers while she was with the captain.

Bish noticed Anita checking her weapons, got up, and went over to her desk. "Ready, kid?" he asked.

"As I'll ever be," she replied, "you?"

"Yep, I'll get the car. Just you and me for now?" he asked.

"Yep. Did you brief the team?"

"Yeah. Hope they don't have to come out. Hope we don't get into a donnybrook."

"Yeah, I'm a bit nervous on this one. I don't know, Bish, but I got a feeling about this. I think it's gonna get dirty."

"Yeah, I feel the same way. You ready?"

She nodded, picked up her equipment, and noticed the room had gone quiet. She looked around the room and every eye was on her. "Okay team, if you're dispatched on this for whatever reason - rely on your training and safety procedures…and each other. I know you'll all do just fine." It was moments like this where words just weren't enough, so she nodded her head, looked at Bish, and said, "Let's go partner."

Anita and Bish gathered their equipment and the warrants and left the office. The others sat looking at each other in silence.

The two detectives loaded their equipment into their car. Both made sure their vests could not be seen underneath their outer clothing, and then climbed into the car and left the garage with Wilson driving. Almost immediately they turned south on Highway 85, otherwise known as South Greely Highway, and made their way to the housing area where the big guy's house was located. Their warrant covered both his home and Helen's home next door. Wilson pulled up in front of the big guy's house and stopped. The piles of snow were still deep in places alongside the roadway and in front of the big guy's home, it was no different.

Bish was watching the homes as they pulled up and as they stopped, he saw the curtains part then rapidly close. "They know we're here; saw the curtains open then close in the big guy's place. We gotta move," he said while opening his door.

They ran up to the door and Wilson knocked and loudly said, "Police, we have a search warrant to search the premises."

There was no response other than the heavy footsteps they could hear within. She knocked again and said the same thing, waited a moment, and then Wilson gave Bish the nod to bust the door.

Bish reared back and flat-footed, jammed his right foot into the door just next to the doorknob. The door flew inward with a crash, the doorjamb splintering wood chips across the room. Wilson was first in as Bish recovered his balance after hitting the door. She hustled towards the kitchen and dining area, Bish now just behind her.

As Anita rounded the corner, she and the big guy ran into each other. She flew backwards after bouncing off the big dude, noticing he was bringing up a handgun, and having already drawn her weapon, began to bring it up. He shook off the impact and was moving a revolver in her direction when Anita yelled, "FREEZE!"

He continued to bring his weapon up and was about to squeeze the trigger when she began firing. Her first round entered just above his pubic bone, rupturing the bladder, and stopping just short of his lower spine. His shot went high and to her left, hitting the wall. Her second shot hit just under his diaphragm, putting a hole through it and lodging in a rib next to the spine; the third hit just right of his sternum, clipping the aorta; the fourth entered just under the right clavicle. The kicker was the fifth round which entered just above his Adam's apple and cutting his medulla, curving upwards into the brain and followed the curvature of the skull cap, cutting a furrow almost all the way around his brain back to his eyes. He sank sideways like a huge water balloon after that and fell into a table with a glass top.

Bish saw all this and more in the fleeting seconds and watched as the big guy was falling face forward into the glass-topped coffee table, which practically exploded as the impact occurred, safety glass shards going everywhere. He saw and heard the report of another weapon on the end of an arm coming out of the hallway and began firing as he dropped to a knee. His first shot went into the shooter's elbow and the arm bent

186

unnaturally with the smoking handgun flying from the numbed hand. The kicker here is Bish had already fired the second round, and as the shooter's grimacing face came around the corner, the second bullet hit him just in front of his right ear, and he followed the big guy into a pile on the floor. Bish saw that it was Daniel.

Bish started yelling to see if Anita was alright. She coughed a few times and yelled back that she was as she ejected her partially used magazine and jacked a fresh mag into her weapon. Bish was still covering the hallway with his weapon and after he got up, helped Anita up. They stood there together, weapons shakily pointed in opposite directions, gulping in huge amounts of air, beginning to shake somewhat from the adrenalin rush.

"You sure you're okay?" he asked her again.

"Yeah, I got hit in the chest; thank God for vests," she said, rubbing her chest and coughing again.

She finally motioned with her weaponless free hand to go down the hallway, so Bish cautiously headed that direction while she covered their rear, still rubbing her chest. Bish edged up to the wall and took a quick peek around the corner looking down the hallway. He brought his head back around and stood there listening. Not hearing anything that was louder than his rapidly beating heart and the ringing in his ears from all the shooting, he looked at Anita and she gave him a bump with her elbow, meaning get going.

Bish pulled a flashlight and with it turned on and his weapon leading, stepped around the corner. Framed photos adorned the walls on both sides, reflecting the light from his beam. Two doors on the right, one to the left, all closed. No telling where the two they'd shot had come from. No light came from the bottoms of the doors and everything remained quiet. The first door on the right was the first they came to so Bish stopped across the hall from it. Anita knelt and he noticed she had her flashlight out. Bish stood there looking and listening and after a moment gave her a tap on the shoulder and motioned towards the door. She stood and moving to the left side of the door, made ready to enter. Bish moved to the right side and would open the door, which obviously opened inward.

She nodded she was ready and he slowly turned the knob and gave the door a gentle push in. She immediately went in to the right, gun, and light leading and Bish ducked in to the left behind her. Both of them had their backs to the wall on either side of the door, panning their lights and weapons around an empty bedroom with no furniture. An open door to his left was a small empty walk-in closet and three-quarter bath. Bish looked at Anita and she nodded back to the hallway.

Bish led once again and headed to the door on the left. They did the same entry again into another near empty bedroom with a bed, closet, and full bath.

The last door to the right was next. They readied themselves and when Anita gave him the nod, Bish turned the knob and pushed…locked! She knelt, weapon up and turned off her light. He took two steps back from the door down the hall and turned his light off, too.

"You want to knock or should I?" Anita quietly asked.

"How 'bout I just kick it in?" he responded.

"…and take a shotgun blast to the chest…yeah, right," she retorted. She then got flat and bringing her weapon up, knocked on the door next to the door knob. In quick succession, three neat, round holes from twelve gauge shotgun blasts of buckshot appeared in the middle of the door and one in the wall next to the door, the buck shot hitting the wall and doorframe on the opposite side.

Anita began blindly firing rounds into the room through the bottom of the door, Bish also firing through the door and wall. The noise was deafening in the confined space, and after they'd fired eight or nine rounds together, they held up, listening. No more shots from the room. Anita rolled from in front of the door and Bish stepped over her and gave it a kick and entered. She was right behind him. He'd gone right she went left to the interior wall.

They turned their lights on and for the most part the room was empty. Three empty shotgun shell casings were against the far corner on the floor. The interesting thing was the big hole in the floor next to the back wall. Both lights were on the opening.

Bish looked at Anita then pulled his radio and keying the mike yelled, "Blue fire…blue fire…blue fire, Detectives Bishop and Wilson in officer involved shooting situation. Two down and another loose with a shotgun. Officers unharmed. We're requesting SWAT, backup, and medical immediately to our location. Blue fire…blue fire…blue fire, out." The Blue Fire code was officers in a critical position with active shooter or shooters, and needing backup immediately. That meant every available officer, local, county, and state that heard the call and being directed by dispatch would be heading their way, and the SWAT unit would automatically be formed and dispatched to the location. The county dispatch center immediately began broadcasting the address of the incident.

Almost instantly they could hear a siren off in the distance. Bish looked at Anita again and motioned for her to get down. He slid down the wall himself, but kept his quivering light and weapon glued to the hole in the floor. They would wait for the backup to arrive before proceeding.

From Anita, Bish heard, "Crap, crap, and crap."

"You Okay?" he asked her, still not taking his eyes off the hole.

"Yeah, the adrenalin has me pumped to the hilt s'all," she admitted. "I'm beginning to shake - I hate that crap; and my chest feels like I was kicked by a bull."

"Can the language and settle down…I never heard you say stuff like that before," he told her sternly. "And you would probably prefer being kicked by a bull. We're fine. We'll just keep low until the rest of the people get here, and then we'll go down and take names. Take a few deep breaths and settle down will ya?"

Bish could hear her taking in deep breaths and letting them out and said, "Let them out slower. That'll help."

She did and soon she said, "I feel better. What do you think is down the hole?"

"Got me?" he answered. "It's probably another way into the basement. I'm hoping who ever shot at us doesn't come out behind us."

"Nice thought. Want me to take a look down the hall?"

"No, just stay put, will you?"

As usual she didn't listen and lay down on her chest, grunted, and elbow-crawled over to the doorway and peered out. She brought her weapon and light up and shown the light down the hall and said, "All clear for now."

A relief, that. Then they could hear a siren winding down outside and others in the distance converging on their location.

"Better get ready to warn the backup where we are. Don't want any accidents happening," Bish told her.

They could hear the door open and a shout, "CHEYENNE POLICE DEPARTMENT! Detective Bishop, you there?" the voice yelled.

"Back here!" Bish yelled his answer. Anita was still on the floor with her weapon and light pointed down the hallway, his still on the hole.

A voice from around the corner next to the two dead guys said, "Police, don't shoot," and a badge in a hand came slowly around the corner.

Anita said, "Clear!" and stood up, grimacing. Two officers came around the corner with weapons drawn and lights shinning. "Come join the party, boys. Bish is in there." She stepped back and the two officers stepped over the two bodies, eased down the hall, and entered the room. "I want you two to stay in here and cover that opening in the floor," she directed. "Whoever had the shotgun went that way. Don't go near the hole, stay back, and just cover it. We're going out to discuss the tactical situation with everyone else that responds."

"Yes ma'am," one of the officers responded.

Anita and Bish went down the hall and he checked the two bodies - both dead – then went outside and waited for the rest of the responders to arrive. He kept looking at her out of the corner of his eye. The next two squads that arrived they sent to the next blocks over to cover those roadways, stop traffic, and keep civilians off the streets. SWAT arrived next and an ambulance. Then the team showed up, tires screeching in the dirt as the two cars slid to sliding stops. The SWAT commander met with Wilson and Bish, as did the ambulance crew, and Anita directed the ambulance team to set up across the street and to notify the medical examiner about the two bodies inside, and then she told the SWAT commander the events that led to the Blue Fire code going out.

First thing he did was yell MEDIC! As the paramedics got there he directed them to check out Anita, then said, "Okay, while you're getting checked out, I'll brief my team and we'll enter through both the hole in that room and the basement door if there is one," the SWAT commander said. "We'll throw flash-bangs then rush the openings. If it's okay with the medics, I'd like for you both to follow on with any other officers that show up. Good briefing. We'll get ready."

Anita wanted the medics to leave her alone, but Bish stepped in and said, "If you don't let them check you out, I'll hold you down and let them."

She gave him a look that said, *I'd like to see you try*, but relented and they found that the bullet had caused the softball sized hematoma it made to rupture – she was bleeding some. The medics cleansed the wound and bandaged it and let her get back to work.

The rest of the team had arrived and she waived her them over, then she, Bish, and the rest went back up and around the porch and waited. She put her last fresh magazine in her weapon and Bish followed suit. Several other squad cars and Sheriff's deputies had arrived by then and Anita directed those officers to take positions in the back and sides of the house after giving them the plan.

Detective Michael Hicks put his hand on her shoulder and asked, "You sure you're okay? You really got hit hard…"

She gave him a smile and answered, "I'm fine, Mike. I'll be okay."

"You're kinda pale looking, that's why I asked," he responded, sheepishly.

The SWAT team was about ready when the captain pulled up and got out of his Crown Vic and began running towards Wilson and Bish. The Sheriff was right behind him. Knowing she had been hit, they went straight to Wilson and found out she was for the most part fine, then went to talk with the SWAT commander, and were briefed on the plan. The Captain then looked up at Anita and Bish, smiled and gave them a thumb up.

The SWAT team entered the house and found the basement door. When they opened it no gunfire came up at them so they split the team. The commander and three SWAT team members would go down the stairs; the other three members would go down the hole in the bedroom after the second flash-bang exploded. Anita, Bish and the rest of the team would follow down the stairs.

When everyone was in position, the SWAT commander keyed his throat mike and said, "Go… go…go." Pins were pulled on the flash-bangs and both were thrown, one down the stairs and the other down the hole in the bedroom floor. Everyone quickly closed their eyes, opened their mouths and held their fingers in their ears and waited for the detonations.

Everyone felt the concussions and heard the loud reports from both flash-bangs as they exploded. The SWAT team members immediately reacted and weapons up, charged into the black void below. Anita, Bish and the other team members followed. It wasn't long before a shotgun blast was heard, immediately followed by several rapid firing M-4 Police carbines, and just as quickly it became quiet once again. Then…"Medic!" was yelled and the call was passed along until it reached the ambulance crew outside.

The paramedics flew into the house, down the stairs and found a SWAT team member with a nasty leg wound from the shotgun blast everyone had heard. One of his teammates had set a tourniquet in place. "Dude, two inches to the left and you'd be a eunuch," one of the paramedics told him with a chuckle.

The shooter, not as fortunate as the SWAT team member, died as the three SWAT officers that had opened up on him had about cut him in half. They left a body bag for the coroner.

The paramedics quickly had the officer stabilized and took him out on a gurney. As they passed the SWAT commander they said they would take him to the hospital and order another ambulance to the scene. All of the officers then continued to clear the basement.

"I want all papers, notebooks, computers, phones and anything else we find gathered up on the table in the kitchen!" Anita yelled out to everyone. "This is part of an active investigation and I want everything that's not nailed down…GOT IT?" she yelled and multiple "yes ma'ams" came from every direction, both from around the basement and from upstairs.

Wilson motioned for Bish and together they went over and looked at the third body. "I've never seen him before," Bish said.

"Me either," Wilson said. "Check his pockets and see if there's a wallet or something, and get the rest of the team over here to look at him. Maybe one of them has seen him around here when they were out here on stake-out."

Bish patted the body down and there was no wallet or anything for that matter. "Nothing on this guy," Bish said, looking up at Wilson.

"We'll have to have the coroner print him," Wilson said. "She's pretty good at that and faxing the prints over to us quickly. We'll figure out who he is. She'll do the DNA thing also."

Right then the SWAT commander came up and said to Bish, "Hey guy, we found two more tunnel entrances, one going northwest and one going east over here." He looked at Anita and said, "You okay, lady, you look a little pale?"

"I'm fine, let's go see those tunnels," she answered.

"Come on, I'll show you," and he led the way.

Sure enough, the first tunnel entrance, flanked by SWAT team members with M-4s up and at the ready, was cut in the basement wall and led to the east. "I bet it goes to Daniel and Helen's place," Bish commented. "Now I know why we never see these people coming or going."

"I'll bet you're right," Wilson agreed. "We'll need to follow both and see where they go." She looked at the SWAT commander and said, "You want your men and women to lead?"

"That'd probably be best, ma'am," he answered with a smile. He got the attention of the three men and one woman with M-4s covering the tunnel and gave a hand signal for them to move forward.

Almost instantly, four lights attached to the M-4s came on and lit up the darkness ahead. One SWAT member saw a switch on the wall in the tunnel and flicking it, saw that it powered a strip of lights that ran into the distance. The commander waved them forward and the four began to creep into the entrance. The commander, Bish, and Wilson followed, side arms drawn.

The tunnel did go to Helen's place and dead-ended. One SWAT member slowly climbed the small ladder up to the opening into an empty bedroom. He told the others and they looked at Wilson, who indicated they needed to retrace their steps.

Once back in the big guy's basement, Wilson told the SWAT commander to leave two of his team at this entrance and then they would go into the tunnel that went to the northwest. He directed two officers to cover the east tunnel and the rest of them turned for the other one.

Again, SWAT members led the way with lights and rifles up and ready. They were being very cautious and it took them almost a half hour to reach the ladder that went up into what, they didn't know. The SWAT commander motioned that he would go up. He first ensured his M-4 was charged and put a fresh magazine in just to be sure he had a full load, and began to make his way up the short ladder.

At the top, he hesitated, listening, and not hearing anything, turned his light off and eased the hatch up. He moved it upwards just enough to let his eyes see over the rim. He scanned what he could see, and not observing anything that looked dangerous, raised the hatch even more, enough so he could look to his rear. He saw nothing in the space that looked like a threat, so climbed out. He motioned for two more SWAT members to follow, and then covered their ascent.

Looking around, he didn't see anyone so turned on his light and knew they were in a pole barn of some kind. He saw crates stacked in one corner on palettes - nothing else. He noted two garage doors, one on either end of the structure, and one doorway on what he figured was the east side of the structure.

The other two SWAT officers were out and he directed one to search to the right, the other to the left, and indicated he would cover from there. They moved out and searched the place.

"Clear," from the right hand side.

"Clear," from the left.

"All clear," from the commander, who looked down into the tunnel and said, "Come on up. It's clear."

Wilson was first, followed by Bish, then the other two SWAT officers and the rest of the team. They began to do a detailed sweep of the place, both inside and out. They found nothing else. Wilson told the SWAT team to check the crates for explosives and they found no danger.

"Bish, open one," Wilson said, pointing to the stack of crates.

Bish got his knife out and pried the lid from one of the crates. The wooden box was filled with Styrofoam peanuts. Bish looked at Anita and she pointed and he stuck his arm into the crate. Fishing around for a moment, he pulled out an intricately designed Aztec pottery bowl. He handed it to Wilson, and dug into the crate again. This time he came out with another Aztec piece of art that was a figurine of some kind of god or something. He handed that to Wilson also. The last item he found was an Aztec raven bird sculptured mask, which looked like it was carved from a single piece of granite. It was beautiful in its ugliness.

"Man, I don't know who we'll call about this," Bish commented, holding the bird mask up so the others could see it. "What do you think, Anita?" he asked.

"A museum person I suppose," she answered. "Maybe from the Denver Art Museum; I figure they're closest."

"You think those are real?" the SWAT commander asked.

"Couldn't tell you, friend," Bish answered as he placed the bird mask back into the crate. They placed the other two items inside and closed the lid. Bish counted eight crates on two palettes. "Man, there's got to be a lot of things in these crates. Better get the crime scene guys over here quickly and take an inventory and photograph everything."

Wilson gave a chortle and said, "That's an understatement. Stay here, I'll make the call," and she headed for the door.

One of the SWAT team members had been outside and said that the pole barn was northwest of the house in between a quarter and a half mile away.

Wilson, once outside, got her bearings, pulled her cell phone out and called the captain, told him where they were and what they'd found. He told her to post two SWAT officers and return to the big guy's house with Detective Bishop and their team. She did just that, and they walked back above ground.

Back at the shooting scene, the captain, and a DCI agent that had arrived, started to interview Detectives Wilson and Bishop, first wanting to know how she was, then needing the facts about the incident. After close to an hour, the two were cleared by the DCI agent. "I still need your weapons and magazines for analysis; procedure. I'll get 'em back to you as soon as I can."

Wilson and Bish handed over their unloaded and cleared weapons and the magazines for each, dropping them into an evidence bag the DCI agent had open for the task.

The captain gave Bish his car keys and said, "There two weapons and mags in my trunk. Use them in the meantime."

Helen and the baby were not home. The team searched both homes completely and only found a few burner phones and one laptop computer that might help with their investigation. They also found a listing of supplies and equipment for something, and an atlas that was open to Idaho. Bish and Wilson looked at each other when they found that.

After another six hours of searching, and no sign of Helen and the baby, they were about to pack it in and leave when one of the burner phones began to ring. It was almost comical as every officer in the place looked at one another, wondering what to do.

Bish broke the odd moment by saying, "Well should we answer it or see if it goes to a message?"

"Let's wait and see if it goes to message," Captain Carlisle said.

So, they all waited, looking at the evidence bag the phone was wrapped in. The thing rang twelve times, then silence.

Chapter Seventeen
March
Cheyenne, Wyoming

The investigation was on-going. Everything they found in the big guy's house was photographed in place, and then tagged and bagged. The tagging and bagging of the big guy himself took six men and the body bag wasn't big enough.

Three days after the shooting, Detective First Class Anita Wilson found herself looking at the huge bruise just under her right breast, the point of impact of the Daniel's bullet. She gingerly touched the spot and grimaced with the pain. She was fortunate a rib or two hadn't fractured. She could not take a deep breath, and a yawn when she got up almost put her on her knees. And laugh or sneeze – no!

She finished getting dressed, made herself some toast with peach jam, another cup of coffee, and sat at her small bistro table in the kitchen next to the window, took a sip of her coffee and stared out the dirty glass. *Someday I have to clean the windows* she thought. She took a bite of toast and turned on her phone, starting her internet connection. She wanted to check the local news headlines for any new developments. There was nothing new.

After breakfast, she cleaned her dishes and left for work. She had to meet the Department of Criminal Investigation (DCI) at the big guy's home. They would go over step-by-step her version of serving the warrant and subsequent actions. Bish had gone through the process the day before. The DCI still had their service weapons and the one she wore belonged to the captain.

She pulled up in front of the house and saw two DCI agents standing near the porch. She got out, waived, and walked up to the pair.

"You ready for this?" a captain from DCI asked her.

"Yes, I want to get this over with," she answered. "What's first?"

"How are you?" the DCI captain asked, pointing at her chest.

"Still a bit touchy and please, don't make me laugh," she answered, then, "Thanks for asking.

"Okay, let's begin. What time did you arrive here on the day in question?" the captain began.

Four hours later, the captain and his partner, a detective, said they were satisfied and told Wilson she could go back to her office, and to not speak with anyone about what they had seen and gone over that morning. She signed the letter of agreement and the acknowledgement of investigation for the shooting, shook their hands and left.

To heck with the office, I need a serious stiff and hot cappuccino and a sesame seed bagel with avocado spread. Then maybe the office, she thought. She pulled away from the site and got back onto South Greeley Highway, heading for town. She sent straight to the Starbucks, ordered her coffee and bagel, picked a bistro table, and sat down to wait. The line was longer than usual that morning.

The server brought her items she thanked him along with a smile, and then sat there staring out the window at nothing. She suddenly got the feeling she was being watched looked up and saw Patrolman Constance Dominguez standing with a steaming cup of coffee in her hand.

"You okay, ma'am?" Connie asked.

"Connie, you can call me Anita, I don't mind and it's okay for you to do so," Anita said. "Have a seat."

Connie sat down and looked at Wilson and asked again, "Anita, are you okay?"

"I'll be fine," she said with a slight grin. "I just got done with the DCI at the scene and needed some caffeine, you know what I mean?"

"No, I don't, truthfully, and hope I never do," the youngster answered.

"The perfect answer if you ask me. I hope you never do either."

"Was that the first time you did something like that?"

"I've served warrants before, but that was the first time I've ever used my firearm for real. I'm still kind of shocked by it."

"How's your chest?"

"Please don't make me laugh." Anita looked Connie in the eye and said, "I really don't recommend this. It hurts terribly. I can't take a deep breath, sneeze, or laugh…hurts."

"I bet. I hope everything is okay."

"It is. My doc said no broken ribs or anything, just a huge bruise that'll be painful for ten days or so. I took a hot bath last night and it helped…a lot."

Connie chuckled, saying, "I bet it did. A hot bath always seems to help, with all kinds of issues."

"Yes, I think so, too," Wilson agreed, taking another sip of her cappuccinos.

The two sat there having small talk while finishing their coffees, and Anita's bagel. Once Anita was done, she said, "Well, back to the fort."

Connie got up and followed Wilson out of the Starbucks. "I'll see you there."

"Okay, kid, see you in a few."

Anita sat at her desk and knew Bish was watching her. They were all watching her. She felt rather than saw Bish get up and move her way. She looked up as he approached and gave him a weak smile.

"Everything go well?" Bish asked, referring to the DCI investigation.

"Yeah, it's good," she answered.

He tilted his head questioningly and asked, "You okay, Anita?"

"Sore as all get out, and for goodness sake, don't make me laugh. It hurts terribly. The doc said it would for the next ten days or so. Said the ribs were bruised but not fractured. Still hurts."

He gave a slight chuckle and said, "You should take a day or two off and relax in a hot tub or something."

She looked up at him with a thoughtful expression, reached for her phone, and dialed the captain. Once he picked up, she asked, "Hey, cap, you mind if I take a couple of days off to let these ribs heal some?"

"You done with the DCI?" he asked.

"Yeah, finished about an hour ago," she answered.

"Then get. We'll see you next Monday. If anything interesting comes up, either Bish or I will get in touch with you. Now scoot," and he abruptly hung up.

She hung up the phone while shaking her head. He never just said good bye or have a nice day, just hung up. Funny.

"What'd he say?" Bish asked.

"He told me to get and come back Monday. Said he or you would let me know if something interesting came up."

"Well, that being said, that burner phone…"

"Yeah."

"It keeps ringing, but no message."

"Can they trace it?"

"They're trying. It's a Verizon phone and they're doing their best to try and ping the towers. Nothing yet, whoever is calling doesn't let it ring long enough. They got one tower, the one north of town just west of I-25."

"The one by Little Bear?" she asked. He nodded. "I suppose that's a start. But even with that, we cannot start a search. There's a million square miles out there…it'd take ten years to cover it all."

Patrolman rookie Thomas Alton, Tom, had been listening in while attempting to read the daily-daily's, reports of local incidents all officers read daily to keep informed. He set the papers on the small desk he was using, and brought up his computer. *Maybe I can lessen the time,* he thought.

Bish gave Anita a hand up, helped her put her coat on, and said, "Now get. We'll be okay. You relax and heal up, got it? And, if you need anything, give one of us a call and we'll take care of it for you. Now scoot," he said, giving her a gentle push towards the door.

Everyone else in the office stood up and gave her well-wishes and reiterated they would pitch in to get whatever she might need. She gave them all a wave, left the office and went home.

She was out the door and Bish was just about to sit down when Tom said, "Bish, can I talk with you and show you something for a minute?"

"Sure, Tom, what's up?" Bish asked moving over to Tom's desk.

"You know about Google Earth?" Tom asked looking up at Bish.

"Yeah, it's pretty cool, why?"

"Well, I'm sorry, but I overheard what you and Detective Wilson was discussing a minute ago and I figured instead of us going out and searching, we use Google Earth and just look for something out of the ordinary. It'd save a ton of gasoline and time, you know?"

Bish stood up straight, looking at the kid with wide-eyes, thinking about what he'd just heard. He leaned back down on the desk and said, "That's a swell idea, kid, you keep thinkin' like that. What've you got?"

"Here's the tower you were talking about," he began, pointing to the tower. He then backed out the image and said, "I figure us rookies could do most of this by cutting the area here," he said using his finger as a pointer and making a huge circle from the north of Cheyenne, north to Chugwater, east to Hillsdale, and west to Laramie. "I figure we could each take a look at homes, barns, and stuff made by humans in these areas and mark each that looks - interesting I guess - and then actually go out and take a look at the places, maybe even use a drone to overfly the properties and take closer photos.”

Bish looked at the kid and smiled. He stood up, called Connie, Andy, and Clint over, and said, “Tom here has come up with a good idea. You three are gonna help him. Tom will brief you and give each of you an assignment, with my blessing. You’ll know what to do when he gets done. Tom…” he said and went back to his desk, smiling all the while.

It was only a few minutes when he saw the three other rookies scoot back to their desks and bring up their computers. Bish smiled again as he picked up his phone and called the captain’s secretary, Amanda, and asked, “Hey, kiddo, does the captain have a moment? I have something he needs to hear…okay, I’ll be right up.”

He stood, looked at Peter, and said, “I gotta go see the captain, be back in a bit.”

Amanda told him to go right in as he sauntered up. He gave her a smile and a small wave and went in.

“Howdy, Bish, what can I do for you?” the captain asked as he pointed to a chair for Bish to sit in.

Bish sat down, and then explained what Tom had suggested. After he explained the idea and what he, Bish, had told the rookies to do, the captain sat back in his chair and began to rock, looking at Bish, thinking the process through. After several long minutes, he sat up, picked up his phone, and said, “Amanda, get me Merkel from photography. He hung up and waited. Bish kept quiet.

The phone rang and Captain Carlisle said, “Merkel? Yeah, Captain Carlisle here, can you come up right now and see me? Okay, we’ll wait. I have Detective Bishop with me. Okay.” And he hung up.

“He’ll be right up,” the captain told Bish.

When Merkel arrived, the captain made sure the two detectives knew each other, and they did, and told Merkel to sit down. He then had Bish explain the idea that Patrolman Alton had. Once the explanation was done, the captain said, "You photogs still have those big drones?"

"Yes, sir, we have a half-dozen of 'em," Merkel answered.

"I want to know if you can have one of those ready to go at a moment's notice, with a pilot, to go look at whatever Bish and his group finds?" the captain asked.

"Yes, sir, we can do that, uh, you're not talking about a night op are you?" Merkel returned.

Bish said, "If I may, sir, no, in all likelihood just daytime flight operations. It would really have to be an unusual circumstance for us to want a night op."

"Then yes sir, we can be ready. I'll go down now and get two of the birds readied and charged up to fly. It'll take about six hours for them to be ready, but from then until you don't need the service anymore, we'll have two readied at all times. That good enough?" Merkel said.

"That's great," Bish said.

"That'll do, then," the captain agreed. "Merkel, thanks for the help. Bishop here will give you a call if he needs you guys. Thanks again."

Merkel got up saying, "Yes, sir, thank you for the opportunity. Bish, tell that kid great idea," he said as he left the office.

"Bish, get 'er done," the captain said, going back to his paperwork.

Bish got up, said, "See you later, captain, and thank you, sir, for the help."

He got a wave in response.

Back in the office, Bish told Tom and the others what the captain had done, and that the drones would be ready to go the next day if the rookies found anything of interest. He directed the rookies to 'get to it' and sat back at his desk after giving Tom an atta-boy and a thumb up. He was proud of the kid. It was a swell idea.

Monday, day three of the Google idea, Anita came in and saw the four rookies hard at it. "Bish, what're they doing?"

"Oh, hey, how are you doing?" he instead asked.

"I'm much better, thanks, what's up with them?" she asked again.

About twenty minutes later, she was suitably impressed and went over to Tom's desk and thanked him for the great idea. He was all smiles and asked her how she was doing. She asked if they had identified anything of interest as yet and he explained they had found very little, in fact only two areas that might foot the bill for a fly-over by one of the drones. She congratulated him once again and told him to keep at it.

Back at her desk, she checked her email and read the daily-daily's. After that, she sat back and sipped her coffee wondering if they would be able to act on anything soon. They all were actually wondering the same thing.

Day seven of the Google mission, Tom's head popped up. His head turned side to side as if he was trying to understand what he was viewing on his computer monitor. Bish had seen the movement and was about to ask when Tom said, "Detective Bishop...can you come look at something I found in my sector?"

Bish said sure as he got up and went over. Tom pointed and shrugged his shoulders and said, "I don't have a clue, sir, what that is. Do you?"

"Uh...nah, got me kid. I've never seen anything like it. Anita, come here and look at this will ya," Bish asked her.

At that, almost everyone in the office got up and moved over behind Tom's desk to watch and join in on the session.

Peter was first with an observation, "It looks like an huge underground hot house or something...see here, it looks like plants of some kind, maybe even a tree. It looks like they've sectioned it off into different gardens for some reason. Neat."

"Yeah," Mike said, "I read about a guy up in Montana that did that, make an underground greenhouse and he could keep it at eighty-five degrees all year long. I thought it was cool myself."

"Can you zoom in more?" Connie asked.

Tom zoomed in until it went to street level view and that distorted everything. He backed off until it went back to an aerial view, and they still couldn't determine what it really was.

"Hey, is that a person?" Clint said, pointing to one of the sectioned off areas.

Tom, Bish, and Anita, all leaned in for a closer look.

"Is that a nude woman?" Tom said, tilting his head.

Now everyone leaned in for a closer look. Silence.

"Time for a fly-by," Bish said straightening up and stretching.

"I agree," Anita said, "Bish, make the call. Tell 'em we want to be able to see the feed up here."

"Will do," he said heading back to his desk to call Markel. "Hey, we got a hot target for you. How do we work this so we can see it up here on our screens?"

Markel told Bish what to do to be able to see the feeds. Then he said, "I need a heading, distance to target, and what we'll be looking for."

"What do you mean heading?" Bish asked.

"I got it," Tom yelled and handed a slip of paper to Anita to give to Bish.

Bish read the note to Markel, "Target bearing three-five-one degrees, thirty-two miles distance, and it looks like it may be one of those underground hot houses or something. It's huge; we're thinking about one-hundred by fifty feet or so, so should be easily seen from the air. What makes us want a fly-by is it looked like a nude woman in one of the sections."

"Oh, I'm definitely flying this mission," he said with a chuckle. "These babies have a range of about a hundred miles so once I find it, we'll have about six to eight minutes loitering time over the target."

"How close to the target can you zoom in your cameras?" Bish asked.

"I can count freckles from a thousand feet if you need it," he answered.

"Oh, wow, then we should be able to tell if that's a human or not," Bish said.

"Yeah, and I can measure her areolar if you need it," he said with a snicker.

"Nah, I don't think so my friend, but that is a thought," Bish answered with a snicker himself.

"What did he say," Anita asked tapping Bish on the shoulder.

"When can you launch?" Bish asked.

"Fifteen minutes or so," Markel answered. "Tell whoever is measuring, to measure from our south parking lot's most southern border…I'll wait."

Bish asked Tom to make the measurement and once he had it said, "According to the measurements on Google Earth, thirty-two point one-five miles on that bearing."

"Okay, flight time'll be about twenty-five minutes at five-thousand feet. We'll check with the tower before liftoff to see if there's any other traffic in the area," Markel told Bish.

"What do you mean?" Bish asked.

"Air Traffic Control – we have to check with them prior to launch to both get clearance and to make sure no aircraft are in the area. We don't want a mid-air collision you know."

"I get your point," Bish said. "That would make things kinda muddy."

"Yes. Okay, we'll launch in about fifteen minutes if we get clearance. Talk to you later," Markel said and hung up.

"Okay," Bish said after hanging up, "they'll launch in about fifteen minutes after getting clearance from the Air Traffic Control folks. Want me to inform the captain?" he asked looking at Wilson.

"Yep," she said.

Bish made the call and Amanda said he was out, but that as soon as he returned she'd let him know.

Bish hung up and told the others how to fix their computers so they could watch the show. Anita said for Tom to put it on the big screen, smart television they had on the wall. He jumped up and made the connection with his computer with a USB cord, and opened the program on the big TV.

"Oh, yeah," Clint said sitting down in his chair to watch. The others followed his actions and sat at their desks to watch the show.

At the twelve minute mark, an image popped up on the big screen. Ohh's and Ahh's sounded around the office.

"Anybody have popcorn?" Peter asked.

Chuckles, and from Anita, "Maybe next time, Peter. I have some chips."

"That'll do," he said with a chuckle.

Tom suddenly said, "Look."

The drone was lifting off. They could see right up Pioneer Avenue, looking to the north when the craft began rising. Once it got about a hundred feet off the ground or so, it started off on the bearing Tom had given it, and still climbed. After a few moments, they could see for a long way to the northwest. It was a cloudless day so the view was startling.

As the flight hit the twenty-two minute mark, they could see the complex in the distance. It was off a dirt road called Roger Canyon Road that fed from Horse Creek Road to the east. At least, they could get to it by driving if necessary.

Bish's phone rang and when he answered, it was Markel, "You seeing what we are?"

"Yeah, we're all looking at it on the big screen," Bish answered.

"We're at five thousand and we're going into a hover now," Markel said and they saw the image begin to still. "Want me to zoom in on it?"

Bish had placed the call on speaker and said, "Yes, please, but do so slowly. I'm on speaker so everyone can hear."

"Okay. If any of you want to stop the zoom, or want us to move into a different viewing position, just sing out," Markel said. They all watched as the camera slowly zoomed in on the complex.

They all saw the two story home alongside the underground structure, and there were several out-buildings, probably pole barns as there were horses about.

"What's that big concrete looking thing to the east of that house and the road?" Clint asked.

"Detective Markel, can you zoom in on that concrete looking thing?" Bish asked.

"Sure, hang on," he answered and they saw the feed move to what they could now see was a large concrete block, about twenty-five feet square.

"Is that an old foundation for a home or barn or something?" Clint asked.

"Unknown," Detective Markel answered. "There's something in the middle…we're zooming in on it, hang on."

They all watched as the camera moved in on what turned out to be a large metal ring embedded in the concrete, obviously a lifting point for a large heavy-lift vehicle might use.

"Maybe it was left by a construction company doing pipe laying or something," Mike said.

"Could be," Bish agreed. "It's been there a while by the growth around it."

"Yeah," Mike agreed.

"Detective Markel, can you zoom out and then back in on the complex?" Anita asked.

They immediately saw the change on the big screen TV, and as the camera zoomed in on the complex, they could indeed see that it was a nude female in one of the sections.

"It looks like cubicles," Connie suggested.

"Individual rooms," Clint added. "Maybe a unusual type of home and they have a lot of kids."

Anita looked at Bish and him at her at the same instant. "How many rooms?" they said in unison.

"Looks to be ten that we can see," Connie answered.

Anita and Bish looked at each other again but this time with knowing eyes.

"That's it," they said in harmony again.

"That's what?" Captain Carlisle asked as he walked into the office.

Anita pointed and the captain turned his attention to the big screen TV. "What's that?" he asked.

"I believe that is where we need to go," Anita said.

"I agree," Bish said with conviction and stood.

"What makes you think that is where these kids were taken?" the captain asked.

"Beg your pardon, captain, but can we work on this for a while and give you that answer when we're sure of what we're talking about?" Wilson asked.

Just then, Markel interrupted and said, "Guys, we need to RTB. We're outta time?"

Bish said, "Go ahead, and thanks. We'll want to schedule another flight out there within the next day or so, but If you don't mind, we'll take you out on Horse Creek somewhere and you can launch from there. That way we can have more time on station to view the area."

"Sounds good, let me know, Markel out," and he was off.

The team and the captain watched the return flight since it was something they had never seen before. Once the drone settled on the parking lot, they turned the big screen off and the captain looked at Anita and said, "It's two. I'll give you to four to come see me," and with that he left the office.

"Bish, get April's list out and let's do some figuring," Anita said. April's list as they called it was an Excel spreadsheet they used that had all the pertinent information about the abductees, date taken, city and state, ethnic backgrounds, and such. The two of them sat together at her desk and went over the dates of abductions and figured that the woman they saw in the last room was the girl that had been abducted in April of 2013. If it was, that would make her twenty years old.

"If that's her, that's the kid from Santa Fe, New Mexico," Bish said sadly.

Anita looked at him with sad eyes and wonderment. She thought to herself, *Is this real? Is this really happening? Is that really that little girl from New Mexico from so long ago?*

They stared at one another wondering if they had really found the place where these kids had been taken all these years. And for that matter, were the girls still alive?

They shook off the realization of what they may have found using Tom's suggestion, and put together information they thought pertinent to the case, enough that they might convince the captain they should further investigate the complex.

At ten till four, they left for the captain's office. Amanda told them to go right in. The captain looked up as they walked in and said, "Have a seat. What do you have?"

They showed him the data, the charts, a still of the complex Tom had printed off showing the number of rooms, the house, the barns, and that strange cement slab to the east of the place.

"If what we suspect is right, then that girl we saw in that last room is from Santa Fe, New Mexico," Anita said. "I'm shocked to think it's possible, but looking at the data and the evidence at hand, it really makes me wonder."

"You're telling me he's keeping them? Or whoever this is, is keeping them?" Carlisle queried.

"Yes, sir, we are," Bish answered the question. "For what reason, we're not really sure. Anything we come up with right now is purely conjecture. The girl we saw was nude, so that tells me it may be a sexual thing of some kind." Bish had to look away as every time he thought about that he became angry.

"Captain," Anita began, "all we want to do is observe for now. I don't think we have enough to ask for a warrant to go in and hit the place as yet, and the only way we can do that is through more investigation. Shoot that may have been somebody's wife waiting to have a fling with her old man when he gets home from work for all we know. Maybe she was just getting some sun when we happened along. But all those rooms…. We just didn't have enough time on station watching to see much else. That's why I want to have another flight out there from a closer launch point. That way we can look at each room and see if there are any other people in there. We just might be looking at a place where all those kids are held captive. If so we need to act quickly."

The captain sat back in his chair and began to think. He rocked back and forth, and from time-to-time went from side to side.

"Detective Markel said he could launch tomorrow?" Carlisle asked.

"Yes, sir," Anita answered.

Back to thinking…

"You say you want to launch from a closer location…from where?" he asked.

Bish answered this time with an explanation, "Sir, I figure we can drive up Horse Creek Road past the turn off on Fisher Canyon Road, going up to Laramie County Fire District Station Number Two, which is up near Horse Creek Cattle Company, and launch from behind their building. I figured it would only be a flight of just under eight miles, giving us about thirty minutes of time over the target. That would be plenty of time to zoom in and look into every room, photograph what we can and then return."

The thought processing began again, the room remaining quiet save the squeaking coming from the captain's office chair going back and forth.

"Okay, I'll authorize it," Carlisle said. "But I want frequent updates. No heroics. You do not go in without a proper warrant and for that you better have really good probable cause, hear me?"

"Yes, sir, we understand," Detective Wilson agreed.

Carlisle looked at them for another few moments and then almost rudely said, "Get."

"Thank you, sir," Wilson said, and then the pair got up and left for the CID.

Chapter Eighteen
March
Cheyenne, Wyoming

The dust and debris billowed as the drone lifted off from behind the Laramie County Fire District Two Station house. The volunteer fire chief was on-hand to watch. Detective's Wilson, Bishop, and Markel, were standing behind their truck, which was parked in the shade of the building. They watched the craft as it climbed in altitude. Once it reached three-thousand feet, it leaned to the west and dipped towards the complex. They would be able to stay on station flying above the site for almost a half hour.

It took ten minutes for the craft to fly the eight or so miles to the site. Markel made the craft circle the complex from five-thousand feet, taking shots of the place from every primary compass heading. This would give them a panoramic view of the place when the photog folks put them all together.

"We want to look in each of those rooms if we can," Wilson told Markel. "We want to see if there are any more people, or even children in them."

"Okay," Markel said, "I'll hover and we'll zoom in on each room. That'll probably eat up most of our loitering time."

"It's important. We really need that more than anything right now," Bish told him.

The craft came to a stop directly over the complex, and Markel made the first zoom into the last room on the northwest corner of the complex. The same woman was in there, wearing what looked to be jeans and a tee-shirt. Markel took several photos, and then moved to the room across the central hallway that ran the length of the glass enclosure.

Sure enough, they saw another woman, reclining on what looked like a Chaise lounge, reading a book. Markel moved to the next room and found another woman. Then the next, the next, and the next, and they all had a person in them. Most looked to be adults, but several looked to be children, and even infants in the last two rooms. They zoomed in on each person and took photos. A few who were reclining or sun bathing, they could get fairly clear photos of their faces. Most, however, were oblique shots with no distinguishing features.

"Okay, go to the main house now and take a few shots there," Bishop asked.

"Moving over there now," Markel said.

Wilson and Bishop watched as Markel flew the drone around and took photos from each side of the two-story home. They saw one vehicle, an SUV, and he took several photos of it, and even got a fairly good shot of the license plate. It was a white BMW X-7.

"Anything else right quick; we've about run out of time," Markel asked.

"That slab to the east, if you can get it," Bish said. "We can't figure that out."

Markel moved the craft just a few yards and the cement slab came into view. He took several close-up photos of the thing and then said, "Gotta get back. We're outta time." He turned the craft towards the east and poured on the power to get it back.

They saw the drone before they heard it, watching it as Markel brought it into a hover just below the large propane tank every building had out in the Wyoming boondocks. He gently descended until the drone touched down, killed the engines, and let the dust settle. They could hear the metal in the engines ticking as they cooled.

While waiting for the craft to cool, Markel stowed the monitoring computer, the flight control panel, and his personal hearing protection. He asked Bish to assist taking down the craft itself, stowing the props and engine struts, then the drone body and camera. Closing the cover and locking it, they pushed it back into the bed of the truck, got inside, thanked the fire chief, and departed. It had been a good mission and they had plenty of photographs to study, especially the ones with the peoples' faces.

When Wilson and Bishop got back to their office, the first thing was to copy the photo drive from the mission onto several computers for backup purposes and tag the original as evidence. Everyone gathered around Wilson's desk to hear the results of the drone flight.

"We got a lot of pictures, and to answer your question, yes, there was a person in every room in that complex," she began. "We are fairly certain they're all female. Ten of them, ranging in age from infant to what looks like young adult and everything in between. We also saw a white SUV in front of the home and think we got a good enough shot of the plate to run it."

"What kind of SUV?" Patrolman Clint James asked.

"Bish…?" Wilson looked at him for an answer.

"It was a BMW X-7…why?" Bish said.

"Peter, that was the rig that pulled up to the big guy's home that day…some Hispanic-looking guy got out and went in," James said. "He was in there about twenty minutes, but I remember that gleaming white BMW. Guy had some money to have that thing."

Bish looked at Anita and she said, "Peter, you and Clint get the photos of the plate and run it if you can. Go."

Hicks and James moved over to Hicks' computer and brought up the photo files and began looking for the shots of the plates.

Wilson told the others to concentrate on the photos of the females in the enclosures and try to match them with photos of the toddlers that had been taken. "Wanda's mother, Margaret, still lives in town. She and her husband divorced several months ago. If we suspect that kid in the southwest cube is Wanda, get Margaret in here to try and make a positive identification. Mike, you and Connie take care of that, please."

Mike motioned for Connie and the pair broke from the group and went to Mike's desk. They, too, brought up the photo files and began going through them.

"Bish, I want you working on that slab thing," Wilson told him. "See if you can figure that thing out, even if you have to go down to that cement factory place and show them. See if they know."

Bish moved to his desk.

Wilson looked at the remaining crew members and told them to start going over all the photos and collect the ones that had face shots. She asked them to do their best at matching those with the toddler photos they had on file from the abductions.

As they all moved to their desks, Wilson phoned Captain Carlisle's office. "Amanda, I need to speak with the captain if I may," she asked.

"Carlisle here, what might I do for you," the captain answered a moment later.

"Cap, we had a successful mission over that complex and I have the team going over every aspect of the photos now. The first priority is trying to match those that we got facial photos of with the photos of the toddlers we have. If they even match up just a little, I think we'll have something. The second important find we got was a shot of the plates on a white BMW X-7…we're running them now. That might be a break since Patrolman James remembered the same kind of vehicle pulling up to the big guy's place while we were doing surveillance. That could be another vital piece to this puzzle. Markel did a superb job out there and we were able to stay on station long enough to get every photo we wanted. We have a lot of things to review, but the team is on it right now. If we get anything else important, I'll let you know."

"Good," the captain said. "Keep on it," and hung up.

Anita shook her head as she hung up her phone. *He's not much of a conversationalist,* she thought. She looked up and scanned the room. Every face was glued to a computer screen, going over photos and other information. She smiled, thinking this just may be the break they needed.

El Jefe threw an empty high ball glass against the wall across the room. It shattered into hundreds of scintillating shards. He was very angry about losing three of his people, and most importantly, the people he needed to complete the mission in April. He stewed, wondering if he could find another group as willing and as competent to abduct the child in Idaho. He only had a month and a half before the proper time. He smashed his fist into his palm and cursed in Spanish.

Sims and Isabella cringed in the kitchen where they retreated when he was angry. They tried desperately to stay out of his way when he was like this. They knew he was like an angry rattlesnake during these times and struck at anything that moved. He was extremely unpredictable when he was angry.

"Sims!" Salinas yelled.

Sims quickly went into the room and said, "Yes, el Jefe?"

"I want a full unit called up for this place," he directed. "I want Dante leading. Tell him what has happened and that I want this place protected fully. No mistakes...do I make myself clear?"

"Yes, el Jefe," Sims quickly answered.

Salinas turned for and looked out the front window. Sims did a hasty retreat into the kitchen, picked up the phone, and called the man el Jefe wanted. After several rings a voice answered: "Yes?" was all it uttered.

"Sims here, el Jefe directed me to call you, senior," Sims said.

"What does el Jefe require of me?" the man asked.

"Senior, el Jefe has directed me to inform you…" After Sims had explained what had happened, he waited.

"Dante Black Cloud will comply," Dante told Sims. "Please tell el Jefe a crew will be showing up in less than an hour. I will follow with the rest and will arrive by six this evening."

"Yes, senior, I will do as you bid," Sims assured him. "Will there be anything else, senior?" He was answered by the phone hanging up. He hung up his phone, took a deep breath, and stepped into the front room.

"El Jefe?" Sims said somewhat meekly.

Salinas turned and looked at him.

"Senior Black Cloud asked that I tell you a crew will be here within the hour, and that Senior Black Cloud and the rest of his men will arrive by six this evening," Sims told him.

Salinas turned back to the window without a word. Sims quietly backed into the kitchen. Isabella looked at him and he shrugged his shoulders. Both remained quiet.

The odd thing was that during this brief moment in time, little did Salinas, Isabella, or Sims, know that a drone was above them taking photos of the complex.

Chapter Nineteen
March
Cheyenne, Wyoming

It was March seventh. Salinas, at the complex, was surrounded by over thirty heavily armed men. They had been on site since the first of March, and were commanded by a despicable man named Dante Black Cloud. No one knew if that was his real name, but that's the handle the man went by.

Salinas didn't care what people called themselves as long as they did his bidding when and how he wanted it. The men with him were all just as serious about their business as Black Cloud was. During his waking hours, Black Cloud would himself canvas the grounds Salinas wanted protected and then report his findings to el Jefe.

No one dared attempt to penetrate the security ring Black Cloud's men had set up around the complex. They had set up two towers on the north and south sides of the complex, giving them a three-hundred sixty degree view. They could literally see for miles in any direction. All were linked by throat mike communication gear. They also had scanners they used to listen in on the state and county local law enforcement agencies. Black Cloud appeared to have every nook and cranny covered.

Salinas was actually happy with the arrangements and felt comfortable in the surroundings. The time was rapidly approaching when he would have his way with the twenty-year-old beauty down in the cubicle. He was dearly hoping she would provide him with another son.

They launched the drone from the same place as the last. It rapidly rose to five-thousand feet and then turned to the west for another photo recon mission above the complex.

Detective Wilson kept her eyes glued to the screen. Detective Bishop watched the drone as it sped westward on its mission. Detective Markel was flying once again.

"This time I just want you to do a fly-by, taking video as you go over the complex," Wilson said to Markel. "Go beyond it several miles then come back just to the south of the place. I want to see if there have been any changes since the last recon."

"Yes, ma'am, that we can do," Markel said, smiling. The drone was nearing the complex and Markel activated the video. It would run until told to stop by the pilot.

"Black Cloud, drone flying over," one of the henchmen radioed.

"What altitude?" Dante asked.

"Around five-thousand feet above us, heading to the west; it just went by, continuing to the west."

"Alright, if it stops or turns around, shoot it down," Dante ordered.

"Yes, senior, it will be done."

Dante Black Cloud went back in the house and found el Jefe in the front room. "El Jefe, a drone has overflown the complex. It passed to the west and I've given orders if it should stop or turn and make a return pass over us, it is to be shot down."

"Very good, Dante, you have my blessing," Salinas told him.

Dante gave him a small bow, and then turned and left the room. As he turned for the back door in the kitchen, he heard gun fire, so he ran outside in time to see several of his men tracking and firing their weapons at the drone as it passed to the south of the complex, heading easterly. The drone was moving rapidly and the gun fire failed to bring it down as it passed. Black Cloud wondered if the thing was filming the complex or was just some citizen flying around where they shouldn't be.

"You two," he yelled, pointing to two men, "Get in a vehicle, and follow that thing as best you can."

"Yes, sir," one yelled in answer as the pair ran for a vehicle. One of eight green Jeep Renegades started and spread gravel and small stones as it sped to the east. The small fleet of Jeeps was kept fully fueled and ready to go with keys in the ignitions for almost instantaneous travel.

Salinas came out right then and wanted to know what was happening. Black Cloud explained and pointed at the rapidly receding Jeep. El Jefe watched as the Jeep disappeared over the horizon.

"Will they be able to follow it?" Salinas asked.

Dante looked at him and replied, "If it stays near the trail, they will be able to. If they lose sight of it…" he shrugged his shoulders.

Salinas said, "What will they do if they follow it until it lands?"

"They will destroy it, the camera, the film, or disc."

"What of the pilot?"

A shrug of the shoulders and a small evil smile was the response.

Salinas went back inside, the excitement over.

Five minutes later a radio call came in to Black Cloud, "Boss, we lost it. It crossed Horse Creek Road and continued east. There are no roads for us to use to follow it. What would you like for us to do?"

"RTB," Black Cloud told them, return to base. He went inside and told el Jefe.

Anita and Bish watched as a green Jeep swerved in the turn to the west. Markel kept the drone going east for another three minutes, turned to the north for five minutes, and then turned to the west and flew it back to the fire house.

"Good thing you guys were watching the road," Markel said. "They would have had us for sure."

"Yeah, I'm glad we were watching the feed both ways and saw the build-up of forces. Did you see those two new towers to the north and south of the complex? Viewing guard towers if you ask me. Why would a rancher do that?"

"Well, it ain't for an Indian attack in this day and age, kid," Markel replied, sarcastically.

"If we go in, we'll need everyone," Bish said.

"No kidding," Anita agreed. "We're really going to have to study the maps and have a good plan before going in. I gotta bad feeling about this. How many men do you think they have out there?"

"Don't really know," Markel answered. "We might know more when we view the film on the large screen when we get back. We'll at least be able to count how many we saw shooting at the drone as it passed."

"Okay, pack this thing up and let's get outta here," Anita said. They scrambled and once they had everything stored, drove back to the Cheyenne Police Department.

Salinas was standing on the front porch of the house when Dante Black Cloud eased up to him. It was a moment, and Salinas said, "Yes."

"Everything is quiet, el Jefe. I wish to apologize for missing the drone."

"You and your men tried, Dante. That is enough."

"Thank you, el Jefe."

"Have you made enough improvements for security?"

"I believe so, senior. Along with the two new towers, I have road blocks to the east and west, and listening posts to the north and south. If anyone attempts to get here, we'll know about it long before they arrive, if they arrive, depending on your wishes."

"I want no one on the premises at all."

"I shall give the order, el Jefe."

"You of all people should understand why I wish this," Salinas said, turning to look at Dante.

"Yes, el Jefe," Black Cloud said, meeting Salinas' eyes. He had no fear of Salinas. "What else might I or my men do for you?"

Salinas looked at him, smiled, and said, "I wish for quiet. Tell your men to be quiet. This place is my retreat, my place to relax. Do you understand?"

"Yes, el Jefe, they will be informed and we will try to keep it as quiet as we possibly can, depending on circumstance."

"Yes, circumstance. I understand circumstances might make it impossible, but I wish it to be quiet as much as possible."

"Yes, el Jefe, it will be so."

"That will be all," Salinas said.

Dante Black Cloud turned and left to brief his men.

Back in the CID, Wilson and Bishop loaded the video onto several of the computers, and placed the drive with the first in evidence bags for safe keeping. The entire team began viewing the videos. Wilson had directed Peter and his rookie to look for manned positions and mark them. She told Mike and his rookie, to count people they could see. She told Bish and Connie to try and count number and types of weapons. She and Clint would look at vehicles and terrain.

They were all working away when the captain entered the office, going directly to Anita's desk. "What did you get?" he asked her.

"Shot at, well, at least the drone was shot at," she replied.

"No one hurt, then?" he asked.

"No, sir, no one at all," she answered.

"So, what have you got?" he continued.

"They've added two guard towers, here and here," she answered, pointing. "Here you can see eight additional vehicles. One of those did chase the drone. We were fortunate enough to be watching as the drone returned, saw the vehicle chasing, and told Markel to continue to fly east for another five minutes or so. The vehicle couldn't follow as there were no roads and the land was fenced off."

"What have you got everyone doing?" the captain asked.

"Looking for new additions, defenses and such, vehicles, number of and a type of weapons, number of men around the complex, and terrain features if we feel the need to go in."

"Very good, and to let you know, they found Margaret Pierce. She'll be in at one this afternoon to look at your photos. She'd moved to Greeley, Colorado, after the divorce. She's…well, let's say excited to say the least."

"That's good news. At least we'll get her input. If she verifies the kid is Wanda, how do we proceed?"

"First, we'll reassure her that we're continuing to do all we can. Once she's satisfied, we'll send her home; afterwards, we'll get the teams together and discuss options. I'll be calling in the DA and the Chief County Commissioner."

"That sounds like a plan. I'll let everyone know. Will you bring Margaret up here or do you want to meet in your office?"

"I'll bring her up here. I want her to see the resources we've got on this. I want her to see we have eight officers researching and investigating everything we can on this. I think it'll do her some good."

"Yes, sir, I agree. We'll see you at one."

"Keep up the good work. Tell your team I'm proud of them."

"Yes, sir, will do."

The captain left and she and Clint went back to looking at the screen. At eleven she called a halt, told half of the team to go to lunch and when they returned, the other half would go. She wanted everyone there at one to be available for Margaret Pierce.

"I want you all to look and be busy when the captain brings her in here. But, when they do arrive, I want everyone to stand and give our attention entirely to Margaret. She needs that."

At one-fifteen, the captain and Margaret Pierce walked into the office. Everyone stood as she entered. The captain told her who the people were, and Margaret looked at him and said, "I can't believe you have this many people looking for her."

"Yes, ma'am, we do," the captain replied. "Ma'am…"

"Margaret, please," she interjected.

"Okay, Margaret, let me introduce you to the team leader, and the person that is responsible for all the clues that led us to this meeting. This is Detective First Class Anita Wilson."

Margaret stepped forward and reached up and hugged Wilson. Wilson hugged her back. When they separated, both were in tears. Wilson leaned back and, getting control of her emotions said, "This is my partner, Detective Samuel Bishop."

Margaret latched onto Bish also, and he tried to shy away, eyes wide open in surprise. She finally backed off and said, "Thank you all for the work you've done," and began to sniffle again.

Wilson introduced her to the rest of the team and then said, "Captain, my screen…?"

Carlisle nodded and led Margaret over to Wilson's desk. "Please, have a seat here, Margaret."

Wilson brought up the photos and let Margaret take a close look. Her hand flew to her mouth, covering the sobs that began almost immediately. Mother's knew their children.

After a few moments of tears, she wiped her eyes and said to Wilson, "That's my baby…that's my Wanda. Where is she?"

Wilson looked at the captain and he said, "Actually, she's not far from here, Margaret. Now that you've positively identified her, we'll be taking steps to get her back to you. I hope it won't be long. What you have to understand is, since we found her, we also found what we think are up to nine more captives, possibly more."

Margaret took in a sudden breath and looked at Wilson for confirmation. Anita shook her head.

That's when the DA and Commissioner walked into the CID.

Wilson continued with, "Margaret, because of that and where these captives are located, we have to be extremely careful how we handle this." The DA and Commissioner eased up next to Captain Carlisle and stood quietly, listening. "You see, the complex where they're being held is quite large, and there are a large number of men guarding the place. We'll have to do a lot of planning for this, and we'll have to bring in the Sheriff's Office and the Highway Patrol also. We'll need their assistance. So, I'm asking you not to think that we'll be running out to collect Wanda from a bad man. We want to plan this so we can get her and the others out safely. Do you understand that?"

She looked at her and shook her head. She looked back at the screen, and then asked Wilson if she could have a copy of the photograph. Wilson looked at the captain, and he nodded his head approvingly. Almost immediately, the printer began sending out the photo. Wilson looked at Clint, and he pointed at Andy. Wilson smiled at him and retrieved the photo, giving it to Margaret.

She gingerly took the photo, looked at it, and began to softly cry. The entire office got up to console her. The support overwhelmed her and she began to sob in earnest. The team and the captain, the DA and Commissioner, all stood around her in support, with a few of the rookies looking for support themselves, not knowing what to do.

After what seemed to be an eternity, Margaret, wiped her eyes with a tissue, and said, "Thank you all for your concern. I'll be okay."

The captain said, "Yes, ma'am, thank you also. Please, come with me, Margaret, and we'll go back to my office. Anita, please give the DA and Commissioner a briefing if you would and ask them to come to my office afterwards for a briefing. You join them."

Margaret stood and turned towards the door with the captain holding her arm. She paused just before the opening, turned back to the team, and again said, "Thank you all for what you do. Please be careful when you do go get her and the others. I'll be praying for all of you."

She and the captain left the office and the team stood around looking at each other. Detective First Class Anita Wilson broke the spell, "Alright, quick gawking and get back to work." It sounded like a small stampede. The DA and Commissioner smiled.

Dante Black Cloud pulled into the compound in his GMC truck. He backed up to the place where his men were bivouacked, and he and a few of his men began to unload the supplies and equipment, which amounted to several thousands of rounds of ammunition for their weapons, ten cases of Meals, Ready to Eat (MREs), and a dozen empty, five-gallon water containers. They would fill these before going inside. Other items included twenty-five pounds of jerky, thirty pounds of Folgers coffee, a pack of filters, five cases of canned soups, ten dozen eggs, and forty pounds of bacon. If nothing else, his men were well supplied.

He parked his truck after the unloading, and took a stroll around the complex, checking on his men. Everything was quiet, just the way el Jefe liked it. He was walking towards the house when he stopped and looked at the night sky. Out where they were, away from the city lights and smog, the sky was crystal clear and he could see millions upon millions of stars out in the vastness of space. He watched as two satellites flew overhead. Seeing that sky reminded him of his home in Honduras; he always loved looking at the night sky.

Breaking his revelry, he continued to the house to report to el Jefe. He knocked on the door, and Sims answered. "Please, come in Mister Black Cloud," Sims said upon opening the door. "El Jefe is in the study, sir."

"Thank you, Sims," Dante said and made his way to the study.

"Ah, Dante," Salinas said, "what do you have to report this night?"

"All is quiet, senior," Dante told him.

"Very good. Did you get your supplies?"

"Yes, el Jefe, thank you very much for providing the food and materials."

"Yes, yes, of course. It is for your men, no."

"Yes, el Jefe."

"It is nothing. If you need anything, anything at all, just let me know. I will give you enough money to get it, or make arrangements for it to be delivered. Whatever you might need."

"Short of a direct attack by the United States armed forces, I believe we have everything we need to hold off just about anything."

"That is good; however, if the police do come, and if it is only one or two, go ahead and let them in and I will speak with them. More than that…," he gave a tilt of his head and a shrug of his shoulders, pursing his lips as he did so.

"I want to know who owns that property and how much property are we talking about," Captain Daryl Carlisle told Anita Wilson. "Contact the County Clerk's office, they'll know. I wonder how bad the rattlesnakes are out there."

"I think I can answer that, Cap," Bish said. "We were flying the drone and the altitude Markel was flying that thing was just under twelve-thousand feet above sea level. Since we were at five-thousand feet above ground level so, that makes the complex over seven-thousand feet above sea level. Rattlers don't get much above six grand or so."

"Well, I think we'll still need to be aware of the threat out there," the captain said and that meant it would be briefed to the team before anyone went out there.

"I'll call the clerk's office and find out the answers to your earlier questions," Anita said. "Since we have a positive ID on the little girl, Wanda, we need to act quickly. But planning and thinking first."

"Next week…?" Bish mused aloud.

"We still need a few answers and some planning," the captain said. "I've already cleared an operation through the chief, and he's assured me that he'll support any move we attempt. He will brief the sheriff and the commander of the Wyoming Highway Patrol (WHP). Not sure if we'll get any support from WHP, but we will from the sheriff's office."

"We have eight now, and by the count from the film the other day, they have at least twenty men with what looked to be automatic weapons, AK-47, and M-16 platforms," Anita began. "We saw many of them also had side arms, and we figure they all do. They're wearing combat gear, most likely vests with armor; they all looked to be multiple magazine carriers. It's unknown if they have explosive devices, grenades and such, but I wouldn't rule it out. This will be tough if they decide to fight. I'm of a mind to just go in there with Bish. Just the two of us won't be looked at as a threat. At least we can gather additional intel just by looking around. If we find ourselves in a fight, we can call for the rest of the team. Depending on the tactical situation, we may have to call a Blue Fire event and have everyone respond."

"If we send just the two of you in, I want road blocks here, here, and here, the captain said. "I'll ask the sheriff's office to handle that. When we do this, I want a medical team on site. We'll set up command behind the fire house, where you launched the drones. We'll have back-up and medical there. If we need it, we'll have enough room here, to set up a landing site for Flight-for-Life choppers."

"If it gets hostile, I'll want as much help as we can muster. I want to have Flight-for-Life on standby in case it gets dirty. I think I'll contact the director of the Laramie County Emergency Management Agency (EMA). She can bring the command van out and if we need assistance, that thing can relay assistance requests to just about anybody anywhere. I'll call her and set a meeting. You remember her name?"

"Yeah, Jeanne Best, nice lady, but tough when it comes to EMA issues," Anita told him. "If you need plans done up for emergency stuff, she's the one."

"Good, I'll give her a call here in a few minutes. Get as much information, both physical and speculative, together and I'll arrange a meeting with all the heads and we'll figure out how to get those kids outta there. I'll call you later," and the captain left.

"Okay team let's get all the information we have together," Anita directed. "While we're waiting on when the meeting will be I want you to write down everything you can think of from your point of view on how to best approach this situation. Nothing is far-fetched. And try to remember, if we can think of it, they may have already prepared for it. Let's go."

Chapter Twenty
March
Cheyenne, Wyoming

Two days later, the heads of all the agencies that would be involved were meeting out at the Archer Complex east of town. They were congregating in the LCEMA building, which had a conference room large enough to accommodate everyone. Director Best had gone all out, with a coffee and pastries table set up. There was fresh fruit and tea, also.

Captain Daryl Carlisle found his name placard at the head of the table. There were paper, pencils, and a remote to the large computer screen on the wall. Next to him were placards for Wilson and Bishop. Others around the table included the Director of the LCEMA, Commandant of the Wyoming Highway Patrol, the Laramie County Sheriff, and two of his captains, the Cheyenne Police Department Chief, the DA, and the Chief of the County Commissioners. Detective Markel sat behind Wilson. He was there if anyone wanted further aerial reconnaissance.

At nine o'clock, Captain Carlisle called the meeting to order, and everyone sat down with coffee or tea. The captain used the remote to bring up a huge map of Wyoming, and then narrowed it down to just Laramie and surrounding counties. He pulled a red-laser pointer out of his pocket and pointed to Cheyenne.

"Good morning everyone," he began. "You all know why you're here, and we hope and pray we come to a good solution to this problem we have. I'd like to begin with a slide show, showing the area in question along with some of the evidence we've gathered." He began advancing the photos.

As he advanced, he paused long enough for questions to be asked, comments to be made, suggestions, and etcetera. The session had lasted close to three hours when they decided to break for lunch. Director Best had arranged for that as well, and she had pizzas, salads, and sandwiches delivered.

The meeting began again at one o'clock, and continued until five o'clock. The directors, chiefs, and associates, had come to a viable plan of action, first of which would be to gather more intel, which included another photo recon mission by Markel, and other sources. Teams for each portion of the plan would be gathered, briefed, and sworn to secrecy. Grant money that Director Best had garnered from Homeland Security, would be used for the operation.

The DA and Commissioner, the chief of the Cheyenne PD, the commandant of the Highway Patrol, and the Sheriff, would request a meeting with the governor. They would request support from the Air National Guard for chopper support, both for medical and assault if required.

Wilson and Bishop returned to their office. The team immediately wanted a briefing on what had transpired. Wilson did most of the update. They were surprised to hear the governor might get involved. Anita told them it was going to have to be an all-out team effort for a successful completion of the operation.

They all freaked when she told them she and Bish would be going out there the next day to have a chat with whomever might be there to speak with. They would be going under the premise of lost or stolen construction equipment, and they were looking around the county. They'd ask them questions such as had they seen any suspicious movement of large amounts of construction supplies and equipment in the area. Or if they'd had anyone drop by wanting to sell equipment. Ranchers were always looking for a good deal. The rouse was replete with photos of the missing equipment and, coincidently, a construction site had been burgled the week prior and the sheriff's office had aired a

Crime Stoppers bit on the local networks for several days. That would add credence to the two officers' visit. Based on what the two saw and heard the following day, they would return and discuss a plan of action with the captain.

In all likelihood, another air recon would be made by Detective Markel and his team. They would be taking photos and video from six to ten-thousand feet, and the Wyoming Air National Guard, through a request from the governor, would fly one of their Remotely Piloted Aircraft (RPA) that had thermal imaging for fixed-target surveillance, and incident reconnaissance. The craft was an MQ-9 Reaper and had a loitering time of over twenty-four hours at an altitude of around fifty-thousand feet. It had a top speed of two-hundred thirty miles per hour, and could have a payload of over three-thousand pounds. This RPA has two cameras aboard that can capture full-motion video, as well as still images of objects, both in daylight and night.

When the captain had told them about the Reaper, they wondered what civilians would be doing with a craft that had a payload of over three-thousand pounds. Wilson and Bishop had looked at each other in awe, and knew that meant the thing could carry anything from two-thousand pound guided bomb units (GBU) to anything smaller, short of nuclear weapons. Not to mention the reconnaissance capabilities both during daylight hours and night time operations. One could almost see the pair drooling at the prospects of using a Reaper.

The whole team was suitably impressed with knowing they may have one of the high-altitude crafts at their disposal. They all hoped it would be so, and wondered what kind of weapons it might use helping them. It would remain to be seen.

Dante Black Cloud was making the rounds, checking his men's positions, ensuring nothing would get past them into the compound proper. He was about to walk down the eastern line when he heard a vehicle approaching. His earbud came to life when one of his men reported, "A city police vehicle, two occupants, one male, one female approaching, action?"

After a moment of thought, Black Cloud answered, "Let them pass. No one take any action unless I specifically say so." No acknowledgement came and none was expected. He walked towards the front of the house and watched as the unmarked vehicle pulled up and stopped. Both officers stepped out of the vehicle and looked around.

"Good morning," Dante said, pleasantly. "What can we do for you?"

"Good morning, sir, I'm Detective First Class Anita Wilson, and this is my partner, Detective Samuel Bishop," she introduced them, pointing towards Bish. "May we ask you a few questions about a robbery that took place in Cheyenne? We're investigating it and looking around the county for information."

"Glad to meet you, I'm Dante Black Cloud," he began by introducing himself. "What kind of robbery?"

Wilson pulled out a folder with paperwork and photos and said, "There was a burglary at a construction site and several thousands of dollars of equipment and supplies were stolen. Has anyone approached you wanting to sell construction equipment or any supplies?"

"No, ma'am, no one," Dante answered.

"Would you please look at these photos and tell me if you or any of the folks that work here have seen any of these around the area?" Wilson said, holding out the photos.

"Sure," Dante said, taking the photos and looking them over. "I haven't seen anything like these around here. Sorry. If I do see or hear of anything, can I call you?"

"Absolutely, sir, here is my business card with our numbers on it," Wilson said, taking the photos back and handing him a card. "Thank you for your time sir, we'll be moving along."

She turned for the car, but stopped and turned back to him and asked, "How's the road to the west? We're going all the way to Laramie."

"Gets rough in a few spots, washboards and such, but you should make it with no trouble. Haven't had any rain lately so should be fine," Dante said earnestly.

"Thanks, we'll be on our way," she said and waved at Bish to get in the car. He was driving and he gave a little wave to Dante, who waved back. The pair back in the vehicle, Bish backed up and pulled out to the road and headed west, Dante watching until they were out of sight.

"Notice how you couldn't see the glass enclosures from the road?" Bish asked.

"Yeah, and I saw at least a dozen prepared positions," she said. "I didn't see anyone in them, but I saw where the preparations had been made. There's probably double that many. We definitely need another fly-over and more photos before we make a move."

"I agree," Bish said, keeping his eyes on the road. "I hope we get that Reaper. It'll have infrared so we can see just exactly how many people are on this place."

Wilson was busy placing each of the photos in plastic protective sleeves. This would prevent any damage to finger prints left behind by the man at the house.

"There, that's done," she commented after finishing.

"What?" Bish asked.

"I got those photos in sleeves so we can get prints off of them. I want to see who that guy is."

"You think he's the owner?"

"No. I think he's in charge of security."

"That was my impression also. His hands looked smooth, not like a rancher's hands, no callus. He ain't from around here."

"Yeah, and that wasn't a ranch house or vacation home either."

Bish began to chuckle and said, "You got that right, sister."

It was another hour before they got to Laramie. They stopped at a place called Born in a Barn, and had a burger and fries with sweet tea for lunch. Afterwards, they got onto I-80 and turned east for Cheyenne. Another forty-five minutes and they arrived back at the station. Bish went to the office and Wilson took the photos to the lab, dropping them off and ordering a fast turn-around on the prints, handing the supervisor a copy of the captain's order.

"We'll get 'em done quickly for you, Anita," the supervisor told her with a smile. She left and he and his team got busy.

After drawing gunfire on the last flight, Detective Markel from the photographic unit kept their recon drone at or near the five-thousand foot mark for the entire flight. He made several passes taking still photos, then one pass to the west and one back to the east taking video on both passes. He landed back at the fire house without incident, packed quickly and drove back to Cheyenne. There, he pulled the photo and video cards from the machine and went up to Wilson's office.

"Hey, I got 'em," he said upon his entrance.

Most of the team got up and moved over to Wilson's desk, where Markel handed her the first card, the video card, and watched as she put it in her computer for viewing. She first downloaded and saved the information, then switched to the big screen, and they watched the first pass to the west.

Everyone began writing and talking as the video ran, noting new positions, the work on the towers, and the crates of heaven only knew what stacked behind the house on the southwest corner. The second pass to the east, showed even more new positions and a better shot of the crates. They could see they were military surplus crates, but could not discern what they held or had held. No telling what was in them.

Wilson saved the two videos to her drive, then inserted the photo card and began going through the stills, saving them as well. The team made groaning noises over the new positions. They used red laser pointers to highlight areas of new improvements – what they were now calling fighting positions. There were twenty-four of the things, surrounding the complex. They, along with the two towers, would just about make it impossible to sneak up on the home site. This was cause for concern on a large scale, so Anita called the captain and asked that he come to the office to view what they had, and to discuss what they could do about it.

Chapter Twenty-One
March
Cheyenne, Wyoming

The Wyoming Air National Guard MQ-9 Reaper slowly made a left-hand turn onto the active runway, stopping on the midline. The Honeywell TPE331-10 turboprop engine began to throttle up until it reached running power. The flight operator, or pilot, was in a *can*, a shipping container that held the control computers and flying positions for the Reaper back in Cheyenne. She watched her screen as the craft began gaining speed down the runway. Once the craft reached one-hundred sixty-five miles per hour, the young black Air Force Academy graduate and pilot, dressed in an olive-green flight suit and combat boots, slowly drew back on the flight control, and eased the craft into the air. It was on the first mission to assist in a civilian operation by the Wyoming ANG, an historic event.

Captain Carlisle, Wilson, and Bishop, watched the screen in rapt attention. They would witness a first in Wyoming history.

Once airborne, the drone turned due east, gaining altitude. It continued eastward until it reached Sydney, Nebraska, Then turned northward. Here it was just passing through twenty-thousand feet, and would continue to climb until reaching fifty-thousand. Once there, it would be considered open military airspace and the operator/pilot would be free to operate her aircraft at her discretion. Meaning, she could pretty much do just as she pleased with the several millions of dollars of aircraft she controlled. She turned to the west near Hay Springs, Nebraska, and flew on to Ammon, Wyoming, where she turned to the south.

The pilot, with an Air Force Academy class ring on her right hand, hit a few switches and suddenly they could see the

Wyoming countryside very clearly. The three had never seen anything like that and remained spellbound for several minutes watching the amber landscape passing across the screen.

"How close can you view something with that?" Wilson asked the pilot.

"Ma'am, I can count the freckles on your nose from up there," the pilot said with a smile. "I can clearly see license plates, dogs, and cats, and kids, in both daylight and night time flying."

Bish spoke up with, "Wow, beats our little drone and how. Can you see into next week?"

The young pilot chuckled and said, "No, sir, it's not a time machine...yet."

They all laughed at that.

The captain spoke up next, saying, "How much longer?"

"We're at cruising altitude and speed now," she answered. "Should be there in five minutes or so, and you should see the fire house come into view sharply. I'll turn to the target house when see the fire station. As we circle the place, just let me know what you want to view and we'll make it so."

"Ah, Star Wars, I love it," the captain said, ""Make it so, number one" right?"

"Nope, Star Trek for that quote, sir, Star Trek's Captain Picard as a matter of fact," the pilot said. "I loved that show back when I was a kid."

"*When she was a kid* she says," Bish commented, aiming a thumb at the pilot. This got a chuckle from Wilson and a look from the captain.

"May I ask how old you are?" Wilson asked her.

"Twenty-three, ma'am...just turned that a few weeks ago," she bragged. "And before you ask, I entered the Air Force Academy at age seventeen, graduating at age twenty-one. Two years of pilot and fighter training since then and now I'm flying these things and loving it."

Bish asked, "Have you flown one of these in combat yet?"

Her answer was one of sadness as she said, "Yes, I've already had my share of combat related duty." Combat wasn't something most veterans openly commented on.

The small room became quiet after that, everyone watching the screen. The detail was amazing. The three police officers could see individual rocks and they even saw a small mouse rush across a portion of the screen. It was as if they could reach out and catch the little varmint.

"If we get the authorization to use something to assist with taking that place when the time comes, what might you use?" Bish asked.

"That'll definitely come from a higher authority to grant that wish. However, our armament ranges from two-thousand pounders to these little things that are not much more than five pound bombs. They're little grenade looking things with fins. I can carry one-hundred of the little monsters and drop them individually or in a pickle. We learned that trick from the Ukrainians."

"A pickle?" Anita questioned, looking at the pilot with a puzzled look.

"Oh, that's dropping them in a long string all at one time. It's a sight to see from altitude, but from close up, it's a horrible sight."

"Does it have guns?" from the captain.

"No, sir, not even on pods, just explosives, missiles, and intel gathering equipment," she replied.

The captain looked at the pilot and asked, "Ma'am, those little bomb things…won't they wind up in Nebraska due to the winds around here if you have to use them that is?"

"No sir, they're laser guided, and we can even mount small cameras on them and actually fly them to a target. If we use those, we'll have another person in here called a bombardier. That'll be the person using the lasing equipment or using another control to actually fly the bomblets. They can fly those little buggers right into your kitchen window, they're that accurate."

"Wow, the capabilities you have these days amaze me," Bish said.

"The things we've been discussing aren't even the classified stuff," the pilot commented. "We've got stuff that even amazes me and I'm new."

They were flying back to the east, and Bish saw something that he wanted a closer view of. The pilot adjusted the camera and saw it was a small stand of bushes about a hundred meters from the complex, just to the southeast.

"Can you fly a little more to the south and take a look at the topography from that clump to the southeast?" he asked her.

"Whatever you need sir," she answered, adjusting her controller. They could see the camera move to the southeast some, on the screen.

"Bish, what are you thinking?" the captain asked.

"Sniper…that clump of brush is perfect for a sniper position, sir," Bish answered. "I'm looking at how best a sniper can get to that spot without being seen."

"Ah, good thinking," Carlisle complemented him.

They watched for another few minutes, and then Wilson asked, "On the next pass, can you use that infrared feature you were telling us about so that we can count bodies?"

"Absolutely, just the flick of a switch will do it, and I can give you a wide angle view so you can see everyone in or around the target all at once."

"That'll be perfect," Wilson said. "Will it give us a still to study?"

"If you want a few, I can do that, ma'am," the pilot answered.

"Great, thank you," Wilson said earnestly.

They made several more passes from east to west and north to south and back again. The captain said, "I think I've seen enough - you two?" The pair answered with a pair of yes sirs. "Well that was spectacular, young lady, thank you very much. This has given us what we need to proceed. Those close-ups on the faces of those people will help immensely. We'll be able to

244

use the facial recognition program on them they were so clear. Maybe we'll get lucky and ID a few of those people."

"It's been a pleasure, sir, and I hope to assist you again sometime," the Air Force Academy graduate and pilot answered.

They watched for another few moments while she turned her craft for home. "What happens now?" Bish asked her.

"I'll give the disc to my commander. He'll review it, take down your recommendations and mine, and forward that to the commandant. From there, it'll go to the governor and he'll make the decision if we support you in any other way. Homeland has already given the okay nationally, for the state ANGs to use these to support civilian operations so that hurdle has already been jumped. I'm not sure what'll happen in this case, but I hope we get the chance to help you out. I just can't say how soon that decision might come."

"Well, little lady, I just might be able to get that going since I'm on a first name basis with the governor," the captain said, smiling.

"Thank you, again," Anita said.

"Yes, thank you very much," Bish said, beaming.

"Let's go and yes, thank you very, very much," Captain Carlisle said to the young lady while she piloted her craft home.

"You're more than welcome. Y'all come back, now, ya hear."

Out in the parking lot, a CPD vehicle was waiting for the captain. He looked at Wilson and Bishop and said, "I'm going to see the governor. You two go on back and I'll see you in a while." He climbed into the police vehicle and left.

"How about a bite to eat?" Bish asked.

"How'd you know I was famished?" Anita said smiling.

"Sometimes I call it right," Bish said. "Get in. Where to?"

"Sanford's...I want a bowl of their jambalaya," Anita told him.

"Oh, man, my mouth's watering already that sounds so good," Bish agreed.

They got in their car and went to Sanford's Grub and Pub on 17th Street. They were seated immediately and ordered sweet tea and the jambalaya, Bish adding fries with his. The two very much enjoyed their meal.

Back in their office, they briefed the team on the capabilities of the Reaper and told them how clear the picture was from altitude. They showed them the photos from the infrared camera, and there were several exclamations once the team saw how many manned positions there were around the complex. Additional comments like 'wow', 'neat', and 'that's amazing' came from the group.

Clint was the one who asked the first question, "That's going to be a tough nut to crack, won't it?"

Bish answered, "I'm afraid so, buddy."

"We can't just go in there, they'll cut us to pieces just getting outta the cars," Andy commented shaking his head.

"They're not gonna make us do that are they?" Connie asked with an incredulous look on her face.

Wilson looked at her and saw the fear. "The captain is with the governor right now discussing how we can go in there and rescue these people…those children. None of us want to go in there unprepared. We know and the captain knows what will happen. No one wants to see a front page photo of a bunch of dead cops in Cheyenne, Wyoming…no one! We're going to do everything we can to do this right even if it means outta the box for police work." There was a pregnant pause here, and after several minutes, Wilson took a deep breath and said, "Look, we are going in there to get Wanda. Bryan and Margaret Pierce want their daughter back, and we're going to go get her…soon." She looked at each of them, and then sat down.

Bish looked at all the faces looking at Wilson and said, "All right everyone, back to work. Let's figure this thing out. Look at your data again, the photos, the new infrared photos and see what you can come up with. Let's do it, gang."

All of them were about to sit down when Bish followed up with a bellow, "Clint! Get over here!"

Clint almost broke his neck looking up at Bish, and wondered what he'd done. Tom looked at him and he shrugged his shoulders, not knowing the reason.

The kid slid up to Bish's desk and asked, "Yes, sir?"

"Sir! What? I'm not a sir…sit down," Bish said a little too loudly.

Clint sat down and his heart rate was way over normal. He took a few deep breaths to try and settle down.

"You were in the military, right?" Bish asked.

"Yes, s…uh…I was, in the Army. Why?" Clint asked.

"Did you see combat?"

"Two tours in Afghanistan."

"What did you do in the Army?"

"I was a sniper."

"Were you good at it?" Bish asked already knowing the answer.

Clint hung his head, Bish noted just about like the lieutenant flying that big drone when they asked her the same question about combat.

Clint looked Bish in the eyes and said, "I was so good that if you were within three-quarters of a mile of me, I had you. Didn't matter what you were doing, you were going down. Not bragging, just that good."

"Sixty-one verified targets down, with your longest shot at just under a mile," Bish said matter-of-factly.

Clint's eye contact made Bish's blood run cold, and the kid said, quietly, "That's not for the public to know."

"I understand that," Bish said, just as quietly and with feeling. "How do you feel your skills are today?"

"That kind of training doesn't go away, Bish," Clint answered directly after a moment. "I'll always have the skill, well, until the good Lord takes it away from me I suppose. Why?"

"Good answer. Don't worry, kid, the only people that know your background is Wilson, the captain and me," he said, nodding towards Wilson.

Clint looked that way and saw her looking at them. She winked at Clint. He looked back to Bish and again asked, "Why?"

Bish looked at him for a long moment, sighed, and then said, "I have an idea I want you to consider. Actually, Anita and I both want you to."

The surprise and silence from the kid was palpable. He continued his eye contact with Bish, making Bish somewhat uncomfortable, like a rare T-bone steak being looked at by a hungry pit bull. Bish shook off the feeling and said, "Come on, I want you to look at something and see if what I saw is what you and your training might."

They got up together and moved over to the big table, where Bish spread one of the large photos the drone had provided. It specifically zoomed on the clump of brush. Bish pointed that out to Clint and asked, "Look this over, please and tell me what you think of this clump of brush."

Clint bent over the photo that had been marked with grid squares, and for several minutes stared at it. He looked up at Bish and asked, "What's the scale on this?"

"Each square is two-hundred square feet," Bish answered.

"Ruler, please," the kid asked. Bish went over to Anita, and returned quickly with a ruler, a pad of paper, and a mechanical pencil.

Clint took the lot and settled down, making marks, and taking measurements with the ruler. After almost fifteen minutes, he looked up at Bish and said, "It is suitable. Not the best but would do for a sniper with talent."

"You still have that talent, right," Bish stated rather than asked.

After a brief hesitation, Clint answered, "Yes, I do."

"What will you need?" Bish asked.

The kid swung the pad around and began writing furiously. He finally lifted up and handed the paper to Bish, who took it and read the list.

Bish looked up at Clint, took a deep breath, and said, "Tom, come here please." Then to Clint, while handing him the page, said, "You have an unlimited budget. Get everything you need, Tom will be your spotter. The two of you are now paired."

Tom slid up and said, "Here, Bish."

"From now on, until this is over with, you're partnered with Clint. The two of you will do everything together. Clint is going to train you on a few things. I want the two of you to go…shopping. Clint, get what you need. Go by finance and tell them who you are and they'll issue you a card. Doesn't mean you can go to Vegas for a weekend for two. Get what you need and get back here. Got it?"

"Yeah, Bish, I do. Nowhere in this town will they have this," Clint said, pointing to an entry on the paper. I know for a fact they have them in Sidney, Nebraska, at Cabela's."

"Then the two of you take my rig and go. Explain everything to Tom while you're driving. If they give you any grief, call me. You have my number. Be careful. Now take off," Bish directed handing his keys to Clint.

Clint held his hand out to Tom and they shook hands. Clint smiled and said, "You're in for the thrill of a lifetime."

Bish watched them leave then went to Anita's desk and she asked, "How did it go?"

"I think I surprised him by knowing a lot of information about his past - he gave me a look - I don't want to see that again," Bish answered.

"Where are they going?" she asked next.

"Cabela's, for the weapon. He flat out said that it could not be found in Cheyenne, and that he knew for a fact it was in Sidney. I told him to get everything on his list and then get back here."

"He took our cruiser?"

"Yeah, didn't figure you'd mind."

"Not at all. Sit down and tell me what he said about the map."

Bish sat and smiling, said, "He said I got it right. He said it's not optimal, but would do."

"What do you mean not optimal?"

"He said there could be a bit more elevation, but that he could see a lot from that position."

"What about the range?"

"He didn't say a word about it. And knowing what I do now about his time in the service, I didn't figure he'd even flinch at a measly two-hundred fifty yards."

"So I guess he's okay with it…becoming a sniper for our team?"

"He took Tom, the card and the car and is on his way to Cabela's for that rifle and stuff, so I figure he's in," Bish concluded.

"Okay, Bish, what I want next is for you, Peter, and Mike, to go over all the weapons and gear. Make sure those rookies have the good armor in their vests. Make sure they all have the individual med kits and know how to use them, especially those CAT tourniquets. I want our team prepared for every contingency we can think of and if it's something new, get us all together for a discussion and training on whatever the issue. What is it you always say, that scout motto thing, be ready…"

"Be prepared. That's the scout motto from the old Boy Scouts of America."

"That's what I want, then, for our team to be prepared."

"We will be, Anita."

Chapter Twenty-Two
April
Cheyenne, Wyoming

Enrique Salinas, also known as el Jefe, had himself a two-hour workout in his gym. The final portion of the session was a relaxing thirty minutes in the sauna, basking in the heat. Afterwards, Sims served his usual breakfast on these days. Salinas had just stepped out of the shower when Sims announced breakfast would be served in ten minutes.

"Very good, Sims, I'll be ready," Salinas answered with a beaming smile. Salinas dressed in a pair of Brunello Cucinelli, Flat-Front Italian-Fit Trousers from Saks Fifth Avenue, and a Ralph Lauren, cotton dual pocket Polo shirt, also from Saks, and completing the ensemble, he slipped on a pair of Prada, Saffiano slide sandals.

As he stepped into the dining room, he heard, "You look dashing this morning, el Jefe," Isabella commented with a knowing smile.

"Thank you, Issy, I feel wonderful this morning," Salinas said with an equally knowing smile on his face. "Have Sims serve me please."

"Yes el Jefe," Issy said with a slight bow, and turned for the kitchen to do his bidding.

Sims wheeled the serving cart into the dining room and served el Jefe. On these days, Salinas always had an eight ounce porter house steak, one egg, over easy, and an English muffin. It had been the breakfast of his choice on this day for the past thirty years, and Sims knew how to prepare it to perfection.

"Smells wonderful, Sims," Salinas commented.

"Thank you, el Jefe, fresh coffee?" Sims asked as he set fresh butter in front of Salinas.

"I would prefer orange juice this morning for a change, Sims," Salinas said.

"Right away, senior," Sims said and turned for the kitchen.

Isabella had left the dining room as soon as Salinas had entered, and gone to the red haired, green eyed, beauty waiting for Salinas. She would further prepare the young lady who was by this time already aroused by the thought of what was about to take place.

When Issy entered the enclosure, the young one was pacing, arms crossed, and an expectant smile on her face.

"Isabella is today really the day?" the young woman asked.

"Yes, young one, it is and I just saw him," she answered. "He is very handsome, superbly dressed, and will be here in less than an hour. You must prepare little one."

"I am so excited," the young woman said, beaming.

Isabella led the young woman to the shower and began to prepare her for the day's event, the young woman smiling all the while in anticipation of what was about to happen to her.

"Will that be all, senior?" Sims asked el Jefe as he was finishing his orange juice.

"Yes, Sims," Salinas answered. "I want to be left alone for a while to meditate."

"Yes, el Jefe, no interruptions," Sims replied turning quietly to leave.

Salinas got up from the table and sat in an easy chair near the picture window. He would gaze at the mountains and contemplate the morning's event before going. Isabella would tell him when the young woman was ready.

Back in downtown Cheyenne, Anita and Bish were hashing out a plan of action for the upcoming operation. "Looking at the aerial photos of that place, there's at least ten or eleven captives in those holding rooms," Anita said. "With the positive identification of Wanda by Margaret Pierce, we know of at least one abductee. That is more than enough to get a warrant from the judge to go bust this place."

"I agree whole-heartedly," Bish agreed. "But, with all the armed men around that place, we can't just go barging in like a posse in the olden days. We'd be slaughtered. We've got to plan this out correctly and make it so the captives do not get hurt or worse."

Captain Carlisle said, "We'll have to go in by stealth. We know they have night vision, that's been confirmed by overflight operations. We need to get at least two teams of shooters around the place. They'll need to be in positions that support each other and not shoot towards each other. Bish, where is that clump you and the kid talked about?"

Bish brought up the photo that showed the brush and pointed it out for the captain, "Right here, sir. It's just a bit over two-hundred yards from the complex to the southeast. If we send in a second team, they should set up to the northeast and shoot only to the east, west, and southwest. Looking at this, I'd say about here," he indicated by pointing to a hilltop to the northeast of the complex. "That way, there won't be a danger of them shooting at each other. They'll have set fields of fire and absolutely will not shoot outside of those parameters."

"I agree with that," the captain said. "That kid at Cabela's yet?"

"I can call him and find out," Bish said.

"Do it, and tell him to get two of everything – my authorization – I don't care how much it costs," the captain directed.

Bish pulled his cellphone and dialed Clint, who answered on the first ring. "We're pulling into Sidney right now actually, what's up?"

Bish told him what the captain wanted and Clint said no problem. He then suggested another young officer that had been an Air Force sniper to be the second team shooter. Anyone could be the spotter with a little training.

Bish explained what they had selected as the second position and Clint agreed. Asked about the range and Bish told him less than two-hundred yards.

"He won't have any problem with that range at all," Clint said. "We're pulling into Cabela's now so I'll talk to you when we're ready to leave and see if you need anything else while we're here."

"Okay, I'll explain the plan to Wilson and Captain Carlisle. Talk to you later." Bish shut his phone down and told Anita and Carlisle what was going on, and then went back to studying the map.

How do you take down a facility as big as the one they faced, with that many armed men, and without sustaining any casualties yourself, or creating a casualty of one of the captives? That was the big question of the day.

The small hillock to the northeast was one-hundred eighty-seven yards from the compound. The clump of brush to the southeast was two-hundred forty yards away. The problem was getting four men, two each in those positions and set up without being seen. The southeast approach could be made using the south fork of Horse Creek, as from the creek it was uphill to the clump of brush.

To the northeast, however, there wasn't much cover. They could begin their approach from Horse Creek proper, and have some cover in a small arroyo that ran to the southwest off the creek itself, but they would still have well over one-hundred yards of open territory to cover before getting to the small hill. One-hundred yards of belly crawling over rough, high-desert range, festooned with cactus, sharp rocks, and heaven only knew what else.

"That'll be a tough nut to crack," Bish said to no one.

Captain Carlisle asked, "What will?"

Bish explained his reasoning and pointed out the route he selected for the northeast shooter to take.

"All we can do is prepare them the best we can, and then let them go and hope and pray for the best," the captain told him. "God will certainly be on our side in this. I'm sure of it, so we need to let Him know our plans every step of the way so He can help us out." After he said that, he got up and moved over to the window and looked out, contemplating what he'd just said. After a few minutes, his shoulders drooped a little and one could tell he'd made a decision of some kind.

"A direct assault," he muttered more to himself than anyone.

Anita looked up at him and asked, "What was that Cap?"

He turned and looked at her and after a moment said, "We'll try and serve the papers and if it goes sour, all we can do is a direct assault after that. Once the two sniper teams are in place and ready to go, we'll send you and Bish in with the search warrant in the SWAT vehicle. We hit them at first light with the sun at our backs. If they argue the point, then everyone else has a green light for a direct assault by SWAT. They'll lead with their armored vehicle, taking the brunt of the assault, and we'll follow in our squad cars. I'll make it clear the snipers have a green light to shoot once they see the SWAT vehicle with you and Bish in it. If shooting starts, maybe they can take out some of those people before we get in too deep. I just hope they don't have any rocket propelled grenades (RPG) or light antitank weapons (LAWS)."

"With SWAT's eight team members and our six additional officers, and the four in the two shooting positions, that'll give us eighteen officers for the operation. I'll see if the sheriff can supply another team or two to help out. Their SWAT team has an armored vehicle, too. Maybe we can let them both go in first and then we'll follow. Two would be better than one."

"Maybe they can come in from the other side and box them in," Wilson offered.

"No, it would be better if they went in together," Bish said. "That way it would reduce the risk of us shooting at each other. We would need a road block, here, to the west of the complex where the road goes down into this little arroyo. Stray rounds would go over their heads. I'd say two units, one sheriff's vehicle, and one from us would do."

"That sounds good," the captain said. "I'll arrange that with the sheriff. Maybe Albany County Sheriff's folks will want to get involved since we're close to the county line with them anyway. I'll give them a call, too."

It was always Anita that came up with the odd thoughts and this instance was no different when she said, "I wonder if this guy has any of our people on his payroll?"

Bish and the captain gave her a hard look.

"What…? We have to consider that and that they might be feeding who ever this is with information," she told them.

"If he does and we catch 'em, they better hide whoever it is," Bish said in a low, evil tone.

"Now, now, none of that kind of talk," the captain said. "We'll let the law decide."

Bish gave him a look that would place the fear of God into most. But, he stood straight up and went over to the coffee pot to cool off. Anita and the captain knew how he felt. And for the most part, they felt the same way. If another cop was leaking information about the operation, they would be in trouble. If there was such a person, every cop in Wyoming would want them by the short hairs. The person would not be safe in the Equality State.

Isabella approached Enrique Salinas, gave a small 'ahem', and when el Jefe turned to look at her, she said, "It is time el Jefe." She then bowed and eased out of the room. Salinas smiled, stood, took one more look at the snow-capped mountains, and made his way to the enclosure. It was Monday, the fourteenth of April, 2031. This particular young woman had been taken on April the eleventh, 2011. She was now almost twenty-two years old, and from the time she had been abducted, had been raised, and trained for this moment with Salinas. He was the first man she'd ever seen, and in all likelihood would be the last.

As he closed the door to the enclosure, Isabella flipped a switch and a ceiling curtain was automatically drawn across the room, shrouding the chamber in dim light, creating a suitable environment for what was about to happen. No one would see. Salinas and the girl would be completely alone and unobserved by anyone. It had always been this way.

Chapter Twenty-Three
April
Cheyenne, Wyoming

Enrique Salinas, el Jefe, was through with the girl. She had been as Isabella had said, a very willing and submissive woman. He was satisfied, in more ways than one. He went to his master suite and in his huge bathroom, ran hot water into his jet-tub, turned on the heat pump and the jets. Sims had already left a chilled bottle of Chateau Lafite Rothschild 1982 on the tub. It had an elegant aroma and rich, favorable taste and was perfect for his relaxation.

Salinas tested the water with a tentative toe, nodded his approval, and slowly entered the bath. He sank into his seat until the water was above his shoulders, gave an approving groan, and settled in for a long soak. It was several minutes before he poured himself a glass of the Rothschild, which he sipped as he eased back into the water, emitting another audible moan.

He spent almost an hour in the jet-tub, finishing the bottle of wine as he climbed out of the bath. He dried himself, selected a pair of jeans, a silk tee-shirt, and leather moccasins to wear. After he dressed, he went and sat in his recliner, gazing at the snow-capped mountains to the south in Colorado. He had a book in his lap, a signed, first edition of Ernest Hemingway's *Old Man and the Sea*. A classic work of fiction Hemingway published in 1952, and a Pulitzer Prize winner. He gently opened the book, took a sip from his last glass of the Rothschild, and began to read.

He'd been reading for several minutes when he noted a shadow cross his view. One of the guards was passing his window on his rounds. El Jefe did not appreciate the interruption and called for Sims.

"Yes el Jefe?" Sims asked upon entering the room.

"Please instruct Black Cloud that his people will not pass my window here," he instructed, pointing to the window. "I don't want to be disturbed."

"Yes, el Jefe, I'll see to it immediately," Sims answered.

"See that you do," Salinas said as Sims departed, quickly.

"What the h…," Black Cloud almost responded to Sims' direction from el Jefe. "Yes, okay, I'll comply. Please convey my apologies for upsetting el Jefe."

"Yes, sir," Sims answered and went back to his station in the kitchen.

What in the world does this guy think I'm doing here…? Black Cloud thought to himself. He wondered if the guy was nuts or something. He'd have to have the men in the south tower keep a sharper eye to the south to cover the area. No more sentries walking rounds on the south side of the complex. *What will be next!* he thought as he stomped off to do the bidding of el Jefe.

Several of his men attempted to argue the point, but Black Cloud just held up his hand and said, "Don't go in front of that window on the south side again…period! Just keep a sharper eye to the south from the tower. We should be able to see anything that approaches from that direction. Now get to it, men."

The group dispersed with a few grumbles still to be heard. Black Cloud smiled to himself and shook his head. He had great respect for his men, and they for him. A tall man, Black Cloud standing six-three, and two-hundred ten pounds, with a broad chest, thick arms, and a profound chiseled, dark-skinned face woman drooled about. He had one small, horizontal scar, just under his left eye. His background was a well-kept secret. No one knew his past, not even el Jefe. Many supposed he was ex-special forces, maybe an Army Ranger, or perhaps an ex-Navy Seal. There was no doubt the man was very well trained in all phases of protection services. He had a standing rule with his men, that if any of them could beat him in a physical fitness test, he would buy them lunch at their place of choice…anywhere in the world. He rarely lost, and the men who had beaten him, had become permanent members of his organization. Not that they were better than he, just that they were good - plain and simple, good.

Bish and Clint had finished loading their equipment and spares into the armored vehicle of the SWAT team. It would be hauled into the compound to have as they needed it. No verification could be made on whether the security team around the complex had RPG or LAWs at their disposal. That made the SWAT commander nervous.

With the Cheyenne PD and the Laramie County Sheriff's office SWAT armored vehicles ready for their use, they had a considerable advantage unless those men had explosive rockets available.

The two sniper teams, James and Dalton, would have Alton as James' spotter and Smith, Dalton's. Timothy Dalton, a five foot, ten inch, one-hundred seventy-five pound patrolman was a prior service, Air Force security forces sniper. He'd selected Patrolman Willie J. Smith, a two-hundred pound, six foot, black American, as his spotter. Smith once said to Bish that he was a black American, not an African American, as he'd met a guy that had been born and raised in Africa, who was white as snow. Willie had never even been to Africa, so didn't feel the African American handle was for him anymore. That had made sense to Bish.

Anyway, with the two sniper teams, the two SWAT teams and their armored vehicles, along with the remaining six officers on Wilson's team, and another team from the sheriff's office of four men and one woman, they now had a force of twenty-seven officers to make the assault if it became necessary. The sheriff would have two more, two-man teams ready for back up, one to the west blocking the road, and another on the east. CPD had two more two-man teams at the eastern roadblock. All together thirty-five officers available for the assault, with the captain and the command team made up of the Laramie County Emergency Management Agency command van and personnel, and representatives from Homeland Security and the FBI. They would handle radio communication and direct resources as requested by the respective SWAT commanders. Medical personnel and two ambulances would be on standby at the fire station. They had not been authorized the use of the Reaper for the assault.

It was Tuesday, the fifteenth of April, 0200 hours. Clint and Tom had been dropped off on State Highway 228, some two miles in to the west. They crept along the banks of the South Fork Horse Creek, making their way along the creek for almost a mile and a quarter before turning to the north and finding and crawling the almost half mile to the clump of brush. There they rested and set up their equipment.

At almost the same moment, Tim Dalton and Willie Smith were dropped off to the north on Horse Creek, and made their way for just over a mile to the point where they turned south, following a fork of the creek to the south. They quietly made their way another half-mile and set up on the little hillock selected for the task. They rested also and waited for the operation kickoff time.

The western blocking force set up at 0400 hours. The eastern force along with the command unit and the medical unit, set up at about the same time. The assault force had gathered just over the horizon from the complex, just west of the eastern roadblock. Everyone on the assault team began loading weapons and ensuring their extra magazines were ready to load in their rifles. They checked each other's protective equipment and by 0500 were ready to go. Sunrise was slated for 0539 hours, and they would begin their assault a moment before that as they needed to travel only a half-mile.

Wilson called the team together. Once everyone was there, she keyed her mike and said, "Prayer time." She received a half-dozen radio clicks in response, and then said, "Dear Heavenly Father, we come before you today to make war on people that have done terrible things to children, your children, Father. We ask that You be with us today, protect us, guide us, and place your protective hands around us. Thank you, Father. We ask these things through Your Son, Jesus, Amen." She heard six quick Amen's over the radio, in response to her prayer. "Everyone get ready, over."

She looked at Bish and without hesitation, reached over and pulled him to her and gave him a hug. He hugged her back. Both held the hug for a few moments. After they parted, he looked her in the eye, and she him. He finally nodded, and went to his position inside the first SWAT vehicle. He and the SWAT commander would serve the search warrant papers, if they could, peacefully. Wilson gave the SWAT commander of that vehicle a thumb up, and walked back to her position in the second SWAT armored vehicle. It was 0525 hours.

Wilson strapped into her seat and keying her mike, said, "Two minutes. Snipers report."

"South team ready," Clint answered.

"North team ready," Tim answered.

"Command and medical report status," she then said.

"Command ready," Jeanne Best, Director of the Laramie County EMA answered.

"Medical ready," a paramedic answered.

"Detective Bishop, you have the warrant?" she radioed.

"Affirmative," Bish answered.

Anita took a deep breath, looked at her watch. "One minute," she radioed. The two SWAT vehicles started engines. The next radio call would simply be go, go, go.

Dante Black Cloud stepped out of his room, turned for the door and stepped outside. It was 0530. He would be checking the positions around the complex and checking on his men as he did every day at this time. He turned to the south and began his rounds.

Sims was preparing Salinas' breakfast, which was to be served at 0545 that day. He was busy, preparing the plate just so, buttering the toast to his master's liking, and setting coffee on the tray. He was thinking about his upcoming retirement and had a smile on his face.

Isabella had just stepped into the underground compound to begin feeding her charges. The babies would be first, then the older children. She would check on the young woman el Jefe had used the day before and make sure she was okay, as el Jefe might want to have a repeat session with the woman at any time.

Enrique Salinas stretched after he'd turned off his alarm. He smiled, remembering the activities of the day prior. He got up, turned on his shower to let the water get hot, brushed his teeth, and shaved. He stepped into shower and stood, basking in the heat of the water, letting the warmth overtake any stress he might have had. It felt wonderful.

Chapter Twenty-Four
April 15th, 2031
Cheyenne, Wyoming

It was 0529 hours and Detective First Class Anita Wilson gave what she assumed would be the most important radio call of her career, "Go, go, go!"

The snipers chambered rounds in their rifles and their spotters began looking for and reporting targets to their shooters.

The SWAT vehicles surged forward and reached top speed for dirt tracks quickly. Dust flew in the early morning sky, blanketing the second vehicle in a cloud that completely covered the huge vehicle. Every officer in the vans, save the drivers, chambered rounds into their M-4 police rifles and prepared themselves mentally for what was about to happen.

In the command van, Jeanne Best announced the operation had begun. Everyone tensed at that.

The medics turned their attention to the western sky and wondered what the rest of the day would bring after hearing the go, go, go command.

Dante Black Cloud stepped into the open area to the south of the complex, ensuring he was nowhere near el Jefe's window, and inhaled deeply. He thought to himself that the day would be clear and fresh. He smiled, took in another huge breath of fresh air, and crumbled to the ground as the bullet passed through his head. The south sniper team had claimed their first kill, and didn't realize it happened to be the leader of the security force around the complex.

The SWAT vehicles crested the hill above the complex just as the sun rose. Those men around the complex looked to the east upon hearing the sound, and between the brightness of the sun and the dust rising, they could not make out what was coming.

In the north tower, the guard turned towards the sound of approaching vehicles to the east, and seeing the huge dust cloud rising over the crest of the hill, brought up his rifle and took aim and fired. The bullet hit the lead SWAT van in the driver's windshield and starred the bullet resistant glass, causing the driver to flinch. That was the last thing the shooter in the tower did as he dropped in a heap as a bullet from the north sniper team took him out.

When the bullet had hit the SWAT van, Bish radioed, "Blue Fire, Blue Fire, Blue Fire, lead SWAT receiving fire. All officers cleared hot." That had been a pre-arranged call to alert everyone to an active fire zone.

Several of the men in positions around the complex rose to see what the noise to the east was. At almost the same time, two dropped back into their positions, having been dropped by the sniper teams.

Seeing this, several of the men began firing haphazardly around the complex. A few began shooting at the SWAT vehicle in the lead again, as it was the only one they could see.

The snipers fired as targets presented themselves and the other security team members realizing what was happening, dropped down into their positions for protection.

The SWAT vans entered the complex, one going to the south, the other stopping in the front of the building. The doors opened and officers spilled out, yelling for Black Cloud's men to drop their weapons and get their hands up.

The man, who had been hiding in the south tower, rose up and fired a half magazine from his automatic weapon at the police vehicles, but quickly dropped from a round from Clint James' rifle.

One black-clad officer was hit and went down yelling for a medic. Three team members rushed to his aid and begin first responder first aid on their comrade. Shooting had become sporadic at that point.

Sims dropped flat upon hearing gunfire. He looked around and crawled over to his butler's desk, opened an access portal and withdrew a Ruger M&P 15, inserted a full magazine and chambered a round. He took two additional magazines and placed them in his pockets. The rifle had been illegally modified to fire fully automatic. He assumed he would be well protected with the firearm. He crawled over to the door and opening it, stuck the rifle barrel through and waited.

Isabella also heard the gunfire and shook her head disgustedly, thinking Black Cloud's men were having another early morning practice session. She wondered why she hadn't been informed and went about her business.

Enrique Salinas cocked his head listening intently. He thought he'd heard gunfire, and wondered what Black Cloud was up to, having his men shooting this early. He finished dressing and was about to call for Sims when a bullet went through the glass in the bathroom and shattered the mirror next to him.

He quickly went into his walk-in closet, and from a hidden cabinet, withdrew an automatic AK-47 and several magazines. He inserted one into the weapon and chambered a round. He then withdrew a pistol belt with a Glock 17 and four magazines and belted it on his waist. He drew that weapon and chambered a round in it.

He moved to his living room and peered out of the large picture window to the south. He saw no one or anything moving, but could hear sporadic gunfire. He also heard the engines of vehicles pulling into the front of the house.

Ensuring he had chambered a round in his rifle, he left his sleeping quarters and headed for the front door, easing in that direction from cover to cover.

Bish was down, having been the officer hit in the initial exchange of gunfire by the man in the tower. He was bleeding badly, and the three officers were frantically working to stem the flow of blood from the through-and-through wound. He'd been hit in the right lower quadrant of his abdomen, and they worried his liver had been hit.

One of the officers broke radio silence procedure and said, "We need medical here STAT! Officer down, gunshot wound to the RLQ. Immediate response is requested."

Two paramedics jumped into their ambulance and without lights or siren, sped to the dirt road, and began that direction.

Jeanne Best radioed the eastern roadblock to let the ambulance through without slowing it down.

Wilson and her team had made it to the front of the house and were about to enter when she heard the call for a medic. Someone had been hit. She shook the thought from her mind and nodding to the SWAT commander, ordered him to enter the home.

A SWAT officer with a battering ram slammed the door. The frame exploded in wood splinters and the SWAT team flew into the home.

Salinas saw the door explode inward and also saw the SWAT officers enter the home just as he brought up his AK-47 and squeezed the trigger.

The expected gunfire from within drove the SWAT team flat, with one returning fire in the direction he'd heard the fire coming from. Round after round left his weapon as he blindly fired in that direction.

Sims opened the kitchen door after hearing Salinas' AK going off and fired several bursts at the portal of the missing front door. He quickly withdrew after pulling the trigger five times, as many rounds were now chewing the kitchen door to pieces. He stopped, using the refrigerator as cover, ejected his spent magazine, and reloaded, and then fired single bursts of three or four rounds through the door, hoping one would hit whoever was shooting at them.

Isabella knew the sounds she was hearing were wrong. Now it seemed as though the gunfire was inside the house, and she could hear several different types of firearms. She moved over to her nurse maid's desk and withdrew a Smith & Wesson .357 magnum from under the drawer, along with a box of shells. She turned for the entrance to the underground complex and waited, gun pointing that direction. The children were crying or yelling for her in fear, not knowing what was happening.

The sniper teams were running for the complex, afraid of shooting now as they might not be able to tell friend from foe. Gunfire continued as the police force cleared the positions of Black Cloud's security force. Many surrendered; several did not and paid the ultimate price. Once the area around the complex was cleared, the prisoners were corralled near the second SWAT vehicle and cuffed together. Four guards stood watch over the captives.

The rest of the SWAT team made their way to the front door and reported to Wilson. She directed them to enter to the left and right, and told them where to concentrate their fire. She radioed the SWAT commander already inside and told him the others were coming in. She got an okay from him, and she gave the team the green light to enter.

The last man paused, bent to her ear and said, "Your man Bishop, is the one that's hit," and turned to enter.

Anita turned pale and looked over her shoulder where she could see the three officers working on the injured man that she now knew was Bish. She steeled herself and remained in her position as she was the on-site commander for this operation. A tear ran down her cheek and she quickly wiped it away. She got ahold of her emotions, taking in deep breaths and turned back to the task at hand.

Salinas was on his third magazine and only had two more in his pockets. He would pop up and fire a short burst in both directions he knew had men. He wished Black Cloud would take care of these people, but didn't know that he'd been the first casualty. He knew something was wrong since the gunfire outside had come to a stop.

He popped up and emptied his third magazine into the front room, then retreated to his bed chamber. He opened the portal again, withdrew a satchel of loaded magazines, and threw it over his shoulder. He also pulled out a fully loaded Benelli M3 tactical shotgun and an additional bandolier of fifty rounds of double-aught buck shot, slinging it over his head.

He turned for the door and fired the shotgun several times through it first, leaving huge holes in it. As he neared the riddled door, he heard who he figured was Sims, firing on full automatic from the kitchen into the front room. When the fire stopped, he crawled out of the bedroom and over to the southwest corner of the room, near the huge picture window. He could see several bullet holes in the large pane of glass and that angered him even more. His anger would be his downfall. He was boiling inside that someone was ruining his home and tearing up his paradise north as he called it.

He raised the shotgun over his head and fired it several times in the direction he now knew were policemen. They kept yelling to drop their weapons and come out with hands up. *What a laugh*, he thought and continued to fire. When he was empty, he quickly followed up with a few rounds from the AK-47, and then reloaded the shotgun.

Sims was firing once again, short bursts through the door. Salinas saw a man get up when Sims stopped firing, most likely to throw a flash-bang into the kitchen, and raised up and fired the shotgun three times at the man, who was blown back flat to the front room floor.

For several minutes all gunfire had ceased. Once again, someone from the police called for them to drop their weapons.

This man also told them all the security men were under arrest and in custody.

This infuriated Salinas even more. Several gunshots came his way, with another hitting the window, leaving a starred hole in it. He felt the heat of his anger rising and with it, rose, and unleashed a barrage of fire from both the shotgun and AK-47 at one time. Bullets and buck shot flew everywhere. The Benelli held six rounds, and with nine double-aught buck shot pellets per round, fifty-four lead balls wreaked havoc on his home. When the shotgun was empty, Salinas dropped it and continued to fire the AK.

The SWAT commander of team two, the first to enter the house, was getting angry himself. These guys would not stop firing and he had one man down. They could not render assistance because of all the gunfire. He made a tactical decision and told his men to begin throwing flash-bangs in the direction of the incoming fire. Maybe they would drop the shooters. He told several to begin firing their handguns in the direction of both shooters and for others to throw the stun grenade devices.

When he gave the signal, the police began shooting into the two areas that Salinas and Sims were shooting from. The others prepared and threw a total of six flash-bang devices in those two directions. The SWAT commander yelled for his team to cover up and it was only another few seconds the noise and flashes from the devices began going off.

Salinas knew what was about to happen and he slipped back into his bedroom. Sims on the other hand, was not so fortunate. Two of the flash-bangs actually hit him prior to detonating, and landed at his knees. He looked down wondering what they were when they detonated. He was out of the fight

Salinas was at the portal of his gun case again. He reloaded his AK-47 and pulled out another Glock 17, ensured it was loaded, slipped it into his waist band and turned for the door. The flash-bangs had gone off, and his ears were ringing somewhat, both from the gunfire and the exploding devices. He waited. He could hear men going into the kitchen and heard someone yell 'clear,' then all was silent. He knew he was next and decided he would not be taken alive, that he would fight until the end. He readied the AK-47 and then moved over to a spot behind his huge bed and waited, lying both Glock 17s on the bed for quick access.

The SWAT commander radioed Wilson they had taken one of the shooters and that the man was injured from the blasts of the flash-bangs. He told her they were moving on the second shooters position and would lead off with another barrage of the exploding devices. Wilson gave the green light.

Isabella was beginning to worry. All the gunfire and all the explosions were troubling to her. She was confused as to what she was supposed to do in a case like this. Only once, many years earlier, had she and el Jefe discussed what she should do to the captives if this were to happen. Salinas had told her to kill all of them. The more she thought about that, the more she knew she wouldn't do such a thing. She had become fond of all 'my' children as she was want to say.

Still, she figured that she would do all she could to protect her babies from whomever was doing this. She held the big .357 magnum up shakily, and pointed it towards the entrance and waited.

Three flash-bangs came through the holes the shotgun had put in the door and in rapid succession, exploded. Salinas was indeed stunned, but had been expecting such a tactic and had opened his mouth, closed his eyes and placed his fingers in his ears, ducking behind the bed. He rose up with the AK-47 and began firing into the doorway. When the rifle was empty, he grabbed both handguns and continued firing, yelling all the while.

He emptied both handguns and was in the process of reloading a magazine when the M-4 fire almost cut him in half. The battle was over in an instant. Silence reigned once again.

The officer that had killed Salinas yelled, "CLEAR!" and entered the room, kicking the handguns away from the mess on the floor.

The SWAT commander radioed Wilson and she entered the home. A handcuffed Sims was being half carried half dragged by two officers. A crowd had gathered at the doorway to a back room, and she moved that direction. She made her way through the crowd of officers and saw the remnant of Salinas in a heap on the bedroom floor, blood and gore everywhere. She shook her head and turned for Bishop.

The SWAT commander got his men under control and told them to sweep the house and find the entrance to the underground complex. This they did, and after a brief exchange of pleasantries, talked Isabella into coming out with her hands up. She was taken into custody without incident.

Anita Wilson dropped at Bish's side, the uninjured side, and held his hand. He was awfully pale and breathing shallowly. "Bish...Bish, can you hear me?" she said quietly.

His eyes flickered and he gave a weak smile knowing it was her. "I guess I got shot," was all he got out. He passed out.

"Ma'am, we gotta get him outta here...ma'am, let go please, ma'am," the paramedic said in a pleading manner.

She reached down and gave him a kiss, and then finally let him go, got up and got out of the way as they put him on a gurney and practically ran to the ambulance. It was only a moment later, and they were off to the fire station. They had called for Flight-for-Life chopper and it would meet them in the back parking lot of the fire house. Bish would be in the

Cheyenne Regional Medical Center's trauma center within the next half hour.

Anita stood, stunned. It took her another five minutes to get her emotions under control, and then asked about the other officer that had been hit. Sadly, he hadn't made it. One of the three shotgun blasts from Salinas had hit they young officer in the left armpit, with several of the buck shot hitting the heart and left lung. He'd died before they could even begin care.

She hung her head, saying a short prayer for him and his family. The SWAT commander came over and told her they had the underground complex under control and that they were bringing out the captives. She asked where, and he pointed. She moved over and saw an officer coming out with a baby. It was Wanda, and she was smiling at the officer, who had great, happy tears running down his cheeks.

The next several hours were a blur for Detective First Class Anita Wilson. The captain, chief and the incident command chief, Jeanne Best, had come down to the scene and were asking loads of questions. Anita told Carlisle that the paperwork was gonna take years to complete. He laughed at that and told her another chopper was waiting to take her to the hospital so she could be there when Bish came out of surgery. He told her Bish had been in surgery for almost three hours already and for her to get, taking her by the shoulders and giving her a shove towards his Crown Victoria.

She drove to the fire station, climbed aboard an Army Guard UH-60 Blackhawk the governor had sent for her and they lifted off for Cheyenne. She was crying.

Chapter Twenty-Five

Barbados

The sun was setting over the western edge of the Atlantic Ocean. The reds, yellows, oranges, and touch of white were actually pleasing to the eye. The fiery orb was just touching the far ocean horizon. One might think they could hear the sizzle as the sun settled into the ocean's edge so far away.

It was sinking rapidly, and just before it sank fully, Bish touched the shutter on his camera and froze the image for himself forever. He thanked God for allowing him to be alive for this moment.

Almost ten months earlier, Bish had been shot in the abdomen. He almost died from the blood loss and the damage done to his liver. Hundreds of people had gathered at the blood donation lab to voluntarily donate their blood for the stricken officer. The surgery had lasted nine hours and he was in recovery for another four before the surgeon sent him to the ICU. He was kept in a medically induced coma for another five days, allowing his body to heal while he was immobilized.

He was moved from the ICU on the tenth day. The hospital put him in a corner room that looked to the southwest. He was able to see the snow-covered mountains from his sixth floor room, a favorite view of his, the mountains.

Anita had stayed in the hospital for two days following the gun battle. She had come to the realization that her feelings for Bish were way beyond friendship. She loved him. The nurses caught her crying on several occasions, and sat with her offering their support while she waited for word. Would Bish pull through?

The whole gang from her crew stopped by frequently. They always approached her quietly, almost reverently, not really wanting to disturb her, but did so nonetheless. She was always happy to see them and was always thankful of their support.

The morning of the third day Bish's surgeon actually ordered her out of the hospital. Patrolman Clint James just happened to be there that moment, grabbed her by her elbow, and led her out, she protesting all the while. Once in his car, he radioed Detective's Peter Donaldson and Michael Hicks, and asked them to go keep an eye on Bish as he took Wilson home to clean up and get some rest. They wholeheartedly agreed.

"Here you are ma'am," he said as they pulled up to her apartment. "I'll be waiting out here until you're ready to go back. You clean up, get something to eat, and some rest, then I'll take you back to Bish. You go on, now. Get some rest. You'll need it for him."

As she opened the car door, she paused, looked back with tears rolling down her cheeks, leaned over, and gave Clint a peck on the cheek, then went inside. It took every bit of strength he had not to bust out crying himself, his hands gripping the steering wheel so tightly, they were white.

Captain Daryl Carlisle kept officers on either side of Bish's hospital rooms at all times. He wasn't taking any chances. No threats had come in, but one never knew after an incident like the one they had been through. He had all the paperwork done for Wilson to sign, and for when Bish woke to do the same. He didn't want his officers to worry about paperwork when a life was way more important. He and the crew gathered and prayed for Bish and Anita every day. All of them knew the two were in love.

The most beautiful part of the story was the family reunions with the children. Margaret Pierce melted in her emotions when she was allowed to hold Wanda once again. Bryan even flew in and had a more or less happy reunion with his ex-wife and daughter.

The other children and young adults were reunited with their families as the Cheyenne PD was able to figure out who went where. The young adults and older children were in awe at what they saw of the world for the first time having never been out of their captive enclosures their whole lives.

The reunifying of the families was confusing to say the least. The children did not understand, and the parents were hesitant at best when the meetings actually took place, wanting to love, but seeing strangers. Most were happy endings – others not so much since their family units, like the Pierce's, had been destroyed by the abductions.

The Salinas crime organization came to a crashing halt. The information found in the Wyoming and Colorado homes, amounted to hundreds of arrests. Millions in stolen merchandise and artifacts like the Aztec artwork found in Cheyenne was recovered. Human trafficking from the United States, both incoming and outgoing, suffered serious setbacks, to the thankfulness of police agencies. Hundreds of children and young adults were now safe. Arrests in other countries were ongoing, especially Canada and Mexico. Drug trafficking also took a healthy hit from the investigation. The fallout from the rescue of the Ladies of Cheyenne, as the rescue came to be known, would have an effect on crime along the I-25/I-80 corridor for a long time.

And the strange cement pad everyone wondered about to the northeast of the Wyoming home finally became a known. The heavy ring in the middle of the pad was a lifting ring. When the investigators raised the huge pad, they found a grave site like no other. Many disappearances were solved after they raised that thing.

Ultimately, the State of Wyoming opted to destroy the complex in its entirety once the investigation was complete, and filled it in. It's now just another flat spot on the prairie, with cattle using it to graze.

Over a thousand federal, state, county, and city police came from all over the United States, Canada, and Mexico, to lie to rest the SWAT team member that died of his wounds during the confrontation. Many of them dropped in to see Bish and wish him and Anita well, much to the chagrin of the hospital staff.

The line of police cars that formed from Cheyenne Hills Church where the funeral was held stretched for miles and miles. Blue and red lights flashed for what seemed hours. It appeared as though the entire population of Cheyenne turned out to honor the fallen officer as the hearse slowly made its way through town. American and Thin Blue Line flags lined the streets, some with a great black strip of cloth used in mourning.

The Cheyenne chapter of the Combat Veterans Motorcycle Association, surrounded the hearse with their bikes, draped in black and supporting American flags in honor of a fallen comrade. The officer had served two tours in Afghanistan while in the Army, and was a biker himself.

The internment lasted almost three hours, with officers from all over leaving badges, patches, roses, and poppies on the casket.

The second day after Bish had regained consciousness, Anita was visiting him. Clint, Tom, Peter, Michael, and Connie were there also. No doctor or nurse would argue that there were more visitors than they normally allowed. They all had guns after all.

Bish had given a tired smile and said, "Hey guys, quiet down, will ya, I gotta question I want to ask." The room became quiet as they all looked at him expectantly, and Bish turned his eyes towards Anita. He feebly held out a hand for her and when she placed her hand in his, he said, "Sorry, darlin', I can't kneel, but will you marry me?"

Needless to say pandemonium broke out. Doctors and nurses flooded into the room thinking something was wrong with their patient, but were happily relieved to hear what had taken place. Mike was in on the deal and handed the ring to Bish. He shakily put it on Anita and she melted into his arms.

Ten weeks after his release from the hospital, the wedding took place in the Wyoming Capitol building, with the governor officiating. Bish still looked gaunt in his tuxedo, and he almost passed out when Anita turned into the aisle way and walked to him at the podium. Captain Carlisle gave the bride away. Guests were packed clear out of the building out onto Capitol Avenue, lining both sides. After the governor said, "You may kiss your bride, sir," the place erupted. Anita more or less carried a weak Bish down the aisle - he'd refused the wheelchair - and out onto the front foyer of the capitol building. The grounds were covered by people yelling and wishing the happy couple a great life together, literally covering the two with flowers and bird seed.

The governor's decorated limousine waited for the couple at the end of the walkway. Bish insisted on helping Anita in, and then slowly climbed in himself with the aid from the governor's chauffer. They were whisked off to the airport and flown to the Caribbean island of Barbados on a private jet, donated by a very thankful, wealthy, and happy father, who had had his daughter returned to him by the teams' actions.

Bish stretched his tired frame and set his camera back on the small table. He'd been released from the hospital after four weeks, and endured another six weeks of physical therapy and rehab. He'd lost almost fifty pounds after being shot and was still very weak.

Missus Anita Bishop, looked longingly at her husband and said, "You okay?"

"Yes, ma'am, I am," he answered with a smile. "Just stiff, I still ache some, you know?"

"No, I don't know and don't ever want to know," she somberly answered.

"Yeah, I wouldn't wish this on anybody," Bish said. He reached over and took her hand in his, gave it a kiss and sat back in his beach recliner.

"Now, that's more like it," Anita said and leaned back, also.

The sun gone and night rapidly closing in, the pair remained where they were, listening to the surf quietly washing ashore. Anita silently prayed a prayer of thanks for the many blessings of late that God had blessed her with.

Here's an excerpt from Jim's next exciting book:

Murder in the Medicine Bow

Chapter 1

The midnight-blue Jeep stopped several yards from the cabin nestled in the trees and backed into a spot seemingly made for it in the tree line. The man got out as did the woman. She gazed at him with a questioning look.

"Other than the realtor, you're the only other person that knows about this place now," medically retired Cheyenne, Wyoming Police Department Detective Samuel 'Bish' Bishop said with a sly smile. " I bought this property some twenty years ago. The realtor doesn't know about the cabin. Now you, and I, are the only people that know about it," he explained looking at her and her amazed countenance. Sam, a large man looking somewhat gaunt after his near-death experience from a bullet wound to the abdomen in which he lost half his liver and several pints of blood before the doctors in the Cheyenne trauma center could save him. It was the wound that took him out of his more than twenty-three year stint as a police officer and detective with the CPD. He was now medically retired on a full pension. He also received a small disability pension.

Mrs. Detective First Class Anita (Wilson) Bishop, almost out of breath, whispered, "It's beautiful, Bish. Why did you keep this a secret all these years?" Anita is forty years old and looking somewhat haggard herself after Bish's ordeal knocking on death's door and their subsequent wedding, which the governor of Wyoming officiated no less. She was now over her twenty-year mark with the CPD, and had, after The Rescue of the Ladies of Cheyenne as the operation had come to be known, was promoted to Chief of the Detective Division. She now had seven detectives working for her.

"You know all those times I called in for an extended weekend…?" he asked.

"Yeah?" she questioning, returned.

"I was coming out here and building this cabin," he murmured, almost whispering. "This is my retreat…my castle of solitude…my palace in the arboretum. This is where I come for my quiet time, to unwind if you will."

"Most fitting for that," the new missus said in awe taking in her surroundings, eyes wide.

"Come on then, let me show you the cabin," the tall man said. Bish had lost almost seventy pounds since being wounded. He had spent several months in rehab, and was now well on his way to recovery. After the governor-officiated wedding, the pair had been whisked away in a private aircraft to the island nation of Barbados, where they had spent an all-expense paid honeymoon together - a time in their lives they would never forget and be forever grateful for. A very rich father of one of the abductees paid for the works.

Together they climbed the stairs onto the porch. He gently grabbed her shoulder stopping her from going inside, stepped forward and opened the door, then swept her off her feet and carried her into the one-room enclosure. He sat her down and with a wave of his hand said, "Here you go."

"You're still in recovery. You shouldn't be picking me up. What if you'd undone something they fixed during your surgery?" referring again to his recent severe wounding in the gun-fight. He almost died from the blood loss. Both detectives along with their entire team, which included six rookies, took on a force of thirty hired professionals employed by one Enrique Salinas, also known as el Jefe, the Boss, who had been abducting two-year-old girls since the sixties, and doing horrific things to them. That operation became known as the Ladies of Cheyenne rescue. One other officer was wounded and one, tragically, killed in the action.

"I'm fine, really," Bish told her.

She shook her gaze away from him and looked the room over quickly and replied, "Well, I'm not going to say it needs a woman's touch because for what this is used for, it's perfect…it's really perfect."

"You haven't seen anything yet. Wait 'till tomorrow and I take you on a tour of our forty acres. You're gonna love it."

"Forty acres…that'll take all day'"

Other Novels by James W. Murphy
The *I'm Tired of Zombies* Series Books 1 - 4

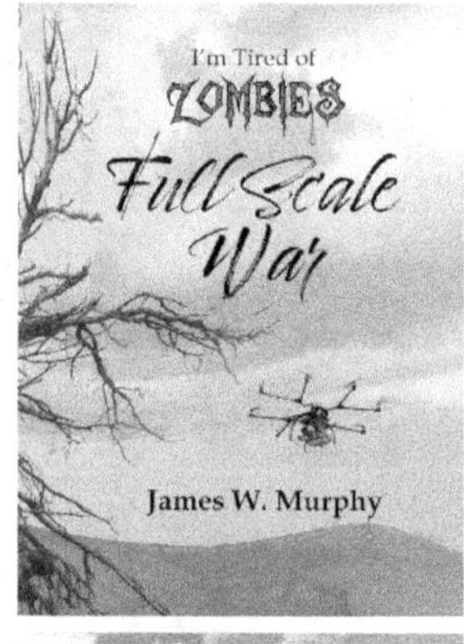

Crashed Wagon Canyon

About the Author

James 'Jim' Murphy was born in Rabat, Morocco, North Africa. After a few years, the family moved to Louisiana, then to Puerto Rico. There, he found Jesus and was baptized at age seven, and shortly afterwards became an American citizen in San Juan in 1960. In 1969, the family moved to Bunker Hill, Indiana. This is where God led James to his soul mate, Jean. They became high school sweethearts, and were married in 1974, and have been happily married since. They have three grown daughters, eight grandchildren, and one great grandson.

James served his chosen country, The United States of America, for over twenty-three years in the Air Force. He was a medic specializing in Aerospace Medicine. He has an Associate's Degree in Science from the Community College of the Air Force, an undergraduate certificate in Biblical Studies from Colorado Christian University, and is currently enrolled in the Dallas Theological Seminary, with a course of study in Biblical Studies. He and Jean moved to Cheyenne, Wyoming, in 1996, and have resided there since on the Nickle 'J' Ranch.

www.ingramcontent.com/pod-product-compliance
Lightning Source LLC
Chambersburg PA
CBHW071557150726
48000CB00004B/1497